The anatomy of IT projects: why they're hard, and why they fail

A guide to the complexities, and how to negotiate them

Mark Seneschall

ISBN: 978-1-291-71758-7

PublishNation, London
www.publishnation.co.uk

CONTENTS

Acknowledgements

Thanks to everyone who worked on all those different projects with me over the years - MOFT, TSP/MOBO, ISPT, STEP, OTIS, Next Gen and all its constituent parts (notably GBO/Sapphire, F&O and Physops), CRT integration, Openbooks, Performance Management System, CSC, CFT, Sigma (the sum of all our risks) Credit, nErgize, PF Iberia, HSP and others with equally uninformative names - from whom and with whom (because as well as everything else these were learning experiences) I learned everything I know (such as it is). This of course includes those who worked on those projects that went awry - given that you tend to learn a lot more from these than from the ones that go swimmingly (though I'm not sure that there were many which you'd describe as actually having gone 'swimmingly') – so thanks especially to you. Wouldn't it have helped if we'd all known then what we know now? Can I also take this opportunity to apologise to you all for being so grumpy. Special thanks finally to Graham Ford and Cathy Ryan; Lorraine McCarthy; Howard Green; Doug Riach; the EAO LT; the EAO CFO LT (or whatever we were calling ourselves that week); Peter Garrett, Jane Ball and everyone else at Prison Dialogue; David Morrison at PublishNation for his help in bringing this book to fruition; and of course Marion, Charlotte and Kay (not forgetting Neville and Ralph).

About the author

Mark Seneschall has 30 years commercial experience, mostly in a large British multinational, working in a number of different functional areas and geographies. He spent a large part of his career heavily involved in various capacities - including as process change lead, project manager, and ultimately programme director - in a diverse array of major transformation and 'IT-enabled business change' projects, some of which were global undertakings with multi-million pound budgets. More recently he has worked as a management consultant providing advice and support to different organisations on IT and transformation projects. He is a qualified accountant, and has a Ph.D and a football blue from Cambridge University. He is married with two daughters and lives in Buckinghamshire.

INTRODUCTION: 'THESE THINGS ARE HARD…'

This book is an attempt to distil some of my own experiences while involved in various ways with a number of different IT projects – mostly while in the employ of a large British multinational company – in a form that may be of benefit and hopefully some interest to others who find themselves (for better or worse) engaged in such undertakings. I should probably add that I'm not writing this from the perspective of someone who is an IT professional, because I come from what might be described as a 'general business/commercial/finance and control' background. In many respects I am something of a technophobe. However, some years ago, I found myself appointed to a new role as manager of a small team which had just been provided with a new system with which to perform its activity; the only problem was that the new system didn't work very well, so the challenge I/we faced was to get it to do more or less what it was supposed to do, and to do this somewhat less slowly so that the team could get its work done properly in the time available to them. Although it took the team and me, working with the IT folk, a little while to sort things out, after two or three months we could see some definite signs of improvement, and the system began to perform more or less as intended. Following this initial small success, I established something of a personal niche as a business person who knew a bit about IT – or at least IT projects; as the saying goes, 'In the kingdom of the blind, the one-eyed man is king'[1] (equally of course 'A little knowledge is a dangerous thing'[2]). But to cut quite a long story short – and in a manner somewhat reminiscent of the First Lord of the Admiralty in Gilbert and Sullivan's HMS Pinafore, who 'polished up that handle so carefullee that now he is the ruler of the Queen's Navee'[3] - by the time I departed the large multinational some twenty years later to pursue other opportunities, I could look back on a lengthy list of IT projects (and other change initiatives) I'd worked on or been associated with – including some very large ones with global reach and price tags to match. Some of these admittedly proved more successful than others – but it's generally recognised that if you're paying attention you usually learn more from your failures than your successes. In my case, this provided plenty of opportunity for further learning. But this said, I'd like to think I learned quite well, because my final two roles at the multinational were as programme director for two of the largest and most complex 'IT-enabled business change' projects the business had ever undertaken – both of which we progressed to successful delivery. Meanwhile, following my departure, I've worked on some smaller scale projects in smaller organisations, which have broadened my experience and provided me with further insights. Given all this, I'm inclined to believe, rightly or wrongly, that I may have something moderately useful to say.

Hence, while I don't claim to be an IT professional, I can point to quite a broad range of experience of IT projects. Moreover, in my experience, a substantial part of what is involved in any IT project has very little to do directly with IT. As a result, no-one who reads this book will need to be particularly IT-literate (apologies in advance to those who are especially IT literate, as you're likely to be disappointed - though I'd argue that you should nevertheless read on, since so much of what IT projects are about is not about the IT, and the more this is understood by everyone involved, the better). My primary intended readership, however, is really those with less previous exposure to IT projects, but who in the course of their activities find themselves confronted with the looming prospect of some form of engagement with such an undertaking – or who have recently become entangled with some form of IT initiative, and are wondering what they may have got themselves into.

Two other events also contributed significantly to my decision to try and put pen to paper/fingers to keyboard/thumbs to Blackberry. The first of these took place after I'd left the aforementioned multinational in a meeting with the management team of a much smaller organisation which I had been asked to help out with an IT project that was proving somewhat problematic. Almost the first thing I said during this meeting was 'These things are hard'. To which the management team smiled and nodded. Several months later, at another meeting with the same leadership team, and having spent the intervening period wrestling - with mixed results - with assembling reference data in the format and to the full extent required by the new system, obtaining final business sign-off on requirements (and then specifying a bunch of changes), defining, developing and agreeing a sensible list of test scenarios, managing resistance - and requests for more changes - from some of the users and some of the management team, maintaining reasonably civil relationships with the supplier against a backdrop of growing mutual frustration, and more...(did I mention reference data?), and with the project continuing to prove problematic, I reminded them of what I had said.   And again they smiled, although perhaps rather more ruefully than the first time round.

Musing subsequently on this, I wondered whether when I said 'These things are hard' the first time round they really had very much appreciation of what this meant at all. In a way, I might just as well have been speaking Ancient Greek (not that I speak Ancient Greek). On reflection, in many respects, 'These things are hard' is perhaps not a particularly useful thing to say. 'Hard' (as in difficult) is a relative term, of course. And depends on the context. Lots of things are hard. Long division is hard. Running a marathon is hard. Childbirth is hard (so I'm told). But the nature of 'hard' is different in each case. If you've been through any of them, then you know what the 'hard' in question really means.[4] But if you haven't, you don't. So while I'm certain that my comment was accurate and justified – these things really are hard - it wasn't necessarily very helpful. In fact, in retrospect I'm not entirely convinced that even having been exposed more closely to some of the myriad of intricacies and convolutions that made up the project, the management team really formed a clear view of what it was that made it as difficult as it was proving - and continued to prove – to be. Quite a lot of this devil is in the detail, and to appreciate it you need to get quite close to it – rather closer than many management teams are often prepared to get. At the same time, some of the problems encountered seemed to be connected to quite deep-seated aspects of the way the business in question operated, its internal culture, the relationships between different departments within the organisation, the attitudes towards individual accountability for task delivery, the way differences of opinion got resolved – which the management team often found hard (that word again) to address. For example, it makes it quite difficult to put together a comprehensive set of reference data where this isn't held in any one place, but sits in the heads of a number of different people in different teams within the organisation which normally work in isolation and have no great appetite for co-operation; and where some of the heads involved belong to individuals who see the implementation of the new system as threatening and would prefer to retain the current mode of operation. Hence some of what makes IT projects hard is implicit in the tasks involved; but some of it comes from the wider context, the nature of the organisation undertaking the project, its culture, internal dynamics and modus operandum.

Following from this, the question it raised for me (and raises) is how to provide a sense of this to those embarking or embarked upon IT projects but lacking in a deep appreciation of them. I suspect that this group is in fact the norm rather than the exception – after all, there is widespread evidence to suggest that a significant proportion of such projects struggle to some degree (see below).

But I haven't been able to find a simple way of describing this (no-one who hasn't had to do it really believes that assembling reference data – in the required format – can possibly be all that difficult; tedious, yes, but difficult, no!). Neither have I had much success in finding a good analogy that both works for me and also resonates powerfully with people. There are obvious parallels with engineering and construction projects, of course, and these can be very instructive – not least because of the differences as well as the similarities. But the differences mean that they only provide partial analogies at best.

Given this widespread lack of appreciation of what's really entailed in the successful delivery of even a relatively straightforward IT project, and the challenge in articulating the reasons why such projects should be as difficult as they seem to be, the best solution I could think of was to try and write it down. Hence this book – so that next time I see my audience's eyes start to glaze over, and I see them thinking 'Hard?...whadaya mean these things are hard?...in my job I do lots of things that are hard...I don't see anything here that's all that difficult' (or words to that effect), I can at least have something to hand that I can give them and say 'you might want to read this'.

The final event which contributed to my decision to try and write this book was the publication of a series of articles by Computer Weekly, the on-line magazine, in late 2011, entitled 'The NHS IT project is dead, but why do large IT projects so often fail?'[5,6] (and I have to admit it is very frustrating as a taxpayer to continue to see the repeated failings of public sector IT projects in particular, and the lack of any discernible improvement in the delivery record). The articles were made up of 200 word submissions from various contributors with different involvement in and experiences of IT and IT projects, some practitioners, some academics, some consultants, some IT managers, and so on, offering different perspectives on the question posed. Given my interest in this topic, I attempted to write my own 200 word contribution. Unfortunately, I failed to stay within the 200 word limit – in fact my submission took on something of a life of its own, and over time has developed into this book. And to be honest, while there is much that I agree with in most of the submissions (there were around 30 of these in total), it's quite difficult to form a coherent sense from them of why large IT projects really do so often fail. A wide array of different factors are referred to – a lot more than 30 in fact, because most of the articles refer to more than one factor, and although there is some overlap between some of the submissions, quite a lot of them provide a perspective that is unique. I'm not suggesting that they are wrong in this, in fact I believe that there are all sorts of factors that contribute to the difficulties encountered by IT projects, but if this is the case, it seems to me that what's needed is a framework for organising the material in a more structured way, rather than as simply a list. This is not intended as a criticism of Computer Weekly or the contributors or anyone involved in the exercise (he said hastily), which of course was merely intended as a vehicle for soliciting input. But looking again at the content provided – as well as many other a list of reasons why IT projects have such a chequered record of performance, and of the things to do to ensure these pitfalls are avoided, readily available online via a quick Google search – it seems to me that it would benefit if it could be structured more coherently. This is one of the things I've tried to do in the pages that follow. I wouldn't wish to claim therefore that all of the content of this book – perhaps even very much of it – is especially original; however, what I haven't seen is an attempt to organise this material and thinking and bring it together in this way previously (although it's possible that I haven't been looking hard enough or in the right place).

Finally, before going any further, it is perhaps worth reaffirming that there genuinely does remain a general and widespread issue regarding the disappointing performance of IT projects. After all, the ever increasing prevalence of computers and smart phones and the internet in our lives means that lots of IT-related activities must be taking place successfully. Even so, another quick Google search will reveal any number of articles (of varying levels of authority) that provide some statistics on project success and failure rates. The most oft-quoted analysis is that by the Standish Group in 1995[7], which concluded that only 16 per cent of IT projects undertaken by US companies and government agencies were completed on time and on budget (with the performance of larger companies even worse, at only 9 per cent). 31 per cent of projects were cancelled before completion, while the remaining 53 per cent of projects cost on average 189 per cent of their original estimates. Subsequent Standish Group reports have identified some improvement in performance – for example in 2010, 21 per cent of projects were described as failures, 37 per cent as successful, and 42 per cent as 'challenged'.[8] However, this still means that almost two thirds of projects ran into difficulties. Another study of 5400 large IT projects (defined as those with a budget over $15m) undertaken by McKinsey in collaboration with the BT Centre for Programme Management at the

University of Oxford, concluded that half of such projects exceeded their budgets.[9] On average, the projects ran 45 percent over budget and 7 percent over time, while delivering 56 percent less value than predicted. Seventeen per cent of projects experienced budget overruns in excess of 200 per cent. Thirdly, a study of 1471 projects of all sizes undertaken by Flyvberg and Budzier[10] reported an average cost overrun of 27 per cent. However, in line with the McKinsey analysis, they found that one in six of the projects was what they called a 'black swan', where substantial overruns were experienced – the average cost overrun for these projects being 200 per cent, with an average schedule overrun of almost 70 per cent. Finally – back at the aforementioned NHS IT project (and more to come on this later in the book) - in September 2013 the House of Commons Public Accounts Committee published a report on 'The Dismantled National Programme for IT in the NHS'.[11] This noted that although the programme had officially been closed down in 2011, in reality many of the elements of it remained in place, and these continued to incur significant costs. The total cost to complete these activities remained uncertain. At the same time, the benefits delivered from the programme were described as 'extremely disappointing'. In light of this, the committee expressed reservations as to whether the NHS would be in a position to deliver its new vision of a 'paperless NHS' by 2018. Clearly then it's still hard going at the NHS. (Not to mention at Obamacare[12]...).

So, yes, it seems that despite all the things that have been happening in terms of the technology, a substantial proportion of IT projects continue to encounter considerable difficulties – which would accord with my own experience. Having said this, the types of project I have principally been involved with concerned the implementation (in some cases the development) of systems to manage business transactions through their life cycle, and/or to provide a record of the activities undertaken by the organisation either for accounting or performance measurement and evaluation purposes, or to optimise supply and logistics activities across a network of supply and demand points with different connections between them, or to provide market and other information to support decision making by commercial personnel. Some of the projects with which I have been associated extended across multiple different countries. In the main there was a significant organisational change aspect to the initiatives, and linked to this a sizeable user engagement element. At the same time, a number of the projects also involved a material IT infrastructure component. Even so, there are plenty of types of IT project to which I haven't had a great deal of exposure (for example, none of the major projects I've worked on brought me into any great contact with the internet or the world of 'on-line'). No doubt my experiences have coloured my judgements, at least to some degree. This said, I nevertheless believe that what follows should still be of at least some relevance in connection with the vast majority of IT projects, regardless of their precise nature, scale, cost or apparent complexity, and in almost any organisation, no matter how big or how small.

CHAPTER 1: A DIVERSION - ENGINEERING PROJECTS ARE HARD TOO...

So, where to start? As I was thinking about this, I remembered a comment of a former colleague of mine, who once said to me that when I was standing up and speaking to a gathering of people and trying to whip up a modicum of enthusiasm for the particular project in which we were at that point of time engaged, as was my lot from time to time, the only thing to which people paid any attention were the analogies I drew with other (non-IT) projects (which is of course better than nobody listening to anything at all, so I took this as positive). Whenever I spoke about these, for some reason there appeared to be a general rousing of the audience from its slumbers, and at least some vestige of interest from some of its members. It's certainly true that IT projects per se are not exactly very tangible, and perhaps therefore quite hard to think about. Whereas there's an inherent fascination about engineering and construction projects (how did they do that!?), and they are much more tangible (this might explain why there are TV programmes about Megastructures[1], while we are still awaiting 'Reference Data: The Movie'). They also have the advantage that a number of them are very well documented. And of course there are lots of aspects of these that prima facie would appear to be quite 'hard', and there is plenty of evidence to suggest that these projects often struggle, and some of them may also fail. So in the first instance it seemed that one way into this might be to take a look at some other projects which aren't IT ones, and see what they tell us that might help us think about IT projects.

The following section therefore consists of four short(ish) case studies - I've called them 'mini-studies' - of some well-known engineering and construction projects. To help pull out some of the key themes, I've attempted to structure all of the mini-cases in largely the same way, according to the following headings:

Objective – a short description of what the project was seeking to achieve.

Initiation – this describes the main events surrounding the decision to proceed with the project.

Key Challenges – a listing of some of the principal difficulties facing the project which it would need to overcome.

Cost and Timing – a comparison of the actual and projected costs and time to complete the project.

Resourcing, Procurement and Logistics – this discusses some of the practicalities of how the project was undertaken.

Human and Organisational Dynamics – perhaps surprisingly, one of the common themes that emerges from all of the projects concerns the complex relationship dynamics between some of the participants.

Key Events – a brief outline of the main events that took place as the project unfolded.

Outcomes – the results of the project.

As a result, these are not narrative case studies – in fact, I was originally planning to present them as a table, but I concluded that this required too much abbreviation to the point where it would be unhelpful.

I selected three of the mini-studies – the Bell Rock Lighthouse, the Great Eastern, and the Brooklyn Bridge - because they were featured in the BBC series 'Seven Wonders of the Industrial World' (as well as the accompanying book – see Cadbury, 2004)[2], so in many respects they would be considered highly successful undertakings, quite the opposite of failures. Although all clearly had to surmount considerable difficulties, so it certainly seems reasonable to describe them as 'hard'. I'll admit to a degree of selection bias in the choice of Heathrow Terminal 5 for the final mini-study, because of the supplier relationship and organisational change aspects of the project, which seem particularly pertinent when we return later to think about IT projects. But, with the possible exception of this last one, I think that the conclusions that emerge from the mini-studies would not be altered significantly if I'd chosen a completely different sample. Certainly, in terms of the gestation/evolution of this book, it was from thinking about these non-IT projects in this way that helped me develop the framework that is proposed in Chapter 2 and which is then used as the basis for looking at IT projects employed subsequently.

1. Bell Rock Lighthouse[3] - built by Robert Stevenson for the Northern Lighthouse Board between 1807 and 1811

Objective: Construct a lighthouse on the Bell Rock reef (also known as Inchcape), in the mouth of the Firth of Forth, to warn ships of the presence of the rocks, which made entrance very difficult and dangerous and had claimed many ships over the course of history (one 18th century estimate was an average of 6 wrecks a year).

Initiation: In December 1799 over 70 ships were lost or stranded in severe storms off the East Coast of Scotland, many on Bell Rock, or on the nearby coast trying to avoid it. Ships were unable to use the haven of the Firth of Forth due to the risk of hitting the reef. This led to increased calls for a lighthouse to be built. However, the Northern Lighthouse Board was unable to fund the construction without an Act of Parliament, which was not forthcoming. In 1804 the 64-gun HMS York sank off Bell Rock in a storm. Despite continued procrastination, an Act was finally passed in July 1806. This provided for the Board to borrow £25000 towards the project – which it could then repay from the dues collected from ship owners.

Key Challenges: The location of the rock was 11 miles offshore. The Reef was only exposed for two hours twice a day during the lowest tides – at high tide it was covered by up to 16 feet of water. There were frequent storms, especially in winter, and hence work could only progress during the summer months – but even then it was often interrupted.

Only one offshore sea-washed stone lighthouse was then in existence, the Eddystone Light south of Plymouth in Devon, built by John Smeaton in 1759. This had incorporated many innovations in lighthouse design and construction which could be employed at Bell Rock, for example: use of the 'oak tree' shape; interlocking stone blocks, shaped onshore and then fitted together on-site using dovetail joints and dowels; 'hydraulic lime' – a quick drying cement that would set in wet conditions (which is still used today); a crane able to lift large blocks from ships at sea to considerable heights (which has never subsequently been improved upon). However, unlike Bell Rock, the Eddystone lighthouse was built on a rock above sea level. This meant there were additional challenges facing the Bell Rock project. It would also need to be higher and wider at its base. Builders of the Eddystone light had also been ferried to the site each day, but Stevenson considered this impractical at Bell Rock, and planned to keep them on site, first on a ship, and then on the rock itself in a temporary structure (which became known as the 'beacon house').

Cost and Timing: Stevenson's original estimate in 1802 was £42,685. A similar estimate (£41,840) was also arrived at by John Rennie, a leading Civil Engineer of the day, who had been responsible for construction of the London docks, and who the Northern Lighthouse Board consulted in 1805. The actual cost was £61,331 9s 2d (which equates to £4.2m in 2011 money, based on the GDP deflator method – see measuringworth.com).[4] Given the limitations on the time available for offshore construction due to the weather, the work was effectively completed in four summers.

Resourcing, Procurement and Logistics: Following the passage of the Act of Parliament, in December 1806 the Northern Lighthouse Board appointed Rennie as Chief Engineer, with Stevenson engaged as his assistant. Stevenson took charge of the work on site. Although Rennie developed plans for the lighthouse which closely resembled Smeaton's design for the Eddystone light, he had not previously built a lighthouse, whereas Stevenson had built several. Despite being much younger, Stevenson believed that he was considerably more knowledgeable about lighthouses, and thought that Smeaton's design could be improved upon. He therefore determined to base construction on his own plans.

The project involved 3 main teams of people – the builders, who worked on the actual construction on site on the Rock; the seamen who operated the ships which supported the construction, either by transporting materials out to the Rock, or providing on-site accommodation for the builders during the construction period; and the stone cutters who prepared the stones onshore prior to their being shipped to the site. The total workforce is estimated to have been around 110, made up of about 60 workers and craftsmen, 35 seamen and 15 managers and heads of department.

Workers were paid 20 shillings a week, given generous food rations, and protected from being pressed into naval service. Stevenson preferred to recruit those who had worked for him previously or had been recommended.

A stoneyard was established in Arbroath to dress the blocks to the required shapes. To ensure they would fit together, each course was assembled in the yard prior to transportation out to the rock. Granite, which was used for the outer layers of the lower courses, was sourced from quarries in Aberdeenshire, and sandstone, used for the upper courses as well as the inside of the lower layers, from Mylnefield quarry near Dundee. However, the Mylnefield sandstone was found to split during frosty weather, and a finer sandstone (known as 'liver-rock') from Craigleith Quarry near Edinburgh was used in finishing the structure and building the parapet around the light.

A number of ships were acquired or built to support the construction. These were the Pharos which served as a floating light; the Smeaton, the Alexander and the Patriot, which were used to transport stone from the quarries to the yard at Arbroath, and then the completed stones and other supplies out to the rock; and the Sir Joseph Banks, which provided offshore accommodation for the workers at the rock. Wide, flat-bottomed vessels called praams were also used to complete the delivery of the prepared stones from the ships to the Bell Rock itself.

Human and Organisational Dynamics: The Northern Lighthouse Board was reluctant to appoint Stevenson, who had initially been assistant to his step father as inspector of the Board's lighthouses, to undertake the project, despite him being their Chief Engineer and his having submitted designs for a lighthouse on Bell Rock in 1800 and in 1802 (the latter being close to the final design employed). At that point Stevenson was only under contract to the Board, and was not a fully qualified engineer. This led them to approach other more experienced engineers, firstly Thomas Telford, and then Rennie.

At least superficially, Rennie and Stevenson appear to have worked well together, Stevenson as the resident engineer on site, and Rennie supposedly in overall charge – although he made only three site visits during construction. Stevenson sent Rennie regular reports on progress and requests for advice, to which Rennie replied often in considerable detail, but in practice Stevenson took little note of his comments, and it is generally considered that this was a stratagem on Stevenson's part to keep Rennie at a distance. Although unhappy at their decision to appoint Rennie, Stevenson also ensured he maintained close connections with the Commissioners of the Northern Lighthouse Board. In 1808 his offer to cease any other business and work exclusively for the board as their full-time engineer was accepted. While this did not change the official arrangements covering the Bell Rock project, Stevenson's commitment to the Board contrasted with Rennie's wide variety of other interests. Over time, Rennie's involvement with and influence on the project receded as Stevenson's increased. Stevenson was also anxious to ensure he received full credit for the construction – in the book he wrote following completion of the project, he made little mention of Rennie's involvement.[5] This subsequently resulted in a heated exchange of letters between Stevenson's and Rennie's sons, and a continuing debate about the extent of their respective contributions.

In the main good relations existed between Stevenson and his workers throughout the project. Stevenson worked alongside and endured all the same hardships as his men, and as a result earned their respect and trust. This said, there was talk of a strike by some workers in 1810 due principally to dissatisfaction with the beer ration provided every evening.   Stevenson threatened to turn the men over to the local press gangs if they did not withdraw their demands – which understandably they did. The ringleaders were subsequently dismissed.

Key Events: Work on-site commenced on 18th August 1807 (Stevenson had hoped to start in May, but preparations were not complete), and went on until 6th October 1807 - though work continued on-shore preparing the stone blocks. The primary task during the first season was to begin the construction of the 'beacon house', which would provide a stable platform for work and a refuge in the event of storms. From 1809 it was also used as accommodation for the workers, enabling the men to remain on the rock rather than return to the boats when the tide rose. During the 1808 season, when only 265 hours were spent on the rock, work continued on the beacon house, rail tracks were laid to transport the blocks from the landing point to the lighthouse site, the foundations were prepared (this involved digging out a circular base in the sandstone of the rock, which had to be done by hand, due to the risk of fracturing the rock beyond repair if explosives were used), and 3 courses (layers) of stones (400 blocks weighing a total of 388 tonnes) were laid. As well as the weather, delays were also caused by difficulties in obtaining blocks of granite of sufficient size from which to cut the stones. Work recommenced offshore in May 1809. Progress was delayed for ten days when an embargo was placed on all British shipping due to the war with France, and the supply boats were prevented from leaving port. The solid part of the lighthouse – up to the 26th course - was completed in August 1809, following which work on-site was suspended until 1810, when the 'balance crane' to lift the stones to the required height was installed and the remaining (hollow) courses were laid.   The final (90th) course was completed at the end of July 1810. This left only the internal staircase, the light room and the installation of the light to be completed. Some delays occurred as Stevenson had decided to give the light a distinctive alternating white and red signal, which required sheets of red glass 25 inches in diameter, bigger than had previously been manufactured in Britain. A glassmaker in London undertook to make the glass, which was delivered to the rock on 14th December 1810. After final preparations, the lighthouse entered service on 1st February 1811.

Outcomes: Bell Rock Lighthouse is still standing and in service today, 200 years after it was built. It is the oldest surviving offshore lighthouse in the world – testament to its design and construction.

5 people died in the building of the lighthouse.

2. Great Eastern[6] - built by Isambard Kingdom Brunel, 1852-59

Objective: Build a ship capable of sailing to Australia and returning without refuelling (since at the time there were no known coal supplies in Australia). This would be the biggest ship in the world, over five times the size of any existing ship, and would be able to carry 4000 passengers.

Initiation: Brunel conceived the ship against the background of a wave of emigration to Australia, associated with the discovery of gold and the growing realisation of the continent's agricultural potential. Although designed for the North Atlantic, Brunel's previous ship, the Great Britain, had been transferred to the Australian run, which had proved very profitable. However, the Great Britain needed refuelling en route, which in turn required coal to be transported from Wales to the Cape of Good Hope. In 1852, Brunel and John Scott Russell, the leading naval architect of the day, who Brunel had consulted for advice, presented a plan for the 'great ship' to the Eastern Steam Navigation Company (ESNC). The company had originally been formed to bid for the mail contract to the Far East, but had lost out to the Peninsular and Orient Steam Navigation Company, and as a result was considered likely to be interested in alternative schemes. The company ultimately decided to proceed, but only after a number of directors had resigned, and been replaced by others persuaded to participate by Brunel, who also took a significant personal stake in the venture – although given the scale of what was contemplated, the company was insufficiently capitalised, with £120,000 paid up by December 1853.

Key challenges: Most large ships at the time were still wind powered, less than 150 feet long, and built of wood. No ship had previously been built on anything approaching the scale of the Great Eastern - at 692 feet, and ultimately displacing 32160 tons, the Great Eastern was to be more than twice as long, and over five times larger, than any ship then in existence. This raised some major technical challenges - eg in terms of hull design (the Great Eastern was to have a double hull, and transverse and longitudinal bulkheads), propulsion (a combination of paddle wheel, screw and sail was proposed), steering (Great Eastern was the first ship fitted with a steering engine), construction facilities, and launching. At the time, no dry dock anywhere was large enough to build the ship, and the River Thames in London, which at the time was the centre of British shipbuilding, was too narrow to launch a ship of this length in the normal way. Likewise, there was also a lack of port facilities able to accommodate such a large ship once in use.

Cost & Timing: Brunel estimated that the cost of construction would be approximately £500,000, with additional costs to fit out the vessel. By the time the ship was launched, the total cost stood at £732,000, with £170,000 of this attributable to the costs of launching. Including the costs of fitting out, the total cost of the ship amounted to about £900,000 (which equates to £95m in 2011 money, based on the GDP deflator method – see measuringworth.com).[4]

The launch date was originally planned for October 1855. The ship actually launched in January 1858. She entered service in 1860.

Resourcing, Procurement and Logistics: John Scott Russell, whose assistance Brunel had initially sought to help design the hull, and who was also the owner of a Thames shipyard, was selected to build the hull and paddle engines, while James Watt & Company was contracted to build the screw engines. The total cost of the contracts was £377,200 – which was around 25 per cent lower than Brunel's estimate. Scott Russell seems to have wanted the commission badly, and may have submitted a low bid. Brunel accepted Scott Russell's bid without challenge, given that the two men enjoyed a good relationship and Brunel regarded Scott Russell as a highly experienced shipbuilder.

However, in many respects, the choice of Scott Russell's yard to build the ship was far from ideal. The yard was a traditional one, lacked supervision, and pilfering was rife. Moreover, it was much too small to build a ship of the size proposed. As a result, the adjacent yard, which was vacant (the owners having decided to relocate their operations to the Clyde, which they considered a much better location for constructing iron steamships), was rented by ESNC to provide space for construction. Brunel's original plan had been to construct the ship in a dry dock, but this would require a dock to be built. Scott Russell had quoted from £8000 to £10000 for this, but despite this again probably being optimistic, it was dismissed as prohibitive. This led to a decision to build the ship alongside the river, parallel to the bank, and launch her sideways.

Scott Russell also faced significant financial problems throughout the project. The yard, which was not insured, was severely damaged by fire in 1853, and then twice more in 1855. Moreover, the decision to make part of the payment for the ship in the form of ESNC shares further compounded Scott Russell's liquidity problems. Although the main iron supplier for the ship, Samuel Beale and Company, Parkgate Ironworks, Rotherham, of whom Charles Geach – also a Director of ESNC – was principal partner, was initially prepared to accept the shares as payment to them, this came to an end following Geach's death in 1854. Without informing ESNC, Scott Russell was forced to mortgage the yard, and when in 1856 he was declared bankrupt, work on the ship came to a halt. Ultimately Martin's Bank agreed to lease Scott Russell's shipyard to ESNC, until August 1857, the then expected launch date. Large fees were incurred by ESNC when the launch was further delayed.

As a result of the cost overruns incurred during construction and launching, ESNC had insufficient funds to fit the ship out. Hence a new company called 'The Great Ship Company' was formed, with capital of £340,000. They bought the ship for £160,000 from ENSC, which went into liquidation.

Despite what had transpired previously, and having been declared bankrupt, Scott Russell won the contract for fitting out the ship with a bid thought to have been around £125,000, some £15,000 lower than the other bid received. At the time, however, Brunel was incapacitated, and since Scott Russell was more familiar with the Great Eastern than anyone other than Brunel himself, and still retained the detailed drawings for the ship, as well as the paddle engines which had not been installed, there was considerable logic behind the choice.

Human and Organisational Dynamics: The project was severely affected by a breakdown in relations between Brunel and Scott Russell. Initially there was considerable mutual admiration between the two, but this subsequently gave way to suspicion and antipathy. The two were very different – Brunel the hands-on workaholic, anxious to oversee every detail, whereas Scott Russell was suave and polished and preferred to delegate. Conflicts arose over the payment method; an article in The Observer crediting Scott Russell with the major role in the ship's design, which Brunel believed Scott Russell had instigated, and to which he took objection; the slower than projected progress (partly because Scott Russell had diverted resources to build 6 other ships to aid his cash flow); the method of launching (Brunel insisted on a 'controlled launch' whereby the ship was lowered carefully down to the high water mark and then floated on the high tide, whereas Scott Russell favoured a cheaper 'uncontrolled' launch); Scott Russell's failure to provide Brunel with the information he requested for launch planning; and Brunel's growing suspicions of Scott Russell's financial integrity. Brunel was wintering in Egypt on medical advice (following his being diagnosed as suffering from Bright's disease, now more commonly known as nephritis) when the contract for fitting out was awarded. On his return, the tension between the two men continued, with the project split into two opposing 'camps', and a number of disputes requiring resolution by means of independent arbitration.

Key events: The contract with Scott Russell was finalised in December 1853, and work commenced in February 1854 with the preparation of the site, as well as modifications to the yard and the installation of new machinery needed for the new ship. Construction of the ship began in the summer of 1854. By the time Scott Russell was declared bankrupt in early 1856, only about a quarter of the hull was complete, even though Scott Russell had already been paid £292,295, and after allowing for any extra work undertaken at ESNC's request, there was only about £40,000 still owing on the contract. There was also an apparent disparity between the amount of iron for which the company had paid and the amount that had gone into the ship, while at the same time Beale's, the iron supplier, were Scott Russell's biggest creditor. Following negotiations with the bank and other creditors, work recommenced in May 1856 under Brunel's direct supervision, although without assistance from any of Scott Russell's key associates. Nevertheless, work progressed faster than previously, and in June 1857 Brunel reported that the ship was almost ready for launching. Although the launching arrangements were still incomplete, and none of the testing that Brunel had intended had been undertaken, under pressure from the mortgagees, Brunel agreed to attempt to launch the ship on the next suitable tide on 3rd November 1857. This ended in failure, due to insufficient power of the steam winches and manual capstans employed. One man was killed and four seriously injured during the proceedings. After further failures, Brunel decided to increase the number of hydraulic presses employed, which had already been increased from two to four, to eighteen. Over the course of January the ship was gradually pushed to the water's edge, finally being successfully floated on the high tide on 31st January 1858, and moored at Deptford, on the opposite side of the river. However, the company lacked sufficient funds to fit out the ship, and work came to a halt until the new ownership and financial arrangements were put in place in December 1858. Fitting out was completed in August 1859.

The Great Eastern made underwent her first sea trials in early September 1859. Brunel had suffered a stroke shortly before the ship was due to sail and so was not on board for the first voyage. The trials went ahead, but ended in disaster on 9th September following an explosion in one of the paddle engines, caused by a build-up of pressure due to a stopcock being closed on one of the feedwater system heaters (which heated the water for the boilers while preventing the saloons receiving too much heat from the funnels) when it should have been open, resulting in five deaths. The stopcocks were installed as a temporary measure to permit pressure testing, and served no purpose when the ship was operating; however, those above the paddle engine boiler room had not been removed when the testing had completed. It has been suggested that the accident may not have occurred had Brunel been present given his comprehensive understanding of the ship and its many innovative features, with which many of those on board were not fully familiar (the paddle engines were under the control of Scott Russell and his team, as the manufacturers of the engines, during the trials). Brunel died at his home in London a few days after having been informed of the explosion.

Outcomes: The Great Eastern was a tremendous technical achievement but a commercial failure. She never sailed to Australia, but instead due to the shortage of funds was finally put into service in 1860 as a luxury liner on the Atlantic run. However, partly as a result of damage caused by an uncharted needle of rock while entering New York in 1862 (sustaining more damage than subsequently sank the Titanic, but being kept afloat by her double hull), she lost £130,000 in 2 years. She was auctioned in 1864 for £25,000, and converted to cable laying. She had a successful career in this guise, laying the first transatlantic cable in 1866. However, a purpose built cable laying ship came into service in 1874, making the Great Eastern obsolete. She was considered still too large to be viable as a transatlantic passenger ship, and was no longer suitable for the Australian trade, being too big to pass through the Suez Canal, which had been opened in 1869. She was laid up for 12 years, before a brief period as a showboat and mobile advertising hoarding in Liverpool. She was broken up for scrap in 1889-90, still the largest ship built to that point. It was only a decade later that a ship bigger than the Great Eastern was constructed.

3. Brooklyn Bridge[7] (built by John and Washington Roebling between 1869 and 1883)

Objective: Construct a bridge across the East River between New York and Brooklyn to connect the two cities. This would reduce the dependency on ferries (in 1869 there were up to 1000 ferry crossings per day), which were not sufficient to meet demand, caused congestion, and were disrupted by bad weather (especially when the river froze).

Initiation: The East River froze severely in 1866, preventing the operation of the ferries, and increasing calls for a bridge. A bill creating the New York Bridge Company, with a capital of $5m, and authorising them to build the bridge and buy the land required was passed by the State of New York in 1867. Work commenced in 1869, after $5m funding had been raised ($3m from the City of Brooklyn, a smaller amount from the City of New York, and the remainder from the public).

Feasibility/Key Challenges: The East River was about one third of a mile wide, requiring a span of around 1600 feet. The longest bridge then in existence, at Cincinnati (also built by John Roebling), had a span of 1057 feet. The bridge also had to be high enough so as not to interfere with traffic on the river.

A number of early suspension bridges had failed in high winds (and continued to do so into the following century – eg the Tacoma Narrows bridge[8]). Roebling believed that this required rigidity to be built into the bridge floor.

Even a span of 1600 feet meant that the bridge towers would have to be built in the river; the bedrock was around 40 feet below water level on the Brooklyn side, and 100 feet below on the New York side. To reach bedrock it would be necessary to dig down into the river bed through layers of sand and gravel interspersed with boulders. The construction of the towers would require the use of caissons - large watertight chambers, open at the bottom from which the water is kept out by air pressure and in which construction work can be performed. Although these had been used previously on projects in Europe, they had not hitherto been employed on such a scale and at these depths.

The design provided for the cables to be made from steel rather than iron, due to its greater strength – no bridge then built had steel cables. Ultimately the suspenders linking the cable to the bridge deck and the bridge deck itself were also constructed of steel.

Cost & Timing: The bridge took nearly 3 times as long to build as John Roebling estimated, and at $15 million (which equates to around $300 million in 2011 money[4]) cost around twice as much – in 1867 he had estimated a cost of $6-7m, excluding land (the actual cost of which ultimately was $3.8m).

The Bridge Company initially raised $5m to build the bridge (having received a lower estimate for the work from another engineer).

Resourcing, Procurement and Logistics: The bridge was built by the New York Bridge Company, which was initially a private entity but later became a public body. John Roebling was engaged by the company as Chief Engineer in 1867. He was the leading bridge-builder and wire-manufacturer in the US at the time, and had previously produced proposals for a bridge over the East River. After his death in 1869, his son Washington took over as Chief Engineer.

Washington appointed 6 assistant engineers who were responsible for much of the construction activity – all 6 remained involved in the project until completion.

Numerous third party contracts were let by the company in the construction of the bridge. Key contracts were for construction of the caissons, air compressors for the caissons, the stone for the bridge towers, steel wire for the suspension cables and the suspenders, steel for the bridge deck, lumber for the caisson roofs (which would also provide part of the tower foundations) and for the bridge roadway. The award of these was initially the responsibility of the General Superintendent, William Kingsley, a major shareholder in the bridge company, and an established Brooklyn building contractor. A number of contracts were let to companies in which he had an interest. Other board members likewise appear to have sought to profit from their involvement in the project – most notably when a Brooklyn company was engaged to provide the wire for the suspension chains, despite having a questionable reputation and not submitting the cheapest bid, and was subsequently found to be supplying substandard wire by deceiving the inspection process.

The bridge company employed the on-site workforce engaged in the construction work. The size of this varied over the lifetime of the project. For example, there were over 260 men working in the caissons, 2 day shifts of 112 and a night shift of about 40. There was a rapid turnover of personnel – about one in three left each week. Other crews worked on other parts of the bridge (such as the bridge towers, the cable anchorages, spinning of the cables between the towers and assembly of the roadway). A stoneyard was also established to prepare the blocks for construction. 600 people were working on the bridge when work was halted in late 1878.

Human and Organisational Dynamics: Although the Bridge Company was a private company, many of its directors were highly politically active in Brooklyn and in New York. In 1875 the company reverted to being a public body, overseen by a group of trustees – many of whom however had previously been board members of the private company. The project took place against a backdrop of rivalry between the two cities, political corruption and intense public and media interest. The press were used by the various factions within the board to promote their own views and interests (and often to cause mischief).

Washington Roebling had strong support from a cadre of core directors and trustees, largely from the Brooklyn contingent, but as costs rose and the timescale extended there was also significant opposition, especially during the later years of construction as new participants became involved and there was increased criticism of his lack of on-site presence and his non-attendance at Board meetings – in fact many trustees had never met him – following his severe debilitation as a result of 'caisson sickness' (see below). Throughout this period he continued to direct the work, assisted by his wife Emily, to whom he dictated instructions, and who over time played an increasing role in the project.

For his part, Washington Roebling had little patience with the political intrigues which accompanied the project, and believed that much of the opposition he encountered was motivated by his resistance to any fraudulent schemes (although it seems that he was unable to prevent all of these). Roebling was contemptuous of many of the trustees, few of whom had any great understanding of engineering.

Even though the bridge was almost finished, the schisms in the board and the mutual antagonism between a group of the trustees and Roebling led in September 1882 to an attempt by the new mayor of Brooklyn to replace him as Chief Engineer. This was only narrowly defeated in a vote by the board of trustees.

Key Events: Work began on the project in 1869. However, while conducting surveys for the precise site of the Brooklyn tower, John Roebling trapped his foot between a ferry boat and the dock, contracted tetanus, and died shortly thereafter. Washington Roebling, who had been assisting his father and had also worked on the Cincinnati bridge, was appointed Chief Engineer in his stead.

Construction of the Brooklyn caisson commenced at the Webb and Bell yard on the East River, four miles from the bridge location, in 1869. It was launched in March 1870 and in May was towed downriver and manoeuvred into position, the site having been cleared and dredged to a uniform depth. The first courses of masonry for the towers were then laid on top of the fifteen feet thick wooden and concrete roof of the caisson, which helped to secure it in place on the river bed. Digging proceeded, until in December, with the excavation close to bedrock, fire broke out in the timber of the caisson roof. The caisson had to be flooded to extinguish the fire, which had burned through several layers of wood. Since the caisson roof would provide part of the foundations for the tower, the void created was filled with cement: however, as this work progressed it was discovered that a layer of charcoal remained: all the cement therefore had to be removed, the residual charcoal scraped away, and the entire void then refilled with wood and cement. This caused a 3 months delay to the project.

With bedrock finally reached the caisson itself was filled with concrete, and the foundations for the Brooklyn tower were completed in March 1871.

The New York caisson was launched in May 1871, and was manoeuvred into place for work to commence on the excavations for the second tower in September. At a depth of 45 feet below water level, men started to suffer from the mysterious 'caisson sickness' (also known as 'the bends'). Between January and May 1872 110 cases required treatment, and there were a number of fatalities. Washington Roebling himself was severely afflicted, and as a result for the remainder of the project he was an invalid and unable to be present on-site.

In May 1872 at a depth of 78 feet 6 inches digging in the New York caisson ceased. Although bedrock had not been reached, the sand and gravel was so compacted that it was adjudged to be sufficiently firm to support the tower. Filling of the caisson with concrete was completed in July 1872.

Construction of the Brooklyn tower finished in June 1875, and that of the New York tower in July 1876. Work on the Brooklyn cable anchorage began in 1873, and finished in 1875. The New York anchorage was completed in summer 1876. Later in 1876 the first wire rope was strung between the two towers, and the stringing of the cables commenced in earnest in 1877, completing in October 1878 (additional wires were added to strengthen the cables following the discovery of the substandard wire provided by the supplier).

Most of the work was put on hold for 6 months in 1878, due to financial difficulties caused by the withholding of funds by the New York authorities. This action appears to have been politically motivated, although it was claimed that in light of some serious safety incidents, including collapse of the approach road on the Brooklyn side, the bridge was dangerous, and it would also damage commerce by obstructing navigation. Moreover, by this point, the 'highly experimental' bridge had already cost $9 million, and was still far from finished. It was only after the Supreme Court of New York and then the Court of Appeals ordered the city to release the funds that work was able to progress.

Once work resumed in May 1879, the next activity was the hanging of the suspension wires, starting from each end of the bridge, with the steel lattice bridge deck suspended from these as the stringing of the wires progressed. This work was completed in December 1881.

In October 1881 Roebling submitted a request for an additional 1000 tonnes of steel to strengthen the bridge deck to enable it to carry trains as well as the tramcars previously intended. Despite the additional construction costs, this decision appears to have been made unilaterally by certain of the Brooklyn contingent without consultation and approval by the rest of the board, and led to the vote to replace Roebling as Chief Engineer.

The bridge was completed in spring 1883, and opened in May.

Outcomes: The bridge remains standing and operational today, carrying over 140,000 cars per day (the bridge was remodelled and strengthened between 1944 and 1954 to increase the highway capacity). It remained the longest suspension bridge in the world until 1903, when the nearby Williamsburg bridge supplanted it by just 7 feet. It was made a National Historic Landmark in 1964.

It is believed that around 28 people died in the building of the bridge.

4. London Heathrow Airport Terminal 5[9] – project undertaken by BAA between 2002 and 2008 (although the initial proposal to build a new terminal at Heathrow was first made in 1986 in a Government White Paper).

Objective: The project involved the construction of a new terminal at London's Heathrow airport to reduce congestion and increase capacity. Passenger volumes had risen to 68 million per annum in facilities designed to cope with 45 million. The new terminal was intended to increase the airport's capacity to 90 to 95 million passengers per annum (this without adding a third runway). There had been no major expansion of capacity at Heathrow since the introduction of Terminal 4 in 1986, despite the growth in air travel during the interim, the introduction of bigger aircraft, and the significance of Heathrow both as a global hub airport and in terms of its importance to the UK economy.

Initiation: Planning studies for the terminal commenced in February 1988 and the architect Richard Rogers was selected to design the terminal in 1989. BAA officially announced its proposal for T5 in May 1992, submitting a formal planning application on 17 February 1993. The planning inquiry ran from 1995 to 1999, and reported in November 2000. Consent for T5 to proceed was given by the Secretary of State in November 2001.

Feasibility/Key Challenges:
Planning - the new terminal was subject to the longest planning enquiry in UK history (taking 525 days over a period of nearly 4 years). The enquiry resulted in 700 stipulations impacting both the project and future operation of the airport, including for example decisions affecting the height, coverage and appearance of buildings; the provision of car parking; the times of day during which deliveries could take place to the site during construction; the number and times of flights; and acceptable noise levels.

Project scale – whilst under way, the project was the biggest construction project in Europe. As well as the terminal building and all the facilities associated with this, the project also entailed the extension of the Heathrow Express railway and Piccadilly underground lines; construction of a new road link to connect with the M25 motorway; construction of a new air traffic control tower for the airport; and the diversion of two rivers.

To accommodate the number of passengers, the design provided for a main terminal building 400 metres long and 160 metres wide, all under a single roof (68000 sq metres). For construction, the roof was split into 6 sections each of which took 5 to 7 weeks to lift into place. Prior to the actual lifts, a 12-week off-site trial roof lift was conducted in Yorkshire, which identified 125 areas of improvement.

The baggage system installed would be the biggest in world, incorporating 8km of high speed track, and 18km of ordinary conveyor belts, providing a capacity of 4000 bags per hour. Given that a number of other new airports and terminals had experienced significant problems with their baggage systems (most notably Denver, where opening was delayed over a year), a decision was taken to make use of tried and tested technology for the Terminal 5 system.

The undertaking in its entirety consisted of 18 main projects which were in turn subdivided into a total of 147 sub-projects. To manage this number of different activities, individual projects were given a high degree of autonomy, but this was overlain by rigorous programme management and monitoring of progress.

UK Construction industry problems and performance record – the industry had a poor reputation with a track record of cost overruns and late delivery. It was characterised by low profitability, under investment and poor client relationships. There was a tradition of contractors bidding low to win contracts, and then charging much higher amounts for any scope changes – this led to an aggressive, adversarial approach between contractors and their clients, often requiring the legal resolution of disputes. There was a fear that if the project followed the norm, it would be at least a year late and cost an additional £1 billion. Therefore the project team sought to find a different and more successful mode of engagement with its contractors (see below).

Logistics – as one of the world's busiest airports, it would not be possible to interrupt normal flight operations at Heathrow, so construction needed to take place around this. Linked to this, there were limitations imposed by the planning enquiry on working and delivery times, and also on the supply routes that could be used. There was limited space on-site to store the necessary construction materials. Off-site logistics centres were set up to receive deliveries, and materials were then transported to the site according to pre-booked delivery times as required. Significant use was made of prefabrication. There were also major challenges associated with the transport, accommodation and support of the on-site workforce which peaked at 8000 – as well as managing the number of new workers joining and departing (as many as 1000 joiners and 1000 leavers per month) as the project moved through its different phases.

Cost and Timing: The budget for the project was set at £4.3bn in 2003; the projected opening date of 30th March 2008 was set in 2001 (because it was felt that identifying a date would serve to galvanise the project).

The actual cost was in line with the budget, and the new terminal opened on schedule on 27th March 2008 (the precise date had been changed at British Airways' request for operational reasons) - although this was followed by some serious problems (see below).

Resourcing/Procurement: A key feature of the T5 project was the novel way in which BAA interacted with its contractors.[10] This was a response to previous cost overruns and poor delivery performance of major recent UK construction projects (such as the Millenium Dome, Wembley Stadium, the Channel Tunnel, Jubilee Line extension), as well as BAA's own experience following a tunnel collapse during the construction of the Heathrow Express rail link to Terminal 4 in 1994, which resulted in a crater in the Central Terminal Area of the airport.[11] In response to this incident, rather than seeking to allocate blame and taking legal action to pursue damages from any of the parties involved – which would have been time consuming and expensive - BAA had formed a joint team involving key suppliers to resolve the situation as quickly as possible. In this single team context, BAA concluded that it was infeasible to seek to transfer the financial risk to the suppliers through fixed price contracts for defined pieces of work, as would be the case under normal contracting arrangements. Instead they chose to retain the risk by means of contracts that provided suppliers with a margin on the costs they incurred, while at the same time aligning the interests of the integrated team and BAA by providing incentives to suppliers to encourage speedy resolution of the problems. Ultimately, the Heathrow Express opened on time, and the contracting approach was deemed to have been an important factor in contributing to this.

For the Terminal 5 project, this approach was codified into what was called the T5 Agreement.[12] This was a legally binding agreement signed by BAA and all the 'first tier' suppliers to the project. Under this arrangement, suppliers would receive a guaranteed margin on the costs they incurred (5% to 15% depending on trade) for delivery in line with industry best practice (which was defined, and then work was independently reviewed to ensure consistency with this), while a team incentive plan was put in place which would pay out additional bonuses if all suppliers working on a particular activity achieved exceptional performance. Rules were established to cover changes in requirements and the payment for any rework required. The suppliers' exposure was limited to loss of profit or the cost of insurance excess payments if they failed to deliver. Equally importantly, the T5 agreement also established a set of behavioural expectations, requiring collaborative working, co-location of personnel from different suppliers in the same offices, and an emphasis on solving problems rather than allocating blame.

As part of the arrangements, BAA took an active hands-on role in the project, acting as an intelligent and informed buyer and facilitator. Very unusually for a project of this scale, BAA chose not to use a main contractor to manage and oversee the project on its behalf. Instead, BAA effectively took on this role, employing a large number of staff on-site alongside the different project teams to support them and help resolve problems, and putting in place a sizeable central team to oversee and co-ordinate the integrated teams. A series of Key Performance Indicators (KPIs) were established to which suppliers were subject, with routine monthly reviews of this data with the principal contractors. Suppliers were also required to adhere to an 'open books' policy, under which they made their project financial accounts open to BAA for inspection (which of course was necessary in order to provide for the calculation of the margin), and a cost verification team was established to review all costs being charged to the project. Given the level of risk they were assuming, BAA also took out insurance covering around half of the value of the project. A disputes resolution process was established to deal with any serious disagreements with contractors and avoid recourse to the lawyers.

Ultimately, over 20000 different suppliers participated in the Terminal 5 supply chain, around 60 of whom were of key significance. During the first half of the project, there was a core of 10 to15 key organisations which were in the main established suppliers to BAA, and were therefore well placed to work in a 'partnering' way on the project. Subsequently, with many more suppliers on site, many of whom expected to work in a more traditional manner, there was a greater emphasis on oversight and monitoring of delivery, using the KPIs and cost verification mechanisms previously established. Over the course of the project, only 2 first tier contractors and a dozen subcontractors were removed from participation, and any significant legal cases relating to the project were avoided.

Human/Organisational Dynamics: As well as suppliers, the project had to interact with a with an array of stakeholders and interested parties, including national and local government and government agencies (such as immigration and customs), the public at large, especially those living in the vicinity of the airport, employees and trades unions, financial institutions, the (often critical) media, and airlines, notably of course British Airways (BA) as the sole occupier of Terminal 5. At times the relationship between BAA and BA appears to have been quite challenging. This perhaps is not entirely surprising: while both companies had a common interest in the project delivering on time, the relationship dynamics were nevertheless quite complex, given in particular the likely consequences of any delay or problems, not least in terms of reputational damage. For example, Doherty (a senior BAA employee) notes in her book on the project that BAA were concerned that BA might not be ready on schedule, but would seek to blame this on construction delays for which BAA were ultimately responsible – and in fact in his evidence to the House of Commons Transport Committee following the problems associated with the terminal's opening, BA CEO Willie Walsh pointed to the shortening of the time window available for testing and training due to late completion of the building.[13] BAA also appear to have been unconvinced that BA had access to sufficient major project and change management expertise to perform their role in the project fully. They expressed frustration at the length of time it took BA to decide whether to request BAA to undertake construction of the executive lounges at the terminal, to the point where this could have had an effect on the project's critical path. Equally, BA may have been suspicious that given the pressures facing BAA to complete the construction the airline would be presented with an imperfect facility that was not really ready for opening. While mechanisms and meetings were put in place which were able to provide for a sufficient level of alignment between the two companies for much of the project, and the two companies worked closely together in the immediate aftermath of the terminal's opening to resolve the problems which arose, the (new) CEO of BAA, Colin Matthews, stated in his evidence to the House of Commons Transport Committee that in his view some of the difficulties encountered were attributable to a deterioration in the quality of interactions between the two organisations in the lead up to opening.[14]

The introduction of the new terminal also provided an opportunity to implement new ways of working. This was against a prevailing backdrop of poor labour relations at the airport. The project sought active engagement with the unions in agreeing the changes required, although where disagreements occurred – for example in relation to new work rosters - a strategy of communicating directly with the workforce rather than through the unions was adopted. In evidence provided by union representatives to the House of Commons Transport Committee in 2008 there was a degree of residual resentment towards both BAA and BA that there had been insufficient involvement of unions and workers in determining the new working practices and in the manner of engagement.[15]

Key Events: Construction of the buildings' foundation began in September 2002. In November of the following year, work started on the steel superstructure of the main terminal building. By January 2005 the nine tunnels needed to provide road and rail access, and to provide drainage, were completed. In March of the same year, the sixth and final section of the main terminal roof was lifted into position, and in December the building was made weatherproof. Installation of the baggage system commenced in 2005, and was completed at the end of September 2007. The handover from construction to Operational Readiness took place on September 17th. Ideally all building work except for some retail fit-out would have been completed by this point, but in reality some construction had to be carried over. During the period between September 2007 and March 2008 a total of 68 proving trials, involving over 15000 members of the public and all terminal stakeholders, were undertaken to test the operational readiness of Terminal 5 prior to its opening.

The new terminal became operational on 27th March 2008. From this date onwards, all BA flights formerly using Terminal 1 (mainly domestic and European short-haul flights) were transferred to the new terminal. This was approximately 70 per cent of BA's flights from Heathrow, but only around 50 per cent of passengers and just over 50 per cent of bags. The transfer was a significant logistical exercise and many activities had to be undertaken overnight after all flight departures and arrivals from Terminal 1 the previous day had been completed.

As was widely reported, significant problems were encountered on opening.[16] The immediate cause of these problems was the baggage system reached capacity (10000 bags), and therefore (as designed) automatically shut down, which then also resulted in delays to the check-in process. This meant in the first instance that a number of flights were late taking off or took off without all bags on board; subsequently it led to significant numbers of flight cancellations (636 out of 4095 over the first 11 days) as BAA and BA sought to resolve the problems. Between 27th and 31st March 23205 bags required manual sorting and screening prior to being returned to passengers - although by 7th May only around 125 bags had not been successfully reunited with their owners.

A number of different factors appear to have contributed to this situation. Firstly, many staff arriving for work at the new terminal had difficulties parking their cars. The main car park became full by 4.30am, but there were then delays in redirecting staff to the overflow car park. This led to traffic congestion, which in turn delayed arriving vehicles and buses transferring staff from the car parks to the terminal. Secondly, there were delays in those staff who were employed on the 'airside' of the terminal (in the security controlled area) passing through security. This was due to problems with one of the scanners, which required the northern staff security check-point to be shut down for a period of time, and all staff to be redirected to the southern check-point. Moreover, the number of people seeking to gain airside access was between 40 and 50 per cent greater than anticipated (believed at least in part to have been a result of additional people turning up to spectate and be part of the initial opening, even though they were not scheduled to be present at that time). Further delays in staff reaching their actual work locations may also have resulted from lack of familiarity with the layout of the terminal, and problems with a hand held work allocation tool used by BA personnel - although this had previously been used by some BA staff at other terminals, it was acknowledged not to be working perfectly, and according to union representatives, not all users at Terminal 5 had been fully trained in its operation. These factors appear to have combined to cause a shortage of staff to be on hand to remove bags from the baggage system and place them in the containers which would in turn be taken to and loaded onto aircraft.

Additionally, some software problems were experienced with the baggage system, partly associated with some parameters which had previously been set for testing not having been reset for live operation (although BAA believed that this should only have affected bags transferring from other airlines). A number of difficulties were also experienced with the handheld barcode readers which were used to ensure that the bags and their owners travelling on particular flights could be fully reconciled, including inability of some users to log on (mainly due to password-related and user set-up problems), and lack of working wireless access on a number of aircraft stands, which meant that the devices could not connect to the system.

The combination of these different problems occurring at the same time led to a build-up of a backlog of bags which caused the system to stop. This in turn meant that the automatic re-allocation of bags to new flights where they had missed their original flight had to be turned off and a manual process instigated, which took significantly longer. At 5pm on 27th March BA was forced to suspend acceptance of checked baggage. Passengers were still able to travel, but they were not able to take any checked baggage.

A number of other operational issues were also experienced, although they may not have had any significant bearing on the core baggage backlog problem - for example, there were some difficulties in positioning the jetties correctly for different aircraft (attributed to unfamiliarity with the new equipment), which resulted in them being moved outside their limits, in turn causing them to stop working until they had been reset by an engineer; 28 lifts (out of a total of 275 across the complex) were not operational; and painting of some of the corridors was still in progress.

All parties acknowledged that the problems stemmed from insufficient testing and staff familiarisation and training. BAA stated that there had been over 20 trials of the baggage system when fully loaded. However, they acknowledged that there were three elements to the end to end baggage handling process, namely loading bags onto the system, moving bags through the system, and then unloading bags from it to transfer to planes, and that while the first two of these had been thoroughly trialled, the third had not been tested as rigorously. This was obviously a point of interface between BAA and BA, and the CEO of BAA acknowledged that there had been tensions between the two companies in the run-up to the opening (although he only took over this position on 1st April, after the terminal had opened). BA argued that it had been necessary to compromise on some of the testing due to delays in the building programme.

In terms of preparing staff for the move to the new terminal, a multi-year Operational Readiness and employee engagement programme had been put in place. This had involved a number of stages, beginning with an overview for staff of the benefits of moving to Terminal 5. In some cases the move required changes in roles and operating practices, and led to significant employee dissatisfaction. In the lead up to the opening, activities were undertaken to familiarise staff with the new facility, including visits, training for customer services staff in new working practices, and proving trials. Detailed checklists were developed for the 'go-live', in part because it was recognised that one of the important lessons from other airport openings was that 'It was little details like people going home with keys in their pockets and no one knowing where the spare keys were that caused problems'.[17]

BA staff had been provided familiarisation and training which had taken between 2 and 4 days. Total attendance had been 94 per cent. Attendance by BA baggage handling staff had been approximately 85 per cent. The familiarisation had consisted of an overview briefing about the new terminal, a tour of the buildings, and a detailed introduction to individuals' actual place of work, where people were shown around the area and where they would need to report, how the processes would work, and the equipment that they would be using. However, it was acknowledged that the process had its limitations, principally because the site was not fully complete, and not all areas were accessible. Therefore the building was different on day one from when they had been trained, and it was recognised that as a result many staff did not feel fully comfortable in their new environment. Actual 'hands-on' training with the new equipment was not provided as part of the familiarisation exercise, since this was largely equipment with which staff would previously have been familiar. However, there were some changes to operational procedures at Terminal 5 compared to those used at Terminals 1 and 4 (in light of this, more hands-on training was provided to staff whose activities transferred subsequently to Terminal 5). Ultimately, BA CEO Willie Walsh accepted that BA staff 'were not as familiar as they should have been and that impacted on their performance'.[18]

Although BA admitted that in light of the reduced time available for testing and training they had given some consideration to deferring the opening, this would have caused significant logistical problems both for BA and BAA, especially if such a decision was taken at the last minute. Moreover, from BA's operational perspective, the best time to undertake the transfer to the new terminal was at the beginning of a business season, and after end March the next one of these was end October, which would have resulted in a six month deferral. BA recognised that there were risks associated with going ahead in March, but they believed they were sufficiently prepared to proceed. Ultimately the costs of the disruption that arose and the reputational damage suffered were considered likely to have been lower than the costs of an extended delay (and presumably such a delay would itself also have had reputational consequences). Some consideration had also been given to transferring a smaller number of flights initially rather than the 'big bang' approach that was ultimately adopted, but this was considered to have been too logistically complex given the way flights were organised and aircraft were allocated to flights (likewise, consideration was also given to transferring more activities, including those at Terminal 4, but this was dismissed as too risky).

BAA also noted that in hindsight they may have created an expectation of perfection ahead of the Terminal's opening, and in light of the complexity of the programme and previous experiences at other airports, such as Denver and Hong Kong, they may have been better served by a more 'humble' approach.[19]

Ultimately, the worst of the difficulties were resolved within two weeks of the terminal's opening. BA first operated a full schedule of flights at the terminal on 8th April 2008. The planned transfer of BA long-haul flights from Terminal 4, scheduled for 30th April 2008 was deferred until 5th June, when it took place without serious incident. The opening of the second satellite building (Terminal 5C, containing an additional 12 departure gates), built at a cost of £340m, took place in May 2011, a year later than planned.[20] The delays were partly due to design changes to accommodate the new Airbus 380 'superjumbo' aircraft.[21] During the period prior to its completion, BA were forced to bus around 20 per cent of passengers from the main terminal to and from aircraft parked at stands located away from the terminal; with the opening of the new satellite, this reduced to only 5 per cent.[22]

Outcomes: Despite the problems experienced on opening, and the late completion of the second satellite, Heathrow Terminal 5 appears in retrospect to have been a successful project, delivering largely to time and to budget, and achieving the objective of reducing congestion and increasing capacity at the airport. In 2012, 28.1 million passengers on 193,440 flights passed through the terminal.[23]

CHAPTER 2: A FRAMEWORK FOR THINKING ABOUT IT PROJECTS

Well, that was all very interesting, but the point of looking at what are of course engineering and construction projects, in a book which purports to be about IT projects, is to see what they might tell us that is of relevance in helping us think about IT projects. And particularly, what they can tell us about what it is that makes projects hard.

Implicit in this is an assumption that these projects were indeed hard - and it would seem hard (that word once more) to dispute this. Firstly, at least three of the four would generally be considered major engineering feats, 'wonders of the industrial world', and while the fourth project, Heathrow Terminal 5, might not entirely qualify for such a label, it was while it was underway the largest construction project in Europe, so was certainly no trivial undertaking. Clearly, all of the projects identified had to overcome significant difficulties and obstacles - some expected, some unexpected - to achieve their intended objective. Some of these difficulties are referred to in the 'Key Challenges' section of each mini-study, so it's not necessary to repeat them here. In addition, other difficulties emerged as the projects progressed – for example the fires in John Scott Russell's shipyard, the issues with the launch, or the explosion during the sea trials that afflicted the Great Eastern, the fires in the Brooklyn Bridge caisson, the outbreak of 'caisson sickness', or the wire fraud, or the extent of problems experienced at Terminal 5 on opening. Likewise, none of the projects seem to have been entirely immune from supplier relationships and human dynamics difficulties of one sort or another. Another indication of difficulty is that – with the possible exception of Heathrow Terminal 5 – they all cost more and/or took longer to build than planned.

If then they were indeed hard, the nub of the question is: what was it that made them so?

In the first instance, it might be suggested that they were hard because they were unique. Certainly none of them had been undertaken before in anything resembling the form they took. And in fact most definitions of the term project emphasise the importance of uniqueness as a key characteristic (eg Smith 1995: 'a one-time unique endeavour by people to do something that has not been done that way before'; Project Management Institute: 'a temporary group activity designed to produce a unique product, service or result').[1] Hence, all projects, even relatively unspectacular and mundane ones, appear to have elements of uniqueness about them - for example, while a bridge over a motorway is in many respects just another bridge over a motorway, with no end of previous precedents, the particular location of the bridge, the circumstances surrounding it, and the point in time when construction is undertaken contribute to making it a unique project. Perhaps there is something here about 'degrees of uniqueness' (recognising of course that this may be something of a contradiction in terms), insofar as some projects – like those in the mini-studies – appear to be unique in more respects than others, such as our motorway bridge. This said, even in the case of the celebrated projects referred to in the mini-studies, there were still previous projects that provided lessons and experiences upon which the projects in question could draw: for example Smeaton's Eddystone Lighthouse in the case of the Bell Rock Lighthouse, or the Cincinatti Bridge in the case of the Brooklyn Bridge. And clearly there had been plenty of new airports and airport terminals built and brought into operation before Heathrow Terminal 5. So even these trail-blazing projects were not entirely without precedent. But they all contained or involved unique aspects, without which they would have been that much more straightforward. For example, much of the difficulty faced by the Bell Rock Lighthouse came from the offshore location – it would have been a much simpler project to build the same lighthouse onshore. It might therefore be suggested that the more unique the undertaking, the harder it is likely to be; especially given that human beings by and large get better at doing difficult things the more they repeat them, the more experienced they are at doing them, and the more practice they have. This means that the first time we undertake any particular task – which is clearly always the case for any activity which is unique - is the time we are likely to find it most difficult, as there is no opportunity to build up learned experience. This should resonate with anyone who has ever attempted to assemble a flat-packed wardrobe for the first time.[2]

This said, uniqueness does not appear to be the only factor which gave rise to the difficulties encountered by the projects examined in the mini-studies. A second characteristic of all of these was that they were multi-faceted undertakings, and many of the difficulties experienced were implicit in the myriad of different activities involved, some of which were inherently complex. For example, building further on this point about the degree of difficulty faced by the Bell Rock Lighthouse being reduced had it been built onshore, it's apparent that were this the case the difficulties encountered by the project would not have been eliminated entirely. Clearly, there would still have been difficulties in building a lighthouse with the technology then prevailing regardless of where it was constructed. Some of this would have come from the uniqueness of the particular circumstances associated with any particular construction site; but some of it would have derived from the fundamental complexity involved in building a lighthouse, any lighthouse, irrespective of its situation. Those who are interested are referred to 'The Lighthouse Stevensons', by Bella Bathurst (2005)[3], which - amongst other things - considers a number of different lighthouse construction projects undertaken by various members of the Stevenson family over a period of three quarters of a century. What this shows is that while the precise nature of the challenges faced in each case was shaped by the particular location and context of the lighthouse's construction, many of these challenges were the same in all cases. For example, all the lighthouses involved: the acknowledgement in the first place that a lighthouse was required in that particular location, and obtaining the support and approval for construction to proceed; the sites had to be surveyed to determine the constraints on and the options relating to the design of the lighthouse; the determination of a detailed design and specification of the lighthouse; the provision of funding, materials and labour; the organisation of the activity into a logical sequence; the transportation of materials; any necessary arrangements to support the labour force on-site (potentially including transport, accommodation and food supplies); co-ordination and supervision of the construction activity; measures to ensure the work was of appropriate quality and in accordance with the design...and so on. It seems likely therefore that such undertakings would inevitably involve at least some degree of difficulty even in the most benign of situations, and regardless of the sophistication of the technology available. Hence it appears that there are a set of difficulties – or perhaps 'complexities' is a better word here, since this points to their multi-faceted and potentially interconnected nature (one definition of 'complex' being 'something so complicated or interconnected as to make the whole *hard* to understand or to deal with' – my italics) - inherent in any lighthouse project (and likewise, in any bridge project, or ship-building project, and perhaps therefore any IT project), which are given precise expression by the particular context in which the project takes place.

In fact, we can probably go further than this – many of the items included in the above list of complexities inherent in any lighthouse construction project would also apply to any other project; and in fact, as the mini studies demonstrate, there are a number of what we might call 'sources of complexity' which seem to be common across all of the projects, regardless of the nature of the project. In all cases, a significant part of the project delivery, and of the difficulties encountered, involved a diverse assortment of practical, technical, logistical, organisational and human dynamic-related challenges which needed to be overcome. While the significance of these different challenges, and the precise nature of the difficulties experienced, varied from project to project, none of the projects was immune from these.

What is also noteworthy about the various difficulties encountered is that although the projects featured in the mini-studies were all engineering projects, only some of the facets encountered by them and the difficulties they faced concerned engineering matters per se, or even engineering related matters. While the significance of organisational and logistical issues is perhaps unsurprising, given the emphasis placed on such activities in any project management textbook, perhaps more interesting is the prevalence of 'human factors' in all the projects – since in all cases, the human dynamics between the different participants and interest groups involved with or impacted by the project seem to have provided a significant source of complexity for the project in question.

At this point, it is probably necessary to acknowledge that there may be at least a degree of tautology involved in using 'inherent difficulties/complexities' as part of the explanation for why projects are hard. It might seem that I'm suggesting that projects are hard because they are difficult, which is perhaps not very helpful. But the essential point appears to be that projects are multi-faceted activities, made up of a substantial number of different aspects, some unique to the particular project in question, and some common to many and in some cases all projects. All of these different facets or aspects entail at least some degree of difficulty, which is made more or less severe by the particular context in which the project takes place. This implies that by understanding all of these different facets and the nature of the complexity implicit within them in the context of the particular project in question, we can build up an appreciation of the overall degree of difficulty facing the project. The key challenge therefore is to make these explicit. We will return to this point below.

One further potential category of difficulties emerges from the mini-studies. This might be described, in the words of former Prime Minister Harold MacMillan (although there is some dispute as to whether he actually said this), as 'Events, dear boy, events'.[4] Perhaps inevitably, all the projects referred to experienced things happening which were outside their control, or which were unexpected, or at least

40

unpredictable, to which the project then had to respond. In the former category were things like the severity of the storms affecting the Bell Rock lighthouse – which should not have been entirely unexpected, as storms were certain to occur, and there was a strong likelihood that at least some of these would be severe, although the timing of these was clearly unpredictable. On the other hand, the 'mutiny', or the embargo on ship movements would have been more difficult to anticipate – although this said, given the nature of the activity and the circumstances prevailing, the possibility of such events occurring could perhaps still have been recognised. In fact, it seems that the particular nature of the events which afflicted the projects derived from the context in which they took place (as in the case of the Bell Rock storms), and from the activities being undertaken (as in the case of the mutiny, which resulted from the approach to resourcing and labour relations adopted by the project, again in the context of the offshore location). It is perhaps possible to argue therefore that such events constitute a manifestation of some of the contextual and inherent difficulties encountered by projects.

Once an event has occurred, or a situation has arisen, clearly insofar as possible the project will need to take action to respond to it; in some cases in the mini-studies, where there was no way of influencing the situation, the response was what might be termed 'passive', for example the clearing up and rectification of the site following the storms at Bell Rock. But in other cases, it was rather more active, for example in response to the mutiny, or the embargo on ship movements, where Stephenson sought to intervene and shape future events in a way that was beneficial to the project.

Whilst some 'events' are clearly visible and dramatic – such as a storm - there are others which are less obvious and take place over a longer period of time which nevertheless serve to change the situation prevailing and give rise to implications for the project. Under these circumstances, it may be that the response from the project is more obvious than the events which gave rise to it – such as with the decision to reinforce the bridge deck of the Brooklyn Bridge. This was clearly a conscious decision taken by the project in the face of a particular situation, but the changes and events which led to this situation were not especially visible. In terms of our analysis therefore, it is important to distinguish between those events which are themselves the source of difficulty for the project, and those which represent the response of the project to events and changes taking place, which may not always be particularly obvious, at least to the external observer.

As well as the response to such events and changes being a key project management activity, it is perhaps also worth noting that the prediction and avoidance of such events is very often the primary focus of much project risk analysis - perhaps at times at the expense of consideration of some of the broader suite of complexities likely to face the project.

This analysis gives rise therefore to a 'three pronged' framework for describing the various 'sources of complexity' affecting any project. This starts with the unique context in which the project takes place (which reflects its geographical location, the time in which the project is undertaken and the prevailing technology, the political and social circumstances surrounding the project, the mix of individuals involved and so on). Combined with these, are a set of inherent complexities implicit in the activities which make up the project. Some of these may be specific to projects of a particular type (so for example, the complexities inherent in all lighthouse projects will be different from those inherent in all ship-building projects), but some of them – covering considerations like obtaining support and funding, accessing resources to undertake the project, co-ordinating the activities, and dealing with relationship dynamics among the participants - appear to be generic and common across all projects. These are then overlain by another category of difficulties associated with events and changes happening which impact the project which are unexpected, unpredictable, or outside its control – and possibly all three. In the case of any one project, these three categories of complexity appear to be interlinked: in that the complexity inherent in any particular activity combines with the specific context in which it takes place to produce the unique mix of complexities facing the project; and together these shape the particular events to which the project is subject.

Such an analysis seems to have some similarities with a common conceptualisation of project management as being fundamentally concerned with the management of risk and uncertainty (see Turner, 2009)[5]. By and large the greater the complexity and the more difficult the project, the greater the risk of problems arising. This said, in my experience, an emphasis particularly on risk tends to place undue focus on the events component of our framework, and on the identification of potential problems and how these might be avoided, or at least mitigated, rather than on dealing with complexities which are already – or at least should already – be known because they are implicit in the activity being undertaken and the prevailing situation. Perhaps therefore a conceptualisation of project management as the management of complexity provides a more comprehensive description of the broader activity set.

The three-pronged framework proposed here provides a way of thinking about the underlying backdrop to the project and the challenges to be encountered and addressed by it. Building on this, it seems reasonable to suggest that an essential part of project management activity is to understand the complexities that are prevalent or likely to be faced in undertaking the project, secondly to make good choices about how to address these, and then thirdly to ensure that the necessary actions are performed properly to address them. This also emphasises the point that projects are not simply deterministic, technical activities, where a particular need in a particular situation combined with the investment of resources will result in a predictable given outcome. As the mini-studies serve to illustrate, throughout the project process, there are choices to be made; moreover, even in the case of these celebrated, 'blue riband' projects, these choices were not necessarily fully informed, nor were the outcomes of these choices always perfectly delivered.

Probably the most important choices to be made in relation to any project are those made very early in its life, namely whether or not to proceed, and what form the project should take (each of which to some extent informs the other). One might suggest that these choices were somewhat more straightforward in the case of the Bell Rock Lighthouse or the Brooklyn Bridge, given a recognisable need along with significant situational constraints which limited the options available in terms of design and delivery, than in the case of the Great Eastern, where there was a perceived opportunity and then considerable flexibility around how to pursue this (although much of this flexibility was forgone by the decision - itself of course a choice - that the vessel should be capable of making the journey to Australia without refuelling). Moreover, as all the mini-studies show, as the projects progressed, they were faced with any number of decisions and choices, some of which had profound implications for the subsequent evolution of the project. One particular area which seems to have proved problematic for both the Great Eastern and the Brooklyn Bridge relates to the choices made in relation to key suppliers to the projects; in the case of the Great Eastern, this concerned especially the choice of John Scott Russell's shipyard to build the ship; in that of the Brooklyn Bridge the selection of the wire supplier likewise proved a source of considerable subsequent difficulty for the project. While in the latter case those responsible for choosing a wire supplier may have been fully aware of the ramifications of the choice made, Brunel's critical decision to accept Scott Russell's bid to build the ship seems to have been taken somewhat casually, without a full consideration of its implications (such as the small size of the yard, the degree of pilfering prevalent, Scott Russell's financial situation, and the potential consequences for launching). This serves to illustrate that the backdrop of complexity facing the project as described in our framework is 'filtered' by the degree of information and understanding of that backdrop on the part of those responsible for the project – and perhaps also by their motivations, which as the case of the Brooklyn Bridge wire supplier selection decision suggests, may not always be aligned with the successful and efficient completion of the project; in turn, these factors may contribute to sub-optimal choices.

In practice, of course, no project protagonist – even one as brilliant, gifted and experienced as Brunel - is ever likely to have a comprehensive appreciation of all the facets of a complex project (despite having previously built two ships, the Great Western and the Great Britain, Brunel was not a shipbuilder as such, and he had in fact engaged Scott Russell initially because he needed advice on ship hull design). Additionally, given their uniqueness, and hence an absence of precedents, projects will inevitably be faced with unknowns and uncertainties (of course, the greater the degree of uniqueness, the fewer the applicable precedents and the greater the uncertainty). This said, even if there are no direct precedents, the extent of the unknowns and the degree of uncertainty is likely to be reduced the greater the applicable knowledge and prior experience of those responsible.

In terms of our framework, these seem to imply a second aspect to the model, relating to the quality of the project activity in response to the difficulties encountered, as determined by things like the understanding of the circumstances and the difficulties being faced, the wisdom of the choices made, and the level of funding and resources available in light of these difficulties. Much of this appears to be underpinned by the expertise and experience of those involved with the project. Combining this with the three-pronged 'sources of complexity' construct gives us a two-sided model for thinking about projects. One side concerns the unique nature of the project and the complexities faced by it; the other side relates to the nature and quality of the response to these complexities. These can be conceptualised at an aggregate level as two opposing forces, which ideally should be in equilibrium for the project to achieve a successful outcome. If the response is insufficient to address the complexities, the project will fail – or will at least struggle until the response is increased in terms of quality and/or quantity (eg of resources) to a level commensurate with what the project demands; however, if the response is greater than required given the complexity encountered (the project equivalent of a sledgehammer to crack a nut), the project will cost more and consume extra resources than it really needed to. This said, in practice, the opposing forces construct probably works at a more detailed level within the project, in that each individual facet or component of the project needs to be understood and addressed effectively with a response commensurate with the degree of difficulty in question. Ultimately, the project needs to achieve a 'passing grade' in dealing with each element of complexity it encounters; otherwise it will fail. The definition of 'passing grade' probably depends on the criticality of the aspect - that is to say, the more important this is in terms of the project as a whole, then the more demanding the achievement of a 'passing grade' becomes. Thus in all the projects referred to, ensuring that there was a feasible design was clearly critical to the project's success, and without this the project would unquestionably have failed. On the other hand, the problems experienced by Brunel in connection with his relationship with Scott Russell, or the fact that in the aftermath of the Brooklyn Bridge wire fraud it proved possible to strengthen the bridge cabling by adding extra wire suggests that there may be a degree of flexibility available in achieving the pass mark in relation to some aspects of the project. This said, the pass mark also needs to be achieved within a set of cost, timescale and quality constraints – and here it might reasonably be argued that the relationship problems between Brunel and Scott Russell on the Great Eastern, and the need to add additional wire to the Brooklyn Bridge cables, contributed to the cost and timescale overruns which both projects suffered. For less important aspects of a project, in some cases a passing grade may be as simple as implementing some form of workaround or 'avoidance strategy' such that the element in question is no longer relevant - but this is still likely to require a degree of attention by the project to arrive at this position (for example, given the difficulties experienced by Stevenson in obtaining the red glass he wanted for the light, he could have chosen to use ordinary clear glass – this would have eliminated a difficulty facing the project, although it would have required a conscious decision, and would also have resulted in a reduction to some extent in the 'quality' of the solution).

This model is shown diagrammatically in Figure 1 below.

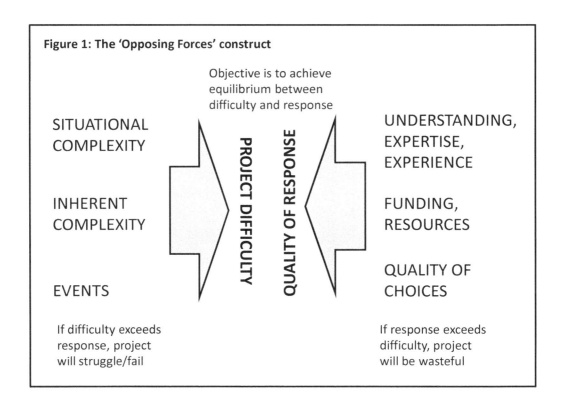

Figure 1: The 'Opposing Forces' construct

Objective is to achieve equilibrium between difficulty and response

SITUATIONAL COMPLEXITY

INHERENT COMPLEXITY

EVENTS

PROJECT DIFFICULTY

QUALITY OF RESPONSE

UNDERSTANDING, EXPERTISE, EXPERIENCE

FUNDING, RESOURCES

QUALITY OF CHOICES

If difficulty exceeds response, project will struggle/fail

If response exceeds difficulty, project will be wasteful

Then, as a test of the model's viability, Table 1 attempts to apply the framework to the Bell Rock Lighthouse project. Building on the mini-study contained in the previous chapter, the table seeks to identify the principal facets of the project which contributed to the complexity encountered, and for each of these to show how that complexity was addressed in the completion of the project.

TABLE 1: ANALYSIS OF THE BELL ROCK LIGHTHOUSE USING THE 'OPPOSING FORCES' APPROACH[6]

Type of Complexity	Specific Aspect	Implication/Response
Situational/ Contextual Complexity (contributing to project uniqueness)	Offshore location	Imposed design and logistical challenges (eg re strength of structure required, transportation of materials and labour, accommodation and provisioning of labour – see below).
	Tidal range	Restricted working to low tide only (until construction exceeded high tide level).
	Weather/storms	Restricted working to summer months only, required suspension of work at other times and provision of safe accommodation on site (on board ships, latterly the Beacon House).
	Geology/bedrock	Required excavation of foundations by hand, due to risk of fracturing rock if explosives used.
	Prevailing technology	Eddystone Lighthouse demonstrated feasibility of offshore construction; also introduced new innovations in lighthouse design and building (eg oak tree shape, pre-shaped interlocking blocks, quick drying cement, balance crane).
	Northern Lighthouse Board	Established in 1876 as the body responsible for lighthouses in Scotland – it was highly political and chronically underfunded. Robert Stevenson was appointed Chief Engineer to the Board in 1800. Board elected to appoint the older and more well-known John Rennie as Chief Engineer for the Bell Rock.
	War with France	Led to difficulties in terms of recruitment/retention of labour (due to risk of capture by press gangs), and provided the backdrop to the 1809 shipping embargo – see below.
Inherent Complexity	Recognition of Need	Ships experienced severe difficulties entering Firth of Forth, and there was a high incidence of shipwrecks (eg HMS York, 1804).
	Support and Approval	Major storms in 1799 and sinking of HMS York in 1804 created 'quorum' of support to proceed; ultimately Act of Parliament passed in 1806 to authorise Northern Lighthouse Board to undertake construction and to raise funds required.
	Site survey to identify suitable site	Largely undertaken by Stevenson (Rennie visited once prior to start of construction). Stevenson's first visit convinced him that a lighthouse on pillars would not be feasible, and a solid stone construction like at the Eddystone would be required, an assessment subsequently confirmed by Rennie.
	Detailed design and specification	Stevenson and Rennie both produced designs, both of which drew heavily on Smeaton's Eddystone Lighthouse as a template. The lighthouse as built closely resembled Stevenson's design.

TABLE 1: ANALYSIS OF THE BELL ROCK LIGHTHOUSE USING THE 'OPPOSING FORCES'
APPROACH (contd)

Type of Complexity	Specific Aspect	Implication/Response
Inherent Complexity [contd]	Provision of funding	Provided by Northern Lighthouse Board, which was permitted to borrow £25000 towards the project.
	Provision of materials	Granite sourced from quarries in Aberdeenshire, and sandstone from Mylnefield quarry near Dundee, and subsequently from Craigleith Quarry near Edinburgh; stoneyard established at Arbroath to shape the blocks; forge established on the rock to maintain tools. Other materials included mortar mixes, cements, wedges and trenails.
	Provision of equipment	Fleet of ships established as part of the project – some of these were purchased and converted (eg *Pharos* – floating light vessel) or built specially for the project – eg *Smeaton* as a tender for the floating light and to transport stone, *Sir Joseph Banks* as floating accommodation for workers on site. Other equipment included rail tracks and wagons, carts, cranes, winches, pumps, jacks, hammers and pickaxes.
	Provision of labour	3 main groups were required – builders, situated on the rock; seamen, to operate the various ships; and stonecutters, to shape the blocks in the stoneyard. Stevenson sought to employ workers who he had employed previously and trusted. Measures were taken to protect the labour force from press gangs.
Events	Storms	Construction was interrupted by frequent storms, which also caused loss and damage to equipment (eg cranes, rail tracks).
	'Mutiny'	Complaints about the beer ration led to talk of a strike – which was averted when Stevenson threatened to turn any strikers over to the press gangs.
	Shipping embargo	Progress delayed for ten days when an embargo was placed on all British shipping due to the war with France, preventing the supply boats leaving port. Stevenson persuaded the Arbroath port officer to take a 'liberal' view of his orders, and permit sailings to resume.

Table 1 suggests that there were at least twenty or so important facets of the project which contributed to the complexity and the difficulty encountered, and which in turn required an appropriate response on the part of those responsible for the project to be successful. From this example, it seems reasonable to assert that the framework has at least some value as a way of helping to organise the way we look at and think about projects and to understand what it is that makes them hard. This said, it might still be argued that the projects referred to in the mini-studies were such obviously extremely difficult and challenging ones – 'Wonders of the Industrial World' – that a framework which is derived from them is unlikely to be particularly applicable to less celebrated and more mundane undertakings, which form the vast majority of projects. Of course, less celebrated and more mundane undertakings rarely – if ever – end up being written about, so it's not easy from readily accessible sources either to confirm or dispute this. However, taking one somewhat unremarkable project known to me (and for which information is available via various on-line sources), and seeking to apply the framework to it, provides at least an indication as to whether the framework has some degree of general applicability. The project in question involved the implementation of a pedestrian crossing to replace a footbridge over a six lane section of dual carriageway on the A40 in Denham, Buckinghamshire – which is just a few miles from where I live.[7] The decision to remove the bridge (which had been built in 1966) resulted from it having been severely damaged after being hit by a mobile crane in early 2011. In the short term the bridge was closed, some parts of it were removed, a temporary crossing controlled by traffic signals was put in place, and the speed limit was reduced to 30mph. Three options were considered in terms of the longer term solution: repair of the bridge, replacement with a new bridge, or replacement with a new 'Puffin' pedestrian crossing involving the installation of traffic signals. In the event the last of these was chosen. Under the circumstances this was felt to be the safest option, as the evidence suggested that the footbridge had not been well used, with most people choosing to cross at ground level. In addition input from local residents participating in a consultation process favoured the Puffin crossing; some (mainly elderly) users of the crossing had found the footbridge difficult to traverse, and other residents considered the footbridge to have been an eyesore which also reduced their privacy. Finally, the ground level crossing was also the lowest cost option, most importantly in terms of lower ongoing maintenance costs - as it was expected that the crane owner's insurance would cover any initial construction costs. As part of the new arrangement, it was also decided to narrow the carriageway to four lanes (two in each direction) and reduce the speed limit to 40mph – which was favoured by residents, although motorists who participated in the consultation process preferred a solution which provided for the restoration of the speed limit to the original 50mph. The consultation and decision making process took a number of months. Works commenced on-site in early 2012. These were designed and undertaken by Transport for Buckinghamshire, with specialist assistance from a third party engineering services and construction company. In early 2012 the bridge supports were removed. This involved overnight road closures for several nights. The work to narrow the carriageways also resulted in a programme of lane closures, sometimes reducing the road to single lane operation in both directions, leading at times to considerable congestion. Further overnight closures were necessitated in mid 2012 to allow for resurfacing of the roadway.

Table 2 below seeks to use the framework to view this initiative. Clearly I'm biased, but it seems to me that this helps reveal the various different aspects of this – apparently relatively straightforward – project, giving a clearer sense of the complexity involved, and providing at least some indication of why it should have taken as long as it did from the damage occurring to the original bridge to the completion of the new traffic crossing.   While one might perhaps argue whether in light of this analysis this project can genuinely be described as 'hard', equally it seems clear that it can't reasonably be considered to have been entirely straightforward – and the framework serves to make the reasons for this explicit. More importantly, though, it does seem from this that the framework has general applicability to a wider variety of projects beyond just those which are spectacular.

But the real question for us here is to understand what this might tell us about IT projects.

TABLE 2: ANALYSIS OF THE FOOTBRIDGE REPLACEMENT PROJECT USING THE 'OPPOSING FORCES' APPROACH

Type of Complexity	Specific Aspect	Implication/Response
Situational/ Contextual Complexities (contributing to project uniqueness)	Severe damage to existing footbridge	Required action to repair/replace; insurance claim pursued to contribute to costs involved.
	Busy 6-lane dual carriageway	Some form of crossing required given the need for pedestrians to traverse the road and the volume of traffic; importance of the route and the volume of traffic imposed constraints on work (eg in terms of road or lane closures).
	Existing footbridge ageing, not well used, and unpopular with local residents	Encouraged adoption of 'ground level' solution rather than repair of existing bridge or construction of new one.
	Legal constraints	Legal duty on the part of the council to minimise risk and safety issues. Requirement to undertake appropriate consultations if crossings on roads for which it has authority are altered.
	Financial pressures	May have encouraged adoption of lower cost solution.
	Local democracy	Local Authority engaged in consultation process with residents and other users (local exhibition of options held).
	Media attention	Traffic disruption, along with high incidence of speeding tickets following introduction of temporary 30mph speed limit, resulted in regular local media attention.
Inherent Complexities	Recognition of Need	Severe damage to existing bridge required action to repair/replace.
	Support and Approval	Approved by Buckinghamshire County Council, with support from Parish Council, local council representatives and local residents (based on input from consultation process - some opposition to chosen solution from road users).
	Feasibility study	Undertaken by Transport for Buckinghamshire – 3 options identified (Repair/New Bridge/Ground level crossing), Ground level crossing recommended.
	Detailed design, specification and scheduling	Undertaken by Transport for Buckinghamshire with third party assistance.
	Provision of funding	Provided by Buckinghamshire County Council (insurance claim used to cover initial costs).
	Provision of materials/equipment	Provided by Transport for Buckinghamshire or their contractor.
	Provision of labour	Provided by Transport for Buckinghamshire or their contractor.

TABLE 2: ANALYSIS OF THE FOOTBRIDGE REPLACEMENT PROJECT USING THE 'OPPOSING FORCES' APPROACH (contd)

Type of Complexity	Specific Aspect	Implication/Response
Inherent Complexities [contd]	Co-ordination/ supervision quality assurance	Undertaken by Transport for Buckinghamshire with third party assistance.
	Progress monitoring and reporting	Undertaken by Transport for Buckinghamshire (project included in 2011/12 and 2012/13 plans, and reported via the 'Transtat' process).
	Media attention	Handled via Buckinghamshire County Council Press Office.

CHAPTER 3: AN IT CASE STUDY - THE NATIONAL PROGRAMME FOR IT IN THE NATIONAL HEALTH SERVICE

And so, armed with our opposing forces complexity/response model, let's - at last - turn our attention to IT projects.

Again, the question that emerges is how and where to start. And again, perhaps somewhat unimaginatively, my answer is: with a case study.

The case study I've selected is the National Health Service's 'National Programme for IT' (NPfIT). In some senses this seems an obvious choice, given that it was the highest profile IT project (or perhaps more accurately, programme, in that it was really composed of a number of separate projects) in the UK in recent years, and was of course the one referred to in the Computer Weekly discussions which formed part of my motivation for writing this book. On the other hand, one might argue that given its scale (it was described as the largest civil computer project in the world)[1], this makes for a somewhat atypical example. However, it is important to note that the purpose of the case study is to serve as a body of source material from which we can extract insights about the sorts of complexity likely to be encountered in relation to IT projects. In this case the scale of the project would seem to be a definite advantage, as it increases the richness of material upon which we can draw.[2] Therefore, the aim is not to tell the full, unabridged, unexpurgated story of the NPfIT - although that would be a very interesting read, and I for one would buy it if someone wrote it. This would however require significant further investigation to go beyond the information already available as part of the public record, which doesn't seem to be necessary for what we need to achieve here. Hence the narrative which follows is based on information which is already in the public domain. In particular, I've drawn heavily on the series of reports produced by the National Audit Office and the House of Commons Public Accounts Committee, which provide a sequence of 'snapshots' of the status of the programme and a critical assessment of its progress over time. This said, the account nevertheless seeks to be quite thorough, so as to provide a comprehensive picture of the complexity the project faced and the way it responded to this. I have also sought to provide detailed references for everything covered in the account, so as to ensure its integrity.

The NPfIT project was the culmination of a series of attempts to establish a comprehensive IT infrastructure, and fully leverage the opportunities provided by greater computerisation, and more integrated computerisation, in the NHS, following the examples set elsewhere in the world, and in response to a belief, which had some justification, that the UK health service was losing out in its use of IT.[3] This meant that it was not taking advantage of the technology to increase efficiency and reduce costs, in terms of things like better management of medical records and improving administrative processes, but also to enhance the quality of care - for example by enabling practitioners to have rapid access to information about the best available treatments for particular conditions.[4]

Various attempts were made from the late 1970s onwards to seek to remedy this situation. In the context of a highly devolved NHS organisation structure, these attempts focused principally on the creation of a set of 'frameworks' by the Department of Health, setting out a series of sequential phases of computerisation which became progressively more sophisticated and which would deliver progressively greater benefits at each stage. The idea was that individual devolved entities within the NHS authorities (of which at the time there were for example over 200 separate hospital trusts, and nearly 9000 general practices)[5] would over time invest in their systems in accordance with the frameworks established, and as the different phases were rolled out, this would ultimately result in the implementation of the comprehensive, integrated state of the art healthcare IT which was the aspiration. To support these investments, the Department of Health provided funding to Health Authorities - although this was not always 'ring fenced' such that it had to be spent on strategic IT investments, and therefore it was sometimes reallocated by them to other healthcare needs. Throughout the 1980s and 90s there were a number of refinements to and variations on this overall approach, but this basic philosophy of setting out frameworks for local healthcare bodies to adopt, supported by funding to help them in doing so, prevailed throughout.

However, the results of all these different attempts throughout the period can be described at best as mixed. Very few authorities were successful in delivering the sorts of solutions that were being sought. While improvements were being seen in terms of administrative systems (eg those used in booking appointments), progress in terms of patient records and electronic support for clinicians was negligible. The approach was also resulting in a patchwork quilt of different solutions in different authorities and sometimes within different authorities. This was partly a result of the devolved decision-making within the NHS, but in addition there was a fundamental dynamic that encouraged suppliers to bid low to win the next bid, seek to establish a presence in the market, and then look to generate a sustainable income stream from future sales. However, with all suppliers adopting this approach, and authorities accepting the lowest tender, it meant that a myriad of different solutions were adopted. A view was also emerging that to achieve the computerisation of patient records and improved management information that were being sought, the IT provided needed to be of genuine assistance to the medical user population, otherwise they would not be motivated to enter and maintain the necessary data required for these other purposes. This implied that in order to achieve the full potential benefits of computerisation, a highly integrated end solution was required. This would enable doctors and nurses to have access to a real-time view of a patient's status and medical history, track case notes, order tests and view results, prescribe drugs, and view essential information about appropriate treatments all on-line, at the same time reducing waiting times, improving clinical outcomes, reducing errors, streamlining the prescription and appointments processes, cutting waiting times and improving diagnoses.

At the same time, it was at least questionable whether many of the authorities, and possibly also some of the suppliers, had the expertise available to deliver the solutions required. While clearly much smaller in scale than the project that was to follow them, the projects to which the strategies gave rise were nevertheless large and complex initiatives in their own right, with significant IT-related and organisational change challenges implicit within them. Any authority or supplier which underestimated the complexity, under-resourced the initiative, treated the activity as a purely IT-focused technical one and failed to appreciate the human factors in implementing such major changes was inevitably going to struggle. Finally, as noted, authorities often believed that they had higher local priorities than investing in IT, leading them sometimes to choose to invest the funds elsewhere.

This lack of progress, despite the level of funding provided, gave rise to perhaps understandable frustration at the Department of Health. There remained a continuing belief that better and wider use of IT provided a means of at least slowing the inexorable rise in healthcare costs, and of improving the quality of the service. The perception in central government appears to have been that the ultimate vision remained entirely appropriate and achievable, but that the problem was with the delivery model. The conclusion was that an approach that relied on the devolved health authorities to lead, manage and deliver the transformations being sought was not viable, and hence in 2002 it was decided to launch the NPfIT, which would be centrally directed and co-ordinated.

The exact background to this decision remains somewhat unclear however. It is claimed that the green light to proceed was in fact given by the Prime Minister, Tony Blair, following a ten minute breakfast meeting with the Department of Health, and was largely based on an assessment conducted by McKinsey, the management consultants (with input also from Bill Gates of Microsoft).[6] McKinsey's analysis has not been made public however. It was also alleged during the 2011 Public Accounts Committee session that at the meeting the Prime Minister had asked how long the project was likely to take. When advised by Sir John Pattison, the senior civil servant responsible for IT in the NHS that this would be 'Maybe three years', the Prime Minister is reported to have responded 'How about two?'[7]

The programme sought in essence to achieve full computerisation of the NHS, covering patient records, provision of medical support to doctors and nurses, automation of administrative processes (eg appointments booking), and better availability of management information. At the same time, this would facilitate and form a key part of the transformation of the NHS, delivering significant increases in efficiency and productivity against a backcloth of rapidly increasing healthcare costs. The table below lists some of the principal aspirations for the programme, based on a number of different NHS policy and strategy statements, which the programme was expected to support.

INFORMATION FOR HEALTH ASPIRATIONS
• Patients and NHS staff caring for them to have reliable, rapid, 24/7 access to relevant personal information to support their care
• On-line access to services, specialists and care to eliminate travel and delay
• Provide patients independent multi-media access to information and advice about their condition
• Provide NHS staff online access to latest guidance and advice on treatment and information to evaluate their work and support their professional development
• Ensure availability of accurate information for managers and planners
• Provide access to multimedia advice on lifestyle and health
• Provide information to support public involvement and understanding of national and local health service policy development
• Develop and make available the Electronic Health Record (EHR) about every individual

INFORMATION FOR HEALTH ASPIRATIONS (contd)
• Implement integrated clinical systems to support GPs and primary care teams
• Provide integrated Patient Administration Systems (PAS) for acute hospitals
• Connect all GP practices to NHSnet
• Provide 24 hour emergency care access to relevant patient records
• NHSnet to be used for all administrative tasks and notification of test resultsClear policy established on core standards eg information management, data structures and contents, telecoms
• Electronic prescribing in place NHS Direct services available to whole population
• Establishment of local Health Informatics System
• National electronic library for health accessible by all NHS organisations

Source: adapted from Burns (1998): Information for Health: an information strategy for the modern NHS; Brennan (2005): The NHS IT Project; Department of Health (2002): Delivering 21st Century IT Support for the NHS[8]

Clearly therefore, there was a compelling strategic logic for undertaking such a comprehensive programme of IT restructuring within the NHS. Equally, however, while the benefits of successful delivery were undeniably substantial, so too were the challenges and risks, given the scale, complexity and ambition of what was entailed, not least in light of the complex mosaic of legacy systems that had been established, and the previous chequered history of UK government IT initiatives both in health and in other arenas. As well as the technical complexities facing the programme, it also faced enormous human and organisational challenges, particularly in terms of the whole structure of the NHS, with so much of the decision-making decentralised to a variety of different bodies. These included:

- 28 existing Strategic Health Authorities (SHAs), which were the organisational entity charged with providing the strategic frame for healthcare in their area, eg by developing plans for service improvement, oversight of local services, and maintaining consistency with national priorities (the number of SHAs was reduced to ten in 2006).

- Over 300 Primary Care Trusts (PCTs) – responsible for ensuring the provision of health services in a local area by GP practices, community nurses, dentists, etc., and as such for managing the bulk of the NHS healthcare budget (the number of PCTs was reduced by about half in 2006).

- Around 250 NHS Trusts (Acute Trusts, Ambulance Trusts, Mental Health

Trusts etc) – responsible for the management of hospitals (Acute Trusts), ambulance services, and other types of secondary medical care.

- A small but increasing number of Foundation trusts – the first wave of 24 of which came into being in 2004. In keeping with the government's attempts at decentralisation of public services they were given greater financial and operational freedom than NHS Trusts, while still remaining part of the NHS.

- GP General Practices –there were nearly 9000 General Practices within the health service in 2002, each of which was in effect a stand-alone business, with its own existing set of systems.[9]

This devolved structure was somewhat at odds with the aspiration to implement a new centrally-driven IT solution. On top of this, the NHS was also characterised by the number of different communities and interest groups which were represented within or around it – for example doctors (themselves subdivided into a myriad of different specialties) and nurses, managers, administrators and other non-clinical staff, and patients, along with an assortment of representative groups and various non-governmental organisations. Finally, such a large and visible initiative would also have to contend with the pressures associated with the politicisation of any attempts at material change in the NHS, and the scrutiny of the media (which was quite likely to be critical even under the best of circumstances).

Notwithstanding the strategic logic, the question remains as to whether the balance between reward and risk really justified a decision to proceed, and whether ultimately the approach taken was the right choice under the circumstance – and after all, a strategy which is not achievable is not a sensible strategy to pursue. At the 2011 Public Accounts Committee hearing, it emerged that a risk assessment undertaken prior to the project's commencement scored the project as 53 out of 72, described as 'very high risk'[10]– although one wonders in retrospect how much more difficult the project could have been, and what would have been required for it to receive a score closer to 72. Additional light on this might be shed by the release of more of the relevant documentation into the public domain, but as noted the government has consistently resisted this (neither has it been made available to Parliament) – which perhaps tells its own story.

The original cost of the programme was estimated at £2.3bn, or £6.1bn taking account of the full value of the lifetime costs of the various contracts awarded (see below), which as well as initial implementation included ongoing operation through to 2013. However, this figure excluded software licensing, networking, infrastructure, hardware at every site, central management costs, project planning, procurement support, the cost of NHS personnel engaged in the project, termination costs for switching off legacy systems, power and other consumables, and overheads. The Department of Health estimated implementation costs of 3 to 5 times procurements, which implied a total expenditure of at least £10bn (even before any cost overruns). Some estimates ran as high as £20bn (although these were disputed by officials). [11]

The programme was to consist of a series of separate but interconnected parts, as follows:

- National data spine – a central database, consisting of three main elements: Personal Demographic Services, which would record basic patient information, as well as individuals' administrative preferences; Personal Spine Information Service, which would contain clinical information on individuals; and the Transaction and Routing Service, which would manage access to the information retained. As such, this would form the repository for, and control the access to, the 'Summary Care Record', which would in particular provide information about the drugs a patient was prescribed, known adverse reactions to drugs, and known allergies (although it was intended that the scope of information included would subsequently be extended). This information would then be available anywhere a patient sought treatment.
- National Network – a broadband network to support all the applications and connect GPs, hospitals and other health and social care providers.
- Electronic Appointment Booking – known as 'Choose and Book', this would enable patients to book their appointments on-line.
- Detailed Care Records - these would consist of the detailed information arising from every aspect of the patient's care – including visits to the family physician, attendance at clinics, hospital admissions, nursing support or any other healthcare interactions, thus replacing the existing paper records. The information would link to the Summary Care Record to provide a comprehensive electronic patient record. This was really the kernel of the programme, and would incorporate a range of functions, including patient administration (managing waiting lists, inpatient stays, document movements etc), order communications (eg requesting laboratory tests and receiving results), clinical data capture, and support for the management of treatment by

means of what were called 'integrated care pathways'. It would require implementation of new systems in all hospitals, other healthcare trusts, and GP practices. Given the scale of this undertaking, it was decided to split the country into five different regions or 'clusters' each of which would have their own Detailed Care Records solutions. The five clusters established – East, London, North East, North West and West Midlands, and South - did not map to any existing administrative structure within the NHS, and instead represented somewhat arbitrary groupings of the 28 Strategic Health Authorities. A 'Local Service Provider' (LSP) would be contracted to provide, implement and operate the systems required to support the Detailed Care Record in each cluster.

- Electronic Transfer of Prescriptions (ETP) – this would replace paper prescriptions, simplifying the transfer of information and the accuracy of prescribing, and enabling a comprehensive record to be maintained of all prescription activity. Provision of this was also intended to be covered by the LSPs.[12]

Some additional areas of activity were subsequently added to the scope of the programme, notably the Quality Management Analysis System (QMAS, which was a tool to provide information on the quality of care delivered to patients), NHSmail (national secure e-mail, calendar and directory service), and Picture Archiving Communications Systems (PACS – electronic storage and on-line viewing of x-rays and scans).[13]

The proposal was that each of the different elements of the programme would be put out to tender, and contracts would be signed with an individual supplier for both the provision of the systems required to support the activity and for the operation of the service through to 2013.

This approach implied both a systems architecture and a delivery model. Clearly this had advantages and disadvantages, and was the source of some of the subsequent criticism to which the programme was subject, and of some of the problems it encountered. The extent to which other alternative approaches were considered is not clear from the information in the public record.

The programme was officially launched by the government in June 2002.[14] In October 2002, the Department of Health established a unit to procure and deliver the systems (in April 2005 this became an agency of the Department called NHS Connecting for Health).[15] Richard Granger, a former partner with the Deloittes consultancy firm who had led the successful implementation of the London congestion charging system, was appointed to the position of Director General of NHS IT, and put in charge of the programme.[16] He established a central programme management team, to support the planning, control and reporting of activities within the programme.[17] This took longer than anticipated, in particular the recruitment of a Chief Operating Officer, which was only concluded in September 2003, and affected the pace of some of the early activity.[18] In January 2003, Professor Aidan Halligan, who was an obstetrician and formerly the Deputy Chief Medical Officer, was appointed to represent doctors and other medical professionals within the senior ranks of the programme.[19] The other key figure in the programme at this stage was Professor Sir John Pattison, Director of Research at the Department of Health, who had been a leading advocate of the approach adopted and had supposedly participated in the breakfast meeting with Tony Blair at which the decision to go ahead with the programme had been taken. He was the chair of the National Programme Board, which was put in place to oversee and govern the programme, and was initially the 'Senior Responsible Owner' (SRO) – the person formally ultimately accountable for the Programme as a whole. [20] In March 2004 he relinquished these roles, and the Director General for IT became one of two joint SROs, the other being the Deputy Chief Medical Officer, who was given the role of Deputy General of Benefits Realisation, responsible for clinical engagement and the delivery of benefits. This sought to recognise that the Director General for IT had no management authority over NHS Trusts, and therefore could not be held responsible for ensuring they participated fully in implementation and realising business benefits. Other SROs were made responsible for individual components of the Programme. In April 2005, this changed again when the Department of Health's Group Director of Health and Social Care Delivery was appointed as overall programme SRO, while the Director General of IT remained SRO for systems delivery. In April 2006, the Acting Chief Executive of the NHS took over as SRO for the Programme as a whole, acknowledging its significance to the overall development of the NHS. He was replaced by the new Chief Executive of the NHS, David Nicholson (later Sir David), on his appointment in September 2006.[21] Nicholson remained SRO for the programme throughout the remainder of its existence.

To reinforce connectivity between the programme and the wider NHS, in November 2004, the Chief Executive of Trent Strategic Health Authority was appointed as Director of IT Service Implementation, reporting to the Department of Health's

Group Director of Health and Social Care Delivery. In May 2005, the then Chief Executive of West Yorkshire Strategic Health Authority took over this role.[22]

In addition, from the outset the structure of the programme provided for endorsement and sponsorship by the Secretary of State, with day to day oversight provided by a Minister from within the Department of Health.[23]

At the cluster level, each cluster had a Regional Implementation Director (RID), as well as a cluster programme board, chaired by the CEO of one of the Strategic Health Authorities (SHAs), and including the CEOs and Chief Information Officers (CIOs) of all the SHAs within the cluster, representatives from the National Programme team, and other regional stakeholders. The Board was intended to provide senior leadership for and engagement in the activities within the cluster, champion the changes being sought, ensure the delivery of the benefits, and help resolve issues. At a more operational level, Programme Management Groups (PMGs) were also established for each cluster, made up of CIOs, programme managers from each SHA, the RID, and other key cluster and LSP personnel. This group was charged with managing and co-ordinating the progress of the programme across the cluster, progress monitoring, issue resolution, risk management, planning, sharing good practice and deploying resources. Within their SHA, individual CIOs were responsible for implementation and the delivery of benefits, receiving direction and support from the PMG, the RID and the programme support team, and reporting back on progress on issues. Further structures existed within the SHAs to provide engagement with medical personnel as well as support for and oversight of the project delivery teams on the ground, which generally consisted of a mix of local, LSP and supplier personnel.[24]

A number of other stakeholder bodies were also connected into the programme, notably:

- NHS Information Authority - this had been established in 1999 to help deliver IT infrastructure and information solutions to the NHS; this was responsible for running all the pre-existing national systems.
- NHS Modernisation Agency – this was set up to support the achievement of the NHS Plan which was put in place in 2000 with the aim of modernising services and improving experiences and outcomes for patients. The agency had responsibility for assisting Strategic Health Authorities manage the change in working practices and realise the benefits of the national programme. (Both the

NHS Information Authority and the Modernisation Agency were abolished in 2005)

- Two new advisory boards, one - the National Clinical Advisory Board - representing health staff including GPs, nurses, consultants, and pharmacists, chaired by Professor Peter Hutton, Chairman of the Academy of Medical Royal Colleges; and a second named the Public Advisory Board which represented patients and carers and included people from groups such as the Patients Association, Help the Aged, Mind and the National Consumer Council. This was chaired by Marlene Winfield OBE, Head of Public Engagement for NPfIT.[25]

- In 2004, the Department established the Care Record Development Board (CRDB), a multidisciplinary group of patients, the public and clinicians, to take the lead in considering ethical issues relating to the Programme.[26]

Additionally, the programme and its various elements would also need to interact with the different organisational entities within the NHS – so for example Primary Care Trusts and NHS Trusts would be required to provide resources (financial and human) to support the roll-out of the programme.[27] Foundation Trusts were given a degree of autonomy as to whether to participate in the programme. However, if they chose to opt out, they had to justify the alternative approach selected.[28] Finally, some form of engagement would also be required with GPs as part of the roll-out of their new systems.[29]

The programme was originally intended to be rolled out in a series of phases and releases over a period of six years between 2004 and 2010. Initially the focus would be on the implementation of the enabling infrastructure and supporting processes, followed by the progressive development and roll-out of the core application systems, and then finally the implementation of more sophisticated technology in pursuit of what was referred to as 'seamless care'.[30]

Formal procurement for the programme started in early 2003. Most of the contracting activity was completed at the beginning of 2004. As well as being notable for its speed, procurement for the programme was also distinctive in that, unlike with most UK government supplier selection, where the department concerned would choose a 'preferred bidder' some time before signing the contract, at least two bidders were kept in the running for each contract as long as possible, to maintain competition and avoid price rises.[31]

The procurement was based on an 'Output Based Specification' (OBS) for the planned systems – a statement of the functions that the solutions were intended to perform. Preparation of the OBS commenced in February 2002 under the auspices of the NHS Information Authority, which established a Design Authority which in turn requested input and assistance from various bodies within or connected to the NHS. Material was provided by 15 NHS bodies which had developed specifications for their own patient record services following the 1998 IT strategy of the NHS Executive. The NHS Information Authority also engaged with Chief Information Officers of NHS bodies such as Strategic Health Authorities, sites which had been part of the previous Electronic Record Development and Implementation Programme (ERDIP), IT directors and the Academy of Medical Royal Colleges Information Group. These groups participated in reviews of the early drafts of the OBS. A revised draft OBS was circulated for consultation in July 2002, requesting feedback on:

- Whether the vision of the NHS Care Records Service was consistent with the overall objectives of the NHS
- What phasing of NHS Care Records Service functions was required to create a long term basis for growth, while meeting specific targets and objectives in the short term
- Whether there were any gaps in the specification which needed to be filled
- Whether the overall level of detail was sufficient for the procurement of such services.
- Whether the standards and national services were appropriate to support implementation of the local services.

Some 190 responses were received from suppliers, clinicians, NHS IT departments and others. The OBS was revised in the light of these comments, and the subsequent draft was refined further with input from some 400 medical professionals, Chief Information Officers and IT managers. The new NPfIT programme unit (which had by this time come into existence), later known as Connecting for Health, then engaged a broad spectrum of NHS stakeholders encompassing leading clinicians, practitioners, policy advisers, health informaticians and managers, including representatives from the Department of Health, the NHS Information Authority, Strategic Health Authorities, NHS Trusts,

Primary Care Trusts, General Practitioners, academic groups and other government Departments. The final OBS was issued to potential suppliers on 1 May 2003.[32]

The contracts which were being let covered both the provision of the systems required to provide the service, and the ongoing operation of the service once these systems had been implemented. Some of the established software suppliers in the healthcare sector submitted bids directly, but most bids were from major systems integration companies such as Accenture, Deloittes and IBM, all of which partnered with specialist healthcare systems companies who would deliver the core product or products as part of their tender. Contractual conditions also included: a requirement to demonstrate and test the proposed systems, and make sure they all worked together; agreement that suppliers would not be paid until their systems were delivered and working, with penalties for delays; and provision for suppliers to be removed if they did not meet performance guarantees.[33]

The National Audit Office subsequently described the selection process as 'vigorous'[34], and noted that the Office of Government Commerce considered there to be many good features in the process which should be adopted more widely in government IT procurement. The process was believed to have resulted in significant savings (one survey estimated these at £4.5bn), and it was argued that it would enable improvements for patients and users to be introduced more quickly, as well as reducing costs incurred by bidders.[35] Nevertheless, many expressed reservations over the speed with which the national programme moved ahead, suggesting that more time should have been spent on defining requirements. In particular it was argued that medical professionals were not sufficiently consulted about the requirements or involved in the contracting process, which resulted in a lost opportunity to engage their support for the programme. These criticisms continued to resound – and be reiterated – throughout the life of the programme (for example, during the 2013 Public Accounts Committee hearing, the comment was made that 'the contracts were let in an enormous hurry, in total secrecy, bound up with huge confidentiality clauses, and it was only after they were all signed— quite rapidly after—that people became aware that the contracts would not deliver what was required'). The Parliamentary Office of Science and Technology in a short overview of the programme published in February 2004 also pointed to suggestions that suppliers may have underbid to win the contracts, leaving them without enough money actually to deliver the services – although they also noted that the similarities in price between successful LSP bids provided some indication that they were indeed realistic. Subsequent events (including the withdrawal of some contractors and the renegotiation of the contracts for others – see below) also suggested that the contracts were underpriced.[36] Some also considered that the procurement process favoured large companies to the detriment of smaller ones.[37]

The main contracts were awarded as follows:

Contract	Value	Period	Contractor	Main application
National Spine	£620m	10 years	BT	
National network	£530m	7 years	BT	
Choose and Book	£65m	5 years	Schlumberger/ Sema (replaced by Atos Origin)	Cerner
LSP North West/ West Midlands	£973m	10 years	Computer Sciences Corporation (CSC)	iSoft
LSP North East	£1099 m	10 years	Accenture	iSoft
LSP East of England	£934m	10 years	Accenture	iSoft
LSP London	£996m	10 years	BT	IDX
LSP South	£896m	10 years	Fujitsu Alliance	IDX

Source: Based on POST (2004), Brennan p5 and p124[38]

Some of these selections came as something of a surprise to observers. The tough contract terms proposed by the NHS, and particularly the threat of penalties given the level of risks they would be facing, were thought to have put off some of the bidding companies, such as Lockheed Martin, who decided to withdraw from the competition.[39] Separately the choice of iSoft and IDX as the Detailed Care Records software system suppliers meant that a number of other vendors, such as McKesson, Cerner, Torex, Siemens, Capula and Epic, some of which were better established than the companies selected, and a number of which would probably have been capable of providing an equally viable solution, were rejected. It was suggested that the selection of iSoft and IDX was a result of their more active and shrewd marketing efforts rather than the superiority of their products. Reservations were also expressed as to whether the LSPs selected had the necessary depth of understanding and experience of the healthcare sector.[40]

Under the contracts, delivery dates were set for the first phase of the programme. These are shown below.

Project	Contract Target Dates
New National Network for the NHS (N3) Prime contractor – BT	Contract set in-service targets of: • 6,000 sites connected by 31 March 2005 • 12,000 sites connected by 31 March 2006 • All 18,000 NHS sites connected by 31 March 2007
National Data Spine Prime contractor – BT	Phase 1 Release 1 – June 2004 Phase 1 Release 2 – December 2004 Phase 2 Release 1 – June 2005 Milestones for later stages to be set later.
Choose and Book Prime contractor – Atos Origin	Target for first booking June 2004. No further public targets were set out for Choose and Book.
NHSmail – email and directory service Prime contractor – Cable & Wireless	Service available for use – October 2004.
Electronic Prescription Service	Target for first deployment by February 2005. December 2005: 50 per cent of all sites should be capable of issuing electronic prescriptions. December 2007: 100 percent of all sites should be capable of issuing electronic prescriptions.
Picture Archiving and Communications Systems (PACS)	Full deployment of 130 PACS by March 2007.
Quality Management and Analysis System	Full deployment January 2005.
LSP: North East Prime contractor: Accenture	Phase 1 Release 1 – June 2004. Phase 1 Release 2 – December 2004.
LSP: London Prime contractor: BT	Phase 1 Release 1 – September 2004. Phase 1 Release 2 – March 2005.
LSP: Eastern and East Midlands Prime contractor: Accenture	Phase 1 Release 1 – August 2004. Phase 1 Release 2 – December 2004.

Project	Contract Target Dates
LSP: North West and West Midlands Prime contractor: CSC	Phase 1 Release 1 – June 2004. Phase 1 Release 2 – December 2005.
LSP: Southern Prime contractor: Fujitsu	Phase 1 Release 1 – September 2004.

Source: NAO 2006, pps 14-23[41]

Dates for subsequent phases were to be set once work on Phase 1 was more advanced and there was a better basis for determining these. The phases and releases referred to were planned to include the following:

Phase 1 Release 1	Installation of systems, hardware and software to form the framework to build future functionality, including Personal Demographics Service, Personal Spine Information Service, Transaction Messaging System and enabling technology for Choose and Book, and Electronic Transmission of Prescriptions.
Phase 1 Release 2	Covered more complex business and message handling processes, including clinical situations. Involved full Choose and Book functionality; outpatient clinic letters; inpatient discharge summaries; report of the single assessment for elderly people; diagnostic imaging and pathology results; screening results; recording of care episode events; and routing of orders for some blood tests and diagnostic images.
Phase 2 Release 1 (Tentatively timetabled for development to be completed by June 2005, roll-out to be completed by December 2006)	This phase was planned to add: National Service Frameworks assessment and review record; secondary uses of Spine data; planning and recording of the total care journey – integrated care pathways; full linking and electronic transfer of correspondence; pathology and image ordering and results communications; and integration of dental services.
Phase 2 Release 2 (Tentatively timetabled for development to be completed by June 2006, roll-out to be completed by December 2008)	Included greater sophistication in the technology available with an increased level of integration and seamless care in three key areas: more sophisticated access control services; extensions of the Choose and Book service; and links to remote care settings. Patients would also be able to place elements of their medical history in a virtual "sealed envelope", allowing them to more closely control access to their data.
Phase 3 (Tentatively timetabled for development to be completed by January 2009, roll-out to be completed by December 2010)	Further enhancement of systems and processes to ensure seamless care. The scope of this phase was deliberately left open to allow a flexible response to ever changing clinical priorities and circumstances.

Source: NAO 2006, p12[42]

It was of course recognised that the programme would need to surmount a number of significant challenges in order to be successful. Some of the most important of these were set out in the briefing document produced by the Parliamentary Office of Science and Technology in 2004, which proved to be extremely prescient.[43] This identified the following:

Managing the transition from the existing IT landscape to the new solution
The paper noted that the NHS had traditionally bought IT systems locally, and hence there was a proliferation of different systems and standards in place across the country, with little interoperability between them. For the first stages of the national programme, the plan was wherever possible to integrate existing systems with the wider programme, and only replace these where they could not be integrated. Managing this transition, integrating and replacing systems as well as converting data from the old systems to the new, would be one of the key challenges facing the LSPs. What was not stated explicitly in the paper, however, was that given the different mix of existing systems in each location, the transition path in each local area would be unique.

Managing change
For the new systems to be successfully implemented, substantial attention would need to be given to non-technical issues, such as rationalising how work was undertaken and helping people to use the new solutions. Previous experience showed that it could cost at least as much to manage the changes arising as to deliver the IT itself. These costs were however not covered by the NPfIT, but would fall instead within the responsibility of the SHAs, supported by the Modernisation Agency. It was anticipated that the funding of these activities, including balancing the provision of central funding via the Modernisation Agency with local support from existing budgets, would therefore be a key issue.

Training
Around 850,000 NHS personnel were expected to use the systems provided by the NPfIT. While suppliers would develop training materials, training would need to be paid for and organised by local SHAs and Trusts, supported by the NHS Information Authority. Trusts would need to make arrangements to cover absences while staff were trained. In addition, there was likely to be an adverse impact on productivity in the aftermath of the introduction of the new systems, until people became familiar with them.

Involving clinicians and users

It was recognised that one of the most common causes of project failure was poor engagement with stakeholders. Although the requirements for the NPfIT had been developed with input from clinicians, surveys suggested that overall awareness of the national programme among medical professionals remained low. There was a widespread agreement that clinicians and other users should be closely involved in the programme, to:

• ensure that the systems delivered what was required
• learn from existing best practice and previous mistakes
• provide local leadership within individual Trusts
• encourage 'buy-in', and overcome scepticism arising from previous IT project failures.

Research had suggested that clinical acceptance would be aided by a rigorous evidence base for the benefits of the programme, support for clinical 'champions' to encourage their colleagues, and ensuring the ease of use of systems during patient consultations.

Health IT Staff

The national programme had ruled out large scale transfers of existing NHS IT staff to suppliers, on the grounds that the purpose of the LSPs was to deliver new services rather than replace existing ones. However, there remained concerns among NHS IT staff, unions and other staff representative bodies that many of the services to be delivered by LSPs would be heavily reliant on current systems and staff familiar with them, and suppliers would need to take on more IT staff who understood healthcare to fill any skills and knowledge gaps. Hence there could be pressure for many NHS IT professionals to transfer to the LSPs, contrary to their wishes and to the detriment of the internal IT function within NHS entities.

Data quality

Much of the patient data for the new systems would need to come from existing records in hospitals and GPs. It would be a major challenge both to collate this data and to ensure its quality and accuracy. A previous initiative, the NHS Electronic Record Development and Implementation Programme (ERDIP), had identified a number of problems both with the quality and comprehensiveness of the existing information, and with extracting this from hospital systems and, particularly, GP systems. This had also pointed to a need for common data standards and incentives to ensure consistent recording of data by clinicians. Ultimately as part of NPfIT it was intended that patients would be able to see their personal care record online.

This would enable them to request corrections for errors, as well as to add information, eg about their treatment preferences.

Security and Confidentiality
A new NHS Confidentiality Code of Practice had been developed setting out data confidentiality requirements for staff, and providing information to patients about how their data would be used and protected. Research indicated that patients were concerned that information should be secure and reliable, protected from viruses and hacking, restricted to the clinicians treating them, and unavailable to non-clinical NHS staff and non-NHS personnel. EURIM, a Parliamentary IT lobby group, noted that while security for paper-based medical records was generally lax, paper records made it very difficult to collate all the data about any one individual. The most common ways to overcome security were still likely to remain low-tech, such as bribery, but the risk of this could be reduced by limiting the information clerical staff were able access. Hence, NPfIT proposed to allow users access to clinical information only where they had:

• An account on the system. Users would need two forms of identification to log-on, such as a smart card and a password. Eventually, a biometric identifier could be used (eg fingerprint or iris recognition).
• A role which permitted them access to clinical information (eg a nurse rather than a receptionist).
• A 'legitimate relationship' with the patient – that is, they would have to be involved in providing care to that patient.
The system would also provide an audit trail, showing who had seen or amended each patient's information.

Nevertheless, concerns continued to be expressed throughout the programme's existence regarding the effectiveness of the security regime and the risk of unauthorised access to medical records.

Consent
The initial assumption was that all patients would have a Summary Care Record on the system, but they would be able to decide whether or not it could be shared if and when they needed care. There were two models for obtaining consent:
• opt-in: patient information would be shared only if the patient gave express consent;

• opt-out: patient information would be shared as a matter of course, unless the patient specifically requested otherwise.

The programme proposed an 'opt-out' approach under which patients would be notified that their Summary Care Record would shortly be created, and giving them a period of time to decide whether they would permit it to be shared. After this period, unless they had opted out, their Summary Care Record would be shared electronically whenever they needed care. However, this proposal remained controversial, as privacy groups believed that individuals should be given the opportunity to opt out of having a Summary Care Record at all.[43]

It was against this background that delivery of the programme commenced in 2004/5. The progress of the programme is well documented, both as a result of a series of periodic reviews notably by the National Audit Office (NAO) and by the House of Commons Public Accounts Committee (PAC), and because of extensive coverage in the press.

The first NAO review was undertaken in 2006, and provided a generally favourable report on the project (subsequently described as 'gushing' by a member of the PAC).[44] The NAO concluded that:

'The Department and NHS Connecting for Health have made substantial progress with the Programme. They have established management systems and structures to match the scale of the challenge. They successfully placed contracts very quickly, after securing large reductions in prices from bidders, and including contract terms that include important safeguards to secure value for money for the taxpayer. Deployments of operational systems have begun and NHS Connecting for Health has taken on, and in some cases already delivered, several additional tasks which were not within the original brief for the Programme. NHS Connecting for Health has adopted many of the key lessons of prior public IT failures. The notable progress and tight control of the central aspects of the programme are to be commended.'[45]

In keeping with this assessment, the report noted in particular:

• The Programme had strong support from government.[46]
• NHS Connecting for Health had put in place sound project management (including use of the Prince 2 project methodology, and regular 'Gateway'

project reviews; in addition an independent review of project management processes by Qinetiq had provided a favourable assessment), and was strengthening its systems for monitoring and managing performance to help deliver the Programme.[47]

- The programme had taken appropriate steps to ensure the systems met the users' needs. This had involved good engagement with stakeholders, appropriate use of previously available sources, and circulation of an initial draft of the requirements to interested parties for comment.[48]

- The standards required for confidentiality of patient records and consent to access and share records had been set out in the Care Record Guarantee. A system of access control had been devised to ensure information remained properly protected, although it was noted that good working practices would be necessary in support of this.[49]

- The programme had ensured there was vigorous competition for the contracts, and maintained this competition after the contracts were awarded. In total, through the contracting process, the final bids accepted by Connecting for Health from the eight prime contractors represented a reduction of £6.8bn compared to their initial bids. A report by Ovum, an independent IT industry analyst, commissioned by Connecting for Health, estimated that central procurement had saved £4.5bn compared to the prices that could have been achieved by individual NHS organisations purchasing the same services separately. The procurement process had been concluded very swiftly. The contracts included strong incentives to deliver – involving the use of both carrot (in that suppliers would only be paid as systems were implemented) and stick.[50]

- The programme had tested potential suppliers' ability to deliver, and had required the final bidders to undertake 'Proof of Solution' tests in a simulated environment with end users, to show whether their systems could meet a number of different scenarios. Appropriate due diligence had been performed on the winning bidders to establish their ability and capacity to deliver the contracts they were to be awarded.[51]

- The programme had adopted what was referred to as 'an intrusive but supportive approach to the management of its suppliers', which it noted was not common in the public sector. As well as transferring financial and delivery risk to its prime contractors (which of course was in contrast with the approach adopted by BAA for Heathrow Terminal 5 – see above), the programme had taken positive action to ensure the contractors – including both prime contractors and the several hundred subcontractors working for them - were managing their tasks well.[52]

The NAO cited a number of examples of this – which also indicated some of the sorts of challenges and complexities which would need to be dealt with if the programme was to be successful - including the following:

o   BT and Fujitsu had separately contracted to use IDX as their supplier to deliver the required care records software. Connecting for Health then agreed with BT and Fujitsu the establishment of a 'Common Solution Programme' to ensure the IDX application was developed just once for the NHS for use by both LSPs. However, by mid-2004 Connecting for Health became concerned about the performance of IDX, and the effectiveness of the supplier management. This led to a review in January 2005 of IDX's capacity and capability to meet the LSPs' requirements. Despite increasing pressure on IDX from Connecting for Health, by April 2005 insufficient progress had been demonstrated and Fujitsu lost confidence in IDX's ability to deliver the Common Solution. Fujitsu requested that they be permitted to replace IDX with Cerner as their solution provider. Fujitsu and BT agreed to dissolve the Common Solution programme, and Fujitsu formally contracted with Cerner to replace IDX. No taxpayers' money was paid to IDX as a result of this change. BT chose to continue to use IDX for delivery of its core solution for the London Cluster. While the replacement of IDX put Fujitsu some 18 months behind schedule for the delivery of the early phases of the programme, it was nevertheless still planned for Fujitsu to have implemented the entire functionality required by 2010 in line with the original contract.[53]

o   A remediation plan had been agreed with CSC for the delivery of Phase 1 Release 1 due to its inability to meet the original target dates. The plan divided the phase into five sub-releases with a revised deployment schedule. Additional delays then led to a second remediation plan being established, resulting in the deployment dates for two elements of Phase 1 Release 1 being pushed further back into 2006, some 19 to 22 months later than originally planned. This second plan sought to introduce an improved software solution delivery model for Phase 1 Release 2 and beyond, including steps to update and agree the strategic solution roadmap and associated interim deployments; increase the development collaboration between CSC and iSoft (the primary software provider), such as through the o   co-location of CSC and iSoft staff in the UK and India; and increase the contractual focus on delivery and adherence to agreed schedules.[54]

o   In early 2005, Connecting for Health advised BT that it was in breach of its obligations under its contract as the London Cluster LSP. BT was given time to make improvements, but these were not considered sufficient by Connecting for Health. As a result an audit of BT's programme was undertaken in August 2005. This concluded that BT's subcontract with IDX did not incentivise IDX sufficiently to provide for the timely delivery of quality solutions. As a result, BT sought to revise its contract with IDX to align it more closely with its own contract with the government. As with CSC and iSoft, BT and IDX were also required to take steps to co-locate their respective teams.[55]

o   Difficulties were also identified in relation to the early implementation by BT of the New National Network (N3) (eg delays in meeting its monthly - but non-contractual - targets for connections, poor communications with NHS sites re the scheduling of visits, complaints from NHS staff that BT did not understand their requirements, criticism of the quality of customer service provided by BT, as well as some local NHS co-operation issues), and regarding BT's failure to achieve the agreed availability requirements for the Spine during its initial deployment. Again Connecting for Health intervened – eg by commissioning audits, increasing oversight, and encouraging improvements – to help address these issues, and again these actions were viewed favourably by the NAO.[55] (Given subsequent events, however, the NAO's attitude towards these difficulties appears to have erred quite considerably on the side of generosity; notwithstanding any interventions on the part of Connecting for Health, it is clear that by the time of their review, the programme was already suffering significant problems and slippages in a number of key supplier-related aspects – later reviews proved considerably more critical).

o   Another intervention concerned the number of GP systems offered by the LSPs from which GP practices could choose. Under the LSP contracts to minimise costs this was limited to just two systems in each cluster. However, this was widely perceived by GPs to be too limited as it meant that most practices would have to change their systems.   In response to GPs' concerns, the Department of Health announced in March 2005 plans to allow GPs to select from any GP system supplied by any of the LSPs, regardless of location. Subsequently, in March 2006 the Department announced its 'GP Systems of Choice' initiative, which gave GPs a wider variety of options to choose from, by using the systems provided either by their LSP, or from an approved set of existing GP system providers. Subject to meeting agreed standards, GPs' systems would be funded either via Primary Care Trusts in the case of eligible existing systems, or via Connecting for Health for systems provided by LSPs.[56]

- Although direct responsibility for communication with staff lay with local NHS units, Connecting for Health had taken steps to inform future users and win their support, such as through the availability of extensive information on the Programme's progress and activities on its website, the publication of numerous leaflets and comprehensive information packs, and the appointment of National Clinical Leads, seven of whom had been appointed in November 2004 to champion four occupational groups: GPs, hospital doctors, nurses, and allied health professionals. Each lead was a well known member of their profession with credibility among practising clinicians. Linked to this, three clinical advisory groups, covering doctors, nurses and allied health professionals, each chaired by one of the Leads had been established to provide a forum for dialogue between Connecting for Health and health care professionals, the Royal colleges, and professional societies and associations. The Leads had assisted the Care Record Development Board in determining the content of the care record and tackling some of the surrounding difficulties, while the GP Clinical Leads had highlighted the demand from GPs for a wider choice of systems and helped resolve some of the issues that this raised. The increased level of dialogue fostered by the introduction of Clinical Leads was highlighted by the professional bodies as a positive development. This contrasted with the lack of consistency and leadership prior to their appointment (subsequently the programme also appointed a full-time Chief Clinical Officer, with a seat on the Connecting for Health Agency Management Board).[57]

- Independent research conducted by Ipsos MORI in July 2005 to track awareness and understanding of the Programme across the NHS found that the majority of staff interviewed were positive about what the Programme was seeking to achieve. They also believed that the services provided by NPfIT would help them in their daily working lives to share information about patients and improve patient care.[58]

- Connecting for Health had established a programme to keep the public informed about the development and deployment of the Care Records Service.[59]

- The report estimated that the total cost of the programme would be £12.4bn over the ten year life of the main contracts to 2013-14. This was not however a budget, it was rather an amalgamation of fixed price contracts, extrapolation of costs beyond the contract periods and provisional forecasts of other costs. Only some of this expenditure was directly managed by Connecting for Health, since local IT expenditure was a matter for the local NHS bodies concerned. Hence Connecting for Health sought to make broad estimates of programme expenditure, rather than maintaining a detailed projection of its total cost.[60]

This extremely positive assessment notwithstanding, the report noted that 'Successful implementation of the Programme nevertheless continues to present significant challenges for the Department, Connecting for Health and the NHS, especially in three key areas:

- Ensuring that the IT suppliers continue to deliver systems that meet the needs of the NHS, and to agreed timescales without further slippage.

- Ensuring that NHS organisations can and do fully play their part in implementing the Programme's systems.

- Winning the support of NHS staff and the public in making the best use of the systems to improve services.'[61]

In respect of the first of these, there had already been some significant changes to project timings and phasing since the contracts had been awarded. These were attributed principally to changes in programme scope following the signature of the main contracts, the problems experienced by some suppliers in meeting the originally targeted delivery dates (see above), and requests from medical professionals for additional piloting of the clinical record before it was implemented more widely. This had led to a new delivery schedule, which gave priority to Choose and Book, the Electronic Prescriptions Service, Picture Archiving and Communications Systems (PACS) and providing Spine compliant local systems for those NHS organisations in urgent need of new or replacement IT systems.

Under the revised schedule, roll-out of the detailed care record was now expected to commence in pilot form in late 2006, and in its full form from late 2007. This was two years later than originally projected.[62]

Linked to this, the report also noted that one key factor affecting the LSPs' rate of deployment of systems was the heterogeneous nature of the NHS, with each NHS organisation occupying single or multiple sites, within modern or older premises, with each having different mixes of functions and specialisations, all potentially employing different systems, different numbers of systems, and sometimes a number of different systems to do the same thing. This meant that the LSPs' solutions needed to be tailored to meet each organisation's specific requirements, in turn meaning that even after a LSP had ensured that its solution was fit for purpose in one organisation, further work was needed to roll-out the solution in every other organisation within its Cluster. This made the task of implementing systems considerably more demanding than in more homogeneous organisations[63] (it is worth noting that this challenge had been alluded to in the Parliamentary Office of Science and Technology briefing paper referred to previously[43], so should not really have come as any great surprise).

The report noted that a key lesson from previous unsuccessful IT projects was that the NHS needed to approach the NPfIT as a business change programme rather than as an IT project.[64] As such, success would require: engagement and support from NHS managers and clinicians for the overall vision and purpose of the programme and the benefits arising from it; the NHS to make clear its priorities in terms of the changes it was seeking, and users to adapt their ways of working in accordance with these; substantial effort on the part of local NHS organisations to install the systems and use them to improve services; and sufficient capability to implement the new systems effectively, including training for the NHS staff who would use them. This remained something of a work in progress. While the NAO believed that there had been good involvement from clinicians and other users in the design of the Output Based Specification (OBS) and in the evaluation of potential vendors, a decision had been taken to conclude the bulk of procurement activities before focusing on communicating and engaging more widely with NHS staff, so as to avoid the risk of creating unrealistic expectations. Connecting for Health also faced severe resource constraints in undertaking such activities. In terms of support for the programme, notwithstanding the Ipsos MORI results referred to above, a survey of GPs and hospital doctors conducted by Medix, an independent healthcare research organisation, in December 2005 and January 2006 found that this had fallen: 26 per cent of GPs and 45 per cent of other doctors who responded were enthusiastic about the programme compared to 56 per cent and 75 per cent respectively in the previous survey two years earlier. The survey also found 6 per cent of doctors responding had never heard of the programme before the survey, while another 50 per cent said they had little or no information about it.[65]

Finally, the NAO also noted that national leadership of parts of the Programme had changed a number of times.[66]

As a result of these findings, the report recommended in particular:

'The Department of Health and NHS Connecting for Health should provide greater clarity to organisations and staff in the NHS as to when the different elements of the Programme will be delivered. NHS Connecting for Health should ensure that it has a robust engineering-based timetable for delivery, which it is confident its suppliers are capable of achieving.

NHS organisations should communicate to members of staff how such a timetable will affect them, and forewarn them of the challenges facing the Programme, so that the setbacks and changes of priority inevitable with a programme of this size do not cause a loss of confidence.

NHS Connecting for Health should continue its strong management of suppliers' performance...

The Department, NHS organisations and NHS Connecting for Health should put in place training and development programmes to strengthen capability, including project management and IT skills available to the wider NHS, continuing its work with the Office of Government Commerce. The shortage of such skills is an immediate risk to the timely implementation of the Programme, and strengthening capacity in these areas will be a long-term asset for the NHS.'[67]

Despite this generally (and perhaps surprisingly) positive report, concerns about the programme had already been raised in a number of quarters. For example, a group of leading UK academics working in the IT field wrote an open letter to the House of Commons Health Select Committee in April 2006. The letter raised the following points:

- While the IT changes being proposed were individually technically feasible they had not been integrated, so as to provide comprehensive solutions, anywhere else in the world.
- Two of NPfIT's largest suppliers had issued warnings about profits in relation to their work and a third had been fined for inadequate performance.
- Various independent surveys showed that support from healthcare staff was not assured.
- There had been delays in the delivery of core software for NPfIT.
- Objective information about NPfIT's progress was not available to external observers.
- Reliable sources within NPfIT had raised concerns about the technology itself.

The writers questioned the wisdom of continuing NPfIT without an independent assessment of its basic technical viability, and raised a number of questions which they believed needed addressing, as follows:

- *Did NPfIT have a comprehensive, robust:*
  - Technical architecture?
  - Project plan?
  - Detailed design?
  - Had these documents been reviewed by experts of calibre appropriate to the scope of NPfIT?

- *Were the architecture and components of NPfIT likely to:*
  - Meet the current and future needs of stakeholders?
  - Support the need for continuous (ie 24x7) healthcare IT support and fully address patient safety and organisational continuity issues?
  - Conform to guidance from the information commissioner in respect to patient confidentiality and the Data Protection Act?

- *Had realistic assessments been carried out about the:*
  - Volumes of data and traffic that a fully functioning NPfIT would have to support across the thousands of healthcare organisations in England?
  - Need for responsiveness, reliability, resilience and recovery under routine and full system load?

The authors proposed that the Health Select Committee help resolve uncertainty about NPfIT by asking the government to commission an independent technical assessment with all possible speed, which they argued would cost a tiny proportion of the proposed minimum £6bn spend on NPfIT and could save many times its cost.[68]

In response, Health Minister Caroline Flint told the House of Commons on 24th May 2006 that the NPfIT was 'already the focus of regular and routine audit, scrutiny and review', and needed no further examination. She went on to add: 'We remain confident that the technical architecture of the national programme is appropriate and will enable benefits to be delivered for patients, and value for money for the taxpayer, without further independent scrutiny.'[69] It subsequently came to light however that by the time the Minister made this statement the project had already failed nine Office of Government Commerce 'Gateway Reviews' (two of which related to the whole programme, while the remainder referred to different component parts of it) in which it received a 'red' rating, requiring immediate action before the project proceeded any further. These were only made public in 2009, with publication of 31 reviews relating to aspects of NPfIT undertaken between 2002 and 2007 in response to a freedom of information request by the Guardian newspaper. Amongst other things, the reviews pointed to:

- Infeasible timescales to complete all the necessary work
- Weaknesses in the project management approach
- Lack of machinery for obtaining clinical input into the programme, and lack of engagement with the hearts and minds of the staff within the NHS at all levels
- Lack of a coherent over-arching design
- Lack of a commercially supported and agreed plan for the delivery of the care records software products, which remained unproven due to development delays
- Lack of a coherent benefits realisation strategy
- Insufficiently rigorous planning for an initiative of such size and complexity
- Insufficient emphasis on the potential impact of the new IT systems on existing practices, procedures and systems
- An undue emphasis on speed, meaning that key staff did not have time to take action in response to recommendations, or learn lessons from other projects

- An 'ivory tower' mentality on the part of programme management - despite the devolved and fragmented nature of the NHS.[70]

Separately, there were also calls from within the medical profession for greater involvement in the national programme. It was argued by many that the mechanisms established to provide for engagement with clinicians had proved ineffective, and that in particular there had been insufficient medical input to the procurement process. It was reported that Professor Peter Hutton, who had resigned as Chairman of the National Clinical Advisory Board after only six months in position had done so because he had been 'frozen out' of the programme after expressing a number of concerns, not only around the degree of consultation with NHS staff, but also over how uniformity and continuity of care would be achieved across the different LSPs, arguing that variations would raise 'major safety and training implications'.[71]

The programme also continued to encounter problems with supplier performance. Early in 2006, Accenture and CSC, the LSPs for three of the five clusters, had together produced a highly critical report on Lorenzo, the Electronic Patient Record software application being developed by iSoft which would provide a core part of the solution they were delivering. The review concluded that 'there is no well-defined scope and therefore no believable plan for releases' - despite the fact that iSoft had stated in their 2005 Annual Report that the product was already 'on the market' and had been 'available' from early 2004. Roll-out of the software was initially intended to begin across the clusters in 2004 – but this had now slipped to 2008 at the earliest (a date which the report considered optimistic). The report also questioned the clinical safety of the tool, and stated that there was 'no evidence for the development, nor testing of, technical procedures that would be required for operation and maintenance of the system...'. Both companies threatened iSoft with legal action, and Accenture stated publicly that it blamed iSoft for missed NPfIT deadlines. It was subsequently reported that Accenture, CSC, iSoft and Connecting for Health had taken action together to enhance the development process, and in August iSoft and CSC resolved their legal disputes with an agreement entitling CSC to take managerial control should Lorenzo delivery fall behind an agreed schedule. Meanwhile, in addition, iSoft continued to face significant financial difficulties, as well as accusations of improper accounting in 2004 and 2005.[72]

In September 2006 it was announced that Accenture was pulling out of its contracts as LSP for the North East and East of England clusters. The company was circumspect about its reasons for withdrawal, but it was reported that they had made a loss of £75m on the two contracts in 2005, and earlier in 2006 had made a £240m provision against subsequent losses. Under the terms of the exit agreement, Accenture was required to repay £63m of the £173m it had been paid on the contracts to date – although this was significantly less than the programme was entitled to claim under the penalty clauses which had been included in the contracts and which had been widely publicised at the time these were signed. Implementation statistics indicated that Accenture had made significantly more progress on the programme than any of the other LSPs, being responsible for over 80 per cent of the system deployments made in the clusters to that point (although it was argued by Richard Granger that this was because they had focused on smaller, primary care deployments rather than on some of the more challenging aspects of the programme which was where other companies had put their emphasis). Accenture's withdrawal led to the two contracts being transferred across to CSC. As part of its exit deal with the NHS, Accenture agreed not to pursue any legal claims against iSoft.[73]

These developments led the academics to write a second open letter to the House of Commons Health Select Committee, suggesting that in addition to the independent technical review previously proposed the committee should themselves conduct an immediate inquiry ahead of the review to establish the scale of the risks facing the programme and identify appropriate shorter-term measures to protect the programme's objectives.

Separately, the group noted that 'The National Audit Office report did not answer any of our concerns and we increasingly felt that the programme appears to be building systems that may not work adequately, and that - even if they worked - may not meet the needs of many health trusts.'[74]

In March 2007 the contract with BT for London was also reset. This followed the switch from GE Healthcare (who had acquired the original sub-contractor IDX in January 2006) to Cerner as the main software supplier. Prior to this point the IDX system had been deployed in one Acute Trust. This change further delayed progress in London. At the same time the value of BT's contract was also increased by £55 million to secure additional functionality requested by the NHS in London.[75]

A second major externally available report on the project by the House of Commons Public Accounts Committee was published in March 2007 – although the committee's principal hearing was actually held in June 2006, following immediately on the publication of the NAO report, which provided the foundation for their review. Despite this, the committee provided a much more critical assessment than that emerging previously from the NAO.[76]

Firstly, in terms of the progress of the programme, the Committee reported the following:

Spine – although this had first gone live in June 2004 as scheduled the achievement of later milestones for increasing its functionality was delayed by up to ten months. Usage of the systems had commenced, but as yet only represented a small part of the overall scheme.

Summary Care Record – the decision had been taken in 2005 to defer roll-out due to 'complexity and the need for wider consultation, for example on patient confidentiality issues'. In the meantime, work had continued on the Care Record Guarantee (the first version of which was published in May 2005, with subsequent versions produced in April 2006 and August 2007). The supporting infrastructure was successfully implemented as part of the Spine.

Detailed Care Record - Patient Administration Systems (PAS): Plans published by Connecting for Health in January 2005 indicated that by April 2007, 151 acute hospital Trusts would have implemented PASs of varying degrees of sophistication. As of February 2007 only 18 had been deployed. These systems provided no care record functionality beyond what had previously been available prior to the programme. In those regions where iSoft was the main software supplier, because the PAS element of the new Lorenzo system was still being developed it had proved necessary to implement an interim solution, which was an old iSoft PAS called IPM which pre-dated the programme (although development work was required to enable this system to connect with other parts of NPfIT such as the Spine and Choose and Book). In those areas in which Cerner was now the main software provider replacing IDX/GE Healthcare there had been delays in modifying the Cerner product so it was suitable for use in England. Meanwhile, a large number of Primary Care Trusts and mental health Trusts who had previously had no corporate patient administration system at all had been supplied with iSoft's old PAS.

Detailed Care Record - Patient Clinical Record: this had not yet been deployed at any location. It was now due to be available in pilot form in late 2006, and in full form a year later, which was two years later than originally planned. The Department advised that the decision to delay had been taken because some suppliers were having difficulty in meeting the timetable and because clinicians wanted to pilot the systems. It was also claimed in evidence submitted to the committee that delivery had also been impeded by delays on the part of Connecting for Health in providing 'Spine message definitions' to suppliers, which were necessary to enable the new systems to interact with the Spine. It was now hoped to have most of the systems implemented by 2010, although no published plans existed for this at the time, and there were concerns around the scale of the implementation and the associated risks.

New National Network (N3) – this was three months ahead of schedule.

Choose and Book – by April 2006 this had been deployed in over 7,600 locations, but it was accounting for only about 20 per cent of referrals from GPs to first consultant outpatient appointments. Some GPs had experienced problems using the system, which were believed to have been attributable mainly to local implementation issues or to the PAS at the hospital where the booking was being sought not being up to date.

Deployment of the electronic prescription service and the computer accessible X-ray systems had also been slower than anticipated, although the Department believed that later deployment targets would be met.[77]

In addition, it was noted that the experience of PAS systems that had been deployed was 'patchy'.[78] Some of the problems encountered were illustrated by the implementation experience at the Nuffield Orthopaedic Centre (NOC) in Oxford, which was the first trust to roll out in the Fujitsu-managed southern cluster, and which was reviewed in some detail in a letter from Sir John Bourn, the head of the National Audit Office, to Mr Richard Bacon MP, one of the members of the committee and included as evidence in the committee's report (see the box below).[79] Trusts had experienced a variety of problems, including inability to report activity statistics, missing patient records and extended shut-down of some systems. Clinical consequences had included waiting list breaches and significant delays in providing inoculations to children.

In light of this situation, the report drew four principal conclusions:

1. 'The piloting and deployment of the shared electronic patient clinical record is already running two years behind schedule. In the meantime the Department has been deploying patient administration systems to

INTRODUCTION OF CARE RECORDS SYSTEM AT NUFFIELD ORTHOPAEDIC CENTRE

Nuffield Orthopaedic Centre (NOC) is an acute specialist teaching hospital in Oxford. It is primarily an elective site where appointments are pre-booked, with no Accident and Emergency department. It was selected as the first trust in the Southern Cluster to receive the new systems as part of NPfIT.

A go-live date of December 2005 was set for the implementation, since the trust's existing PAS was antiquated and expected to reach capacity in early 2006. It was originally intended that the IDX system would be implemented, but following the change of supplier, in summer 2005 this changed to Cerner. Nevertheless, the decision was taken to maintain the December deployment date, as the capacity issue with the existing system remained, preparations were well-advanced – for example, 400 staff had already been trained, the product was well established in the USA and at Newham and Homerton Trusts in London, and hence the risks were regarded as manageable, and any delay would be likely to have knock-on implications for the rest of the programme. Under the circumstances, however, there were some major shortcomings in the preparations for implementation – eg Trust staff were not provided with training on – or even a demonstration of - the system which was to be implemented at NOC; Cerner staff were not at that time available onsite to work with the staff to configure the system for NOC; and staff were not able to visit Homerton to see the system being used.

On go-live of the main system on 20th December:
- the process for initial user log on proved more complex and took much longer than expected. This meant that it was possible to log in only key users initially, rather than all users as intended.
- the system did not start being used until 21-23 December and during that time a range of functionality and data migration issues emerged (the Trust and supplier had not been able to ensure that all data was accurately transferred).
- the system crashed completely on 22 December due to a power failure at Fujitsu's primary data centre, accompanied by the non-operation of the in-built resilience for the power supply. This should have been tested prior to go-live, but the compressed timetable meant that the testing had been deferred to January 2006. As a result, the systems were unavailable for one working day. While contingency plans had been put in place (covering system failures for periods of 24 hours, three days, seven days and one month), these plans were not extensive enough to match the detailed nature and prolonged duration of the difficulties encountered.
- although the system indicated that it was printing appointment letters for patients to clinics, far fewer people were turning up to clinics than expected as they had not received any notification to do so. Equally, other patients were turning up for clinics that they were not recorded as having been invited to. This caused inconvenience to patients, wastage of staff time, a build up of a backlog of outpatient appointments and a need to reschedule appointments. Contingency arrangements again did not adequately provide for this scenario.
- the system was designed such that clinicians participated in the appointments process.

INTRODUCTION OF CARE RECORDS SYSTEM AT NUFFIELD ORTHOPAEDIC CENTRE (contd)

However, this was not the process in place at NOC, where appointments were booked solely by administrative personnel. The use of a different process from the one the system supported made the booking of appointments very slow. This initially resulted in an increased backlog of patients awaiting appointments. Over time, the backlog was eliminated, and a system change requested to accommodate trusts where clinicians did not participate in the appointments process.

- the system was initially unable to generate the performance and activity reports required for the Trust to manage its operation effectively, and the Trust was unable to report externally for three months (these problems were subsequently rectified).

As a result of the problems experienced, which the Trust considered could potentially impact on patient safety, the Trust issued a 'Serious Untoward Incident' report to the Strategic Health Authority on 12th January 2006 (although subsequently the Trust advised that it believed no harm had occurred to patients).

Principal lessons arising were considered to be as follows:
- Only go live with a new system when all data has been migrated correctly and is clean and complete, and that this is assured seven days before the decision to go live.
- Ensure that strong project control is in place so that the introduction of a system does not proceed if critical tasks have not been completed.
- Ensure realistic testing and rehearsal take place for the introduction of new systems, and do not compress the time available for this.
- Test and train for the future working processes that staff will be using with the new system.
- Allow 10 to 12 weeks to train staff on the new system to be implemented, and make sure staff are released for training.
- Migrate enough information from the old systems to allow for a three month contingency period, and put in place contingency plans to deal with prolonged disruptions.

Source: Adapted from PAC 2007, Letter from Sir John Bourn to Mr Richard Bacon, Ev 92-95[79]

help Trusts urgently requiring new systems, but these systems are not a substitute for the vision of a shared electronic patient clinical record and no firm plans have been published for deploying software to achieve this vision.

2. The suppliers to the Programme are clearly struggling to deliver, and one of the largest, Accenture, has now withdrawn. The Department is unlikely to complete the Programme anywhere near its original schedule.

3. The Department has much still to do to win hearts and minds in the NHS, especially among clinicians. It needs to show that it can deliver on its promises, supply solutions that are fit for purpose, learn from its mistakes,

respond constructively to feedback from users in the NHS, and win the respect of a highly skilled and independently minded workforce.

4. Four years after the start of the Programme, there is still much uncertainty about the costs of the Programme for the local NHS and the value of the benefits it should achieve.'[80]

The report also noted the following:

- The loss of Accenture, IDX and Commedica (the provider of PACS applications to CSC in the North West), together with the difficulties the programme was facing in meeting its schedule and its objectives raised doubts over whether the existing contracts would deliver what was required. As a result, the report recommended the Department permit trusts to select from a wider range of patient administration and clinical systems, provided that these conformed to national standards. This approach would have the benefit of speeding up deployment and of making it easier to secure the support of clinicians and managers.[81]

- The report questioned the use of only two major software suppliers (iSoft's Lorenzo application and Cerner's Millenium product) for the electronic patient record, which could inhibit innovation, progress and competition, particularly in light of the fact that Lorenzo, on which three fifths of the Programme depended, was not yet available.[82]

- There was a shortage of appropriate and skilled capacity to deliver the systems, which the Director General of IT acknowledged in his evidence. This had forced the programme to access additional resources in India and the USA in particular, which had caused problems for certain vendors. It was also asserted that the combination of geographical distance and the additional layers of management introduced by the cluster structure impeded the connectivity required between local NHS staff and developers when systems were being implemented. Separately, the withdrawal of Accenture had increased the burden on other suppliers, especially CSC. The report recommended that the Department review with suppliers their capacity to deliver, and also commission an urgent independent review of the performance of LSPs against their contractual obligations.[83]

- Concerns continued to be expressed about the way the Department engaged with NHS staff, especially clinicians. It was noted that the Department had failed to carry an important body of clinical opinion with it. This was attributed in part to the serious problems experienced with systems that had been deployed to date. Evidence from senior clinicians previously involved in the programme which was provided to the committee questioned the way medical professionals had been engaged in the specification process, with the emphasis apparently placed on narrowing the scope of the requirements and closing down the requirements gathering process as quickly as possible. They claimed that the level of real consultation was significantly less than had been portrayed in the NAO report, and some of the consultation was described as 'a sham'[84], not least because 'it was implausible that any valid, sustainable conclusions could be drawn by asking some clinicians to comment on hundred[s] of pages of text in systems-speak' that made up the specification 'in the space of a few weeks'.[85] It was also alleged that communication and engagement with clinical and other NHS staff, as well as with the general public, had been consistently inhibited rather than encouraged, contracts had been placed before the content of the electronic care record had been approved by the National Programme Board, and that suppliers may not have fully understood the requirements of the systems they were bidding for. This in turn raised the question of whether the system as specified would meet the needs of clinicians, and may have contributed to the demands for additional piloting and the implementation delays referred to previously.[86]

- The frequent changes in the leadership of the Department's work to engage NHS organisations and staff were considered to have damaged the Programme and had given the impression that the Department attached a low priority to this activity.[87] By the time of the PAC review, responsibility for the programme had passed between six Senior Responsible Owners.[88]

- The view was again expressed that the leadership of the programme had focused too narrowly on the delivery of the IT systems per se, at the expense of consideration of how best to use IT within a broader process of business change.[89]

- There were ambiguities regarding the responsibility and accountability for the local implementation of the programme. Given the many changes taking place in the configuration of the local NHS at the time, and the range of other initiatives requiring attention, the committee considered it essential that local Chief Executives and senior managers understood their responsibilities for implementation, and were given the authority and resources to allow local deployment to take place without adversely affecting patient services.[90] Evidence presented to the committee suggested that Connecting for Health, and in some cases the LSPs, had at times taken an adversarial attitude towards local NHS entities.[91]

- The report noted that given the rate of progress to date, it was unlikely that significant clinical benefits would be delivered by the end of the contract period (2013/14 for the main contracts). Under these circumstances it was recommended that the programme define precisely which elements of functionality originally contracted for from the LSPs would be available for implementation by the end of the contract period, and in how many NHS organisations it would be possible to have this functionality fully operational. The Department should then prioritise the delivery of those systems which offered the greatest benefit to the NHS, eg local PAS and clinical systems.[92]

- There was no comprehensive record of expenditure on the programme as a whole, and while the programme had always been predicated on the improvement of patient services rather than on the basis that the financial benefits exceeded the costs, uncertainties remained around the benefits case for the programme and whether this would be achieved. It was recommended that the Department publish an annual statement of costs and benefits, and that an independent assessment of the programme business case be commissioned in light of the experience to date.[93]

While the PAC report was being produced (as noted its main hearing was held in June 2006, and the report was published in March 2007), measures were in progress to decentralise some aspects of the programme to the local NHS. In August 2006, the Acting Chief Executive of the NHS appointed the Chief Executives of the 10 Strategic Health Authorities (reduced from 28 in July 2006) as Senior Responsible Owners for implementation of the Programme and realisation of benefits for their part of the NHS. Each Chief Executive was required to appoint a Chief Information Officer to support them in this role. Then in October 2006 the Department initiated the 'NPfIT Local Ownership Programme', to strengthen local ownership and governance and re-position the programme as part of mainstream NHS business, following which responsibility for implementation was transferred to the local NHS in April 2007.[94]

Linked to these changes, the Department and the NHS introduced a new operating model, setting out revised responsibilities for delivering the Programme. Among other things, Connecting for Health remained responsible for the contractual relationship with the LSPs, though the Strategic Health Authorities now had access to the financial and commercial sections of the contracts.[95]

The Local Ownership Programme allowed individual NHS entities a greater role in developing the systems and in the planning and timing of system deployments, working with the LSPs. Prior to the transfer of responsibility, detailed work was done to help prepare the Strategic Health Authorities for their new role, including assessing key areas of risk and developing mitigation strategies. Steps were also taken to boost capacity and capability, and in July 2007 nearly 200 staff and contractors transferred from Connecting for Health to the Strategic Health Authorities.[94] In addition, funding of £25.5 million in 2007-08 and £30 million a year from 2008-09 onwards was transferred to the Strategic Health Authorities to reflect their increased responsibilities.[96]

Mirroring the configuration of the LSPs, the Strategic Health Authorities established three collective groupings - London (where there was one Authority), the South (three Authorities), and the North,Midlands and East (six Authorities) – each of which established a Management Board responsible for co-ordinating and overseeing the Programme in their area, and appointed a Programme Director to work with the Strategic Health Authorities' Chief Information Officers.[97]

Similarly, and in line with the Public Accounts Committee's concerns about the shortage of appropriate and skilled capacity to deliver the systems, during 2007 the programme undertook a procurement exercise to identify a list of suppliers who could provide additional supply capability and capacity should the need arise. In January 2008 the Department signed framework contracts with 38 suppliers, covering information and communication technology services; hardware, infrastructure and associated services; and testing environment and related services. Further contracts for clinical information technology services were awarded in spring 2008. As well as providing contingency for the Programme, local NHS bodies were able to use the listed suppliers to meet new requirements they identified. The framework contracts were not intended to replace the existing Programme contracts – in fact the Department of Health was anxious to avoid the fragmentation of the provision of services - but to supplement the supply capacity and enable new requirements to be met.[98]

Measures were also taken to strengthen the involvement of medical professionals in the programme. In August 2006 the first Chief Clinical Officer for the Programme was appointed, whose role was to enhance clinical leadership of the Programme and ensure that improving the quality and safety of patient care was embedded in every aspect of Connecting for Health's activity. The Chief Clinical Officer was supported by an Office of some 50 staff, including two National Clinical Directors for primary care and secondary care. The Chief Clinical Officer also supervised the clinicians employed to work on the Programme, including the National Clinical Leads, who worked part-time for the Programme while continuing with their clinical work. The Department expanded the network of Clinical Leads from the seven appointed in 2004 to 15 in 2008. As well as Clinical Leads for four occupational groups (GPs, hospital doctors, nurses, and allied health professionals), appointments were made for midwifery, pathology, diabetes care, public health, medications management, ophthalmology and mental health. There was also a National Clinical Lead for patient safety whose role included providing assurance about the safety of the new systems and considering the potential of IT to help address known patient safety issues. The Clinical Leads were intended to act as advocates for the Programme and to facilitate two-way communication between Connecting for Health and staff within the NHS, for example via meetings with professional bodies, presenting at conferences and other events, and producing newsletters. The Clinical Leads also worked with the National Advisory Groups, which included representatives of professional organisations, including the Royal Colleges. These Groups provided a forum for debate, facilitated consultation about the Programme, and offered clinical advice on health IT issues.[99]

Similarly, to reinforce the existing public and patient engagement activity which had been in place since the outset of the programme, in January 2007 a Patient Lead was appointed, with the task in particular of holding Connecting for Health to account for the level of public and patient involvement with the Programme.[100]

In June 2007, Richard Granger, the Head of the Programme, announced his decision to resign from his position by the end of the year (he eventually left in early 2008). Throughout his tenure Granger had been a somewhat controversial figure, aggressively seeking to drive the programme forward, and impatient of anything he perceived as likely to waylay it. In particular, he had been a vigorous advocate of the procurement process adopted, and its speedy conclusion, and had sought to adopt a robust stance in dealing with suppliers – stating in an interview with the *Financial Times* in March 2005, for example, that 'If suppliers cannot do the job, they will be replaced' - as well as with clinicians and NHS staff, politicians and officials, and the media. Shortly before the announcement of his departure, he dismissed much of the debate around the programme as 'complete tosh', adding that 'We would not have got to this point without our dedicated ring-fenced funding. I think that with a bit less whingeing and more support ... we might have even got the programme done quicker.'[101]

In 2008, the National Audit Office published the outcomes of a further review of the programme.[102] This was a rather more critical assessment than the previous NAO report, and mirrored the findings and conclusions of the 2007 PAC report quite closely. The report noted that while it remained difficult to report with precision on the status of all the different parts of the programme, all elements of it were advancing, and some were complete. However, delivering a nationally specified programme into the highly devolved NHS continued to prove extremely difficult. This was most apparent in respect of the Care Records Service, where the scale of the challenge in developing and deploying the systems required had proved far greater than expected and the original timescales had been overly optimistic. This had led to unrealistic expectations, which when not achieved had had a damaging effect on confidence in the programme. There remained considerable uncertainty about when the care records systems would be fully deployed and working across the country, but current indications were that this would now be 2014-15, four years later than previously planned. The North, Midlands and East area did not yet have the strategic system to support its care record service because of the time taken to develop Lorenzo. The NAO nevertheless concluded that the original vision for the Programme remained intact and still appeared to be feasible. [103]

The following actual progress was reported on the programme at the time of the review:[104]

- N3 network: The target to connect 18,000 NHS sites to the N3 network by 31 March 2007 was achieved two months early, in January 2007. By 31 March 2008, there were nearly 23,000 live, serviced connections.
- Spine (comprising eight applications): By the time of the review, the key software releases had been delivered on or ahead of target and the system was expected to be fully complete during 2008.
- Choose and Book: By 31 March 2008, 95 per cent of GPs and 100 per cent of Acute Trusts were live on the system (although 16 per cent of Trusts were not able to take direct bookings). However, utilisation had been lower than originally anticipated - in total 6.7 million bookings had been made by January 2008 against an original forecast of 39 million. Steps were being taken to promote increased usage, by resolving outstanding technical issues and encouraging Trusts and GPs to make the necessary changes to their working practices so as to support broader use of the system.
- Electronic Prescription Service: By 31 March 2008, the first of two phases was underway, with 79 per cent of GPs and 80 per cent of pharmacies able to use the first release of the software. Paper prescriptions would still be required, however, until the second release of the software was deployed. This could only take place once GP and pharmacy systems had been accredited. The second release of the software was due to be piloted in summer 2008.
- Picture Archiving and Communications Systems: Full deployment of the system to 127 Acute Trusts was achieved in December 2007, three months ahead of target.
- HealthSpace: The website was launched in December 2003; and from June 2007, patients in the early adopter areas were able to use the website to view their Summary Care Record.
- NHSmail: The service was available on target in October 2004. By 31 March 2008, some 341,000 NHS staff had NHSmail addresses.

- Quality Management and Analysis System: Full deployment was achieved on target in January 2005, with the first payments using the system made in April 2005.
- GP to GP transfer: The target for 3,500 GP practices to be live on the system was achieved in February 2008, one month early.
- Summary Care Record: after a delay of over two years, deployment began at GP practices in five Primary Care Trusts which were part of an 'early adopter' programme in March 2007. One year later, two of the five early adopters (Bolton and Bury Primary Care Trusts) were in the process of uploading their patient records to the system; the remaining three (Bradford and Airedale, Dorset, and South Birmingham) had public information campaigns underway but had not yet begun to upload any care records. The NAO found that deployment in Bolton had generally gone smoothly, although more slowly than expected. The roll-out had meant substantial extra work for both the Trust and for GPs, who had spent significant time discussing the implications of the Summary Care Record with patients. Although Connecting for Health had provided support, including a dedicated project manager, the Trust's resources were stretched. This situation was expected to continue as more information was added to the Summary Care Record. The Trust was also considering compensating GPs for the work involved.

  Firm timescales had not been set for the implementation of the Summary Care Record in the remaining 147 Primary Care Trusts pending review of the findings from a report produced by University College London into the early adopter programme published in May 2008. It was also necessary to ensure that GPs' care records systems would be compatible with the Summary Care Record, and by December 2007 only two of the main GP system suppliers, covering just a quarter of GPs, had delivered the enhancements needed to provide compatibility.[105]

- Detailed Care Records: progress to end March 2008 is shown in the table below.

Although the most deployments had taken place in the North, Midlands and East by CSC, these were of interim systems pending the availability of the Lorenzo tool. These would subsequently need to be replaced by Lorenzo. The delays in the development of Lorenzo were attributed in part to an underestimation by all parties of the scale and complexity involved in building a new system from scratch

Area	Local Service Provider	Acute Trusts		Mental Health Trusts		Primary care Trusts	
		Number of Trusts	Number of deploy-ments	Number of Trusts	Number of deploy-ments	Number of Trusts	Number of deploy-ments
London	BT	31	4	10	6	31	20
South	Fujitsu	41	9	14	1	31	7
North, midlands and East	CSC	97	21	35	13	90	47
Total		169	34	59	20	152	74

Source: NAO (2008) p8[106]

(despite the claims made previously by iSoft that it was already on the market, and despite the supposedly rigorous product proving process undertaken during the contracting phase). The first release of Lorenzo was now expected to be available for implementation at three early adopter Trusts in summer 2008, with full roll-out planned from autumn 2008. The Cerner Millennium product being deployed in the South and to Acute Trusts in London and the South was already an established product in the United States and elsewhere so development work was focused on adapting it for the NHS in England. Implementation of the first release began in December 2005 in the South and in July 2007 in London, with three further releases of the software due to follow. Most of the clinical functionality was planned for the later releases.

While in the South Fujitsu was also deploying Millennium to Mental Health Trusts and Primary Care Trusts, in London BT was following a 'best of breed' approach by using a different product, CSE Servelec RiO, to Mental Health Trusts and Primary Care Trusts. Further tailoring of the RiO system was being undertaken to meet mental health needs.

Revised implementation timings had been established for London and the North, Midlands and East, which projected the final releases of the care records software to take place between 2009-10 and 2014-15. Plans for the South were still under discussion.[106]

The report also noted that some Trusts remained to be convinced of the benefits of taking up the Programme's care records systems, given the minimal level of additional functionality available relative to their existing systems, and the difficulties in engaging clinicians under these circumstances (especially in light of the likely disruption to the Trust's activities that any implementation would entail).[107]

In terms of project costs, the report estimated these at £12.7bn, which was £300m higher than the previous estimate of £12.4bn, with this increase attributable to additional functionality. However, this projection came with the caveat that it remained difficult to provide a robust estimate of local implementation costs, which made up a significant proportion of the total.[108] Some benefits from the Programme, including financial savings, were starting to emerge, although work to identify and measure all actual and potential benefits systematically was still at an early stage.[109] The review noted that where systems had been rolled out, suppliers had largely met the targets for service availability, though there had been some technical problems using the new care records systems, especially in the period following deployment.[110]

The report also identified 5 main challenges that the programme needed to overcome in order to achieve its objectives. These were: Achieving strong leadership and governance; Maintaining the confidence of patients that their records would be secure; Securing the support and involvement of clinicians and other NHS staff; Managing suppliers effectively; and Deploying and using systems effectively at local level.[111]

Strong leadership and governance[112]
At the time of the review there was a degree of uncertainty in the leadership of the programme, with the announcement in mid 2007 by the Director General of IT that he would be stepping down at the end of the year. This announcement was followed by a review of the management structure for the programme, which resulted in a decision to make two new appointments, firstly a Chief Information Officer, responsible for delivering the Department's overall IT vision, and a Director of IT Programme and System Delivery, responsible for managing Connecting for Health and partnerships with the NHS. These positions had not been filled at the time of the NAO review. In the meantime, the Connecting for Health Chief Operating Officer was temporarily leading the programme.

The report noted that the Local Ownership Programme had been well received by NHS personnel. Although at the time of the NAO's review the new structures were still bedding in and their impact had largely yet to be felt, staff from the Strategic Health Authorities expressed support for the greater control and influence they would now have over key decisions - which in turn required them to recognise their core role in ensuring the successful delivery of the programme. This said, it was generally acknowledged that for the changes to have the desired impact, the Strategic Health Authorities and Trusts needed to have the necessary authority and expertise to fulfil their new role and to ensure that in practice roles were clear and not duplicated. This was especially important given the highly devolved nature of the NHS – hence, in realty, while the Strategic Health Authorities could suggest a timetable for future deployments, in practice decisions about when a new care records system would be implemented lay with Trust Boards and their Chief Executives. [113]

The report also referred to the challenges faced by the programme in maintaining an accurate view of progress and costs, given its complexity, and noted a need for greater openness and realism in presenting what remained to be done as well as what had been achieved. Actions were reported to be under way to provide a more accurate 'roadmap' of progress across the programme.[114]

Maintaining the confidence of patients that records would be secure
While this would have a major bearing on the success of major aspects of the programme, particularly if large numbers of patients declined to have a Summary Care Record on the system, it remained an area of concern. This was despite the continuing interactions with patients groups and professional bodies undertaken by the programme, and the controls and protections that were being put in place – including the use of Smartcards and passcodes, with individuals granted access to information based on their role and level of involvement in patient care, auditing of accesses, and the threat of disciplinary measures and possibly legal proceedings in the event of inappropriate use of health records. It was nevertheless acknowledged that ultimately security depended on the actions of individual NHS staff, and to help provide further assurance about data security and confidentiality, the Department and the NHS had developed a 'Care Record Guarantee', setting out the principles that were to be applied in handling electronic care records. In light of concerns about public sector data protection and particularly the security of information being transferred between locations and organisations, the Strategic Health

Authorities were also undertaking a detailed review of all aspects of data security in their areas.[115]

Securing the support and involvement of clinicians and other NHS staff
The review noted that the most recent survey of NHS staff in May 2007, the third of such reviews carried out by Ipsos Mori, found increases in levels of familiarity with the Programme, while most staff – including 67 per cent of nurses and 62 per cent of doctors – thought the systems would improve patient care. However, the survey no longer included a question on how favourably staff felt in relation to the Programme. The NAO acknowledged that over the last two years Connecting for Health had taken steps to strengthen its mechanisms for clinical engagement, including the appointment of a Chief Clinical Officer to enhance clinical leadership of the programme and extension of the network of National Clinical Leads, who acted as advocates for the Programme and supported communication between Connecting for Health and NHS staff. There had also been increased involvement of clinicians and other NHS staff directly in the development of the programme's systems to help ensure the products were fit for purpose - for example, a team of NHS staff had been established to assist with developing the Lorenzo care record software. Insufficient engagement with users of the systems was nevertheless still seen as one of the main risks to successful delivery, and there was perceived still to be scope to raise awareness and understanding of the benefits arising, for example by more open communications from Connecting for Health and better advance notice of events to make it easier for clinicians to attend them.[116]

Managing suppliers effectively
The three LSPs told the NAO that the scale and complexity of the Programme made it extremely challenging and all had boosted their capacity since the start of the programme - in part prompted by Connecting for Health (eg CSC had reinforced its team with personnel from its United States operations, BT had brought in staff to enhance its programme management capability). BT noted that programmes of the scale and complexity of the NPfIT were rare, and required specific experience and expertise to manage effectively the complex interdependencies between different elements. All the LSPs described how – in a situation where for example an individual Trust may make a hundred or more change requests before it is prepared to sign off the care records system being deployed as meeting its requirements - they needed to be highly flexible to meet the requirements of the NHS, rather than simply 'working to the contract'.[117] (Presumably none of this should have come as

any great surprise). Relations between Connecting for Health and the LSPs were described as 'maturing', with increasing confidence on both sides to work together to deal with the uncertainties and changes that arose during system development and deployment. Relationships were increasingly collaborative and based on partnership, with aligned objectives to deliver the programme. At a local level, the Local Ownership Programme had changed the dynamics between the NHS entities and the LSPs, and relationships were described as still relatively immature but improving. All the LSPs advised however that they had found it difficult to plan and deploy their resources on a programme where progress relied on many decisions necessarily made at local level, although NHS Trusts commented positively on working relations with LSP staff during deployment.[118]

Deploying and using the systems effectively at local level
As part of their review, the National Audit Office visited 15 NHS Trusts which had implemented new care records systems under the programme. A number of common themes emerged from these visits.

Firstly, delivery of the Programme's key objectives was reliant on the local NHS successfully deploying and using the systems. Their implementation (likened by one LSP as equivalent to a major retailer replacing its entire supply chain system) entailed substantial additional work – as well as maintaining 'business as usual', placing a significant burden on both clinical and administrative staff, and required a large resource commitment on the part of Trusts to cover the costs of managing the accompanying major organisational change.

A significant proportion of Trusts had been unable to achieve the timetable for deployment that had been put in place, in some cases suffering repeated delays. One reason for this was the failure of systems to pass successfully through testing. Most Trusts experiencing delays felt that they and their LSP had been guilty of underestimating the time and work required to implement the new system. The slippages had in some cases had a serious adverse impact on staff engagement and training (sometimes requiring training to be repeated). Based on these experiences, LSPs advised that the planning, preparation and testing prior to the go live date should on average be expected to take between a year and 18 months, depending on the complexity of the deployment.

All the Trusts the NAO had visited had sought to involve clinicians in their projects, for example through participation in project boards, in mapping work processes, and in roadshows. Engagement was made more difficult however because of the lack of significant clinical functionality in the early releases of the software. As a result, some Trusts decided not to engage fully with clinical staff until later on in the deployment process to avoid raising unrealistic expectations.

Perhaps inevitably the new care records systems brought advantages and disadvantages compared with the systems they were replacing, and moreover took some time to work as intended following deployment. In some Trusts, the old systems had been developed over many years, often with the direct involvement of Trust staff, and while these systems may not have been able to support the long term aims of the programme (eg in terms of integration with other parts of the NHS) they did meet the specific needs of the Trust. It was therefore common to find that some staff felt a sense of loss in moving from the familiar old system to an unfamiliar new one. This was compounded where the new systems provided a reduction in functionality compared to those previously in use, particularly given the limited clinical functionality available. This had a severe negative impact on the Trust's ability to engage clinical staff in the initiative.

In all the Trusts visited there had been a certain amount of dissatisfaction with the new system in the period following deployment. While over time many staff came to prefer the new system to the one it had replaced, some continued to be dissatisfied, in particular where they had raised issues but these had not been addressed (see below). As well as the level of functionality provided by the new system relative to the Trust's previous one, another factor was the ease of use of the system in helping staff perform their roles. Many staff found that the versions of the systems that had been deployed were less intuitive than they would have liked and it took longer to record initial patient information than previously - in part because more information needed to be captured so that the required reports could be generated. Also, staff at the same Trust often used the system differently, which adversely affected the accuracy of reporting. Some specific areas of difficulty had been identified by the LSPs, who planned to address these in subsequent software releases. It was also acknowledged that there was a need for Trusts to develop guidelines for using the systems consistently and ensuring these were observed across their organisations.

Another common theme was the need for a training environment which accurately resembled the 'live' system being implemented, rather than the 'generic' training environment available, which did not incorporate all the local features and modifications being adopted at the particular Trust in question. Some staff were confused when the system went live as it was different from the one they had trained on. Training proved more successful if it was tailored to reflect people's specific roles, rather than standardised for all staff. Some Trusts also provided basic IT training to help staff who were inexperienced in using computers.

Another issue emerging was the impact of the new systems on the work processes operated by the Trust. While in support of this some Trusts had made efforts to map their work processes prior to the deployment, in hindsight most Trusts considered that they should have devoted more attention to this, which would have identified areas where processes needed remodelling and helped in staff training, thus avoiding potential pitfalls and reducing problems or bringing earlier benefits after the deployment. In some cases staff devised workarounds to make the system work with the processes they used with the old systems, and almost all Trusts found they needed to do additional work post implementation to ensure staff were using the new system as intended.

Migrating data from a Trust's old systems to the new one also proved to be a complex exercise. All the Trusts consulted had performed 'test runs' to ensure data would transfer to an acceptable level of accuracy. Prior to migration, Trusts also carried out extensive work to clean up the records held on their existing systems, so as to avoid migrating duplicate, incomplete, inaccurate or out of date records. Two Trusts felt that they had migrated more data than was needed and that in retrospect they could have been more rigorous about how much historical data needed to be transferred. Some Trusts chose to retain their old legacy systems to minimise the amount of historical data that had to be migrated.

Another implementation task that proved problematic was the issue of Smartcards to staff prior to the go-live date where these were needed to access the new systems. This involved as many as 1500 Smartcards, and was a significant logistical challenge. Some Trusts issued Smartcards in tranches in advance of the go live date to make this more manageable. It also proved helpful to test the Smartcards at the point of issue to check they were working correctly, thus avoiding potential disruption during the critical go-live period caused by faulty cards.

All the Trusts visited experienced some technical problems with the new systems, although the nature of the problems varied. While all Trusts had procedures in place for the raising and reporting of issues to the LSP, the time taken to resolve issues was often longer than anticipated, and in some cases required a later release of the software. A common issue for users was a lack of transparency in the resolution process, so that staff did not understand the timeline for resolving a particular issue or receive feedback on the progress being made. In some cases staff chose to work round issues themselves rather than reporting them.

All the Trusts had also put in place arrangements to provide ongoing support to staff using the new systems, such as employing 'floorwalkers' immediately after the deployment to provide immediate assistance, training 'champions' to act as the first point of contact for queries, and establishing local helpdesks. While in the early deployments Trusts had found that the floorwalkers had themselves not been sufficiently familiar with the system being rolled out, in most of the more recent implementations the floorwalkers were viewed as an essential and effective resource, and some staff felt it would have been beneficial to keep them in place for a longer period. Issues which could not be resolved at local level were referred to the Connecting for Health Service Desk which provided a helpline, e-mail and internet logging facility for technical questions about the programme's systems. During the visits feedback was that the performance of the Service Desk, which was operated by Fujitsu, was consistently poor. Connecting for Health and Fujitsu acknowledged that there had been problems and were taking steps to address these, including ensuring that Service Desk personnel had sufficient knowledge both of the technical architecture of the systems and of the NHS.

Some similar issues were apparent in relation to the roll-out of Choose and Book, which required changes in working practices in both GP practices and Trusts. While usage was increasing, with 50 per cent of new outpatient appointments booked through Choose and Book in recent months, utilisation rates varied considerably, with some Primary Care Trusts above 90 per cent and others below 20 per cent. One Trust visited, which had one of the highest rates, attributed it to the fact that staff had gone out to meet GPs and provided one-to-one training and demonstrations to highlight the benefits of the system.

However, some GPs found the system very slow, and consequently impractical to use during a patient consultation. As a result, those GP practices where administrative staff made bookings tended to make more use of Choose and Book. Connecting for Health had developed a tool to measure the Choose and Book process from end to end, which revealed that although the performance of the central system could be improved, local IT configuration, for example within the GP surgery itself, could dramatically affect the speed with which bookings could be made.

The Trusts visited were positive about the clinical benefits of the Picture Archiving and Communications Systems. In particular, staff felt it aided diagnosis by making it easier to manipulate images, while it was also encouraging changes in working practices, such as with the use of mobile terminals to present scans to patients at their bedsides.[119]

In May 2008 it was announced that Fujitsu, the LSP for the South of England, was withdrawing from the programme. Negotiations to 'reset' Fujitsu's contract had been under way for some time, but it had proved impossible to reach agreement. No decision was taken at this point as to how the activities covered by Fujitsu's contract would be provided.[120]

Also in 2008, to secure greater clinical support for the systems, the Department undertook an engagement exercise with clinicians asking them what they wanted from their IT systems in a hospital setting. This review identified five clinical areas of functionality (which became known as the 'clinical five'), and certain departmental systems, as being the minimum set of requirements considered essential by clinicians. Following this, the programme's approach to the detailed care record was reorientated to focus on delivery of this 'minimum specification of functionality' which comprised:

- a patient administration system capable of integrating with other systems; order communications and diagnostics reporting (eg for things like blood tests or MRI scans); discharge letters, including coding so that all parties involved in a patient's care – hospitals, community care, GPs etc - would know the status of his or her condition and treatment; scheduling for outpatients, beds, tests and theatres; and electronic prescribing, including access to pharmaceutical information;

- five departmental systems – accident and emergency, maternity, community, child health, and operating theatres; and

- core infrastructure, such as case note tracking and data security.

Each Acute Trust would be able to select those aspects of the solution they most needed from a 'menu of modules'. This represented a major change in the overall philosophy of the programme, given that it was originally intended to provide a comprehensive solution covering all aspects of acute health care, and to drive standardisation across the NHS and avoid each Trust putting in place its own unique mix of systems. Instead the programme was now focusing only on a sub-set of acute activities, and gave individual Trusts flexibility to determine which of these they would implement – although Connecting for Health was anxious to emphasise that this constituted 'configuration' based on a set of prescribed options, rather than 'customisation' and hence a free for all.[121]

A further review of the programme by the Public Accounts Committee was published in January 2009 after a hearing in June 2008.[122] The report again referred to the slow progress being made in the deployment of Care Records Systems, which it described as 'very disappointing'.[123] In the five months between the end of March, when the NAO took their latest snapshot, and the end of August, six deployments had taken place, four in Acute Trusts and two in Mental Health Trusts.[124] Lorenzo continued to be a cause for concern. Connecting for Health had undertaken two further reviews of the product, which had led to a number of actions to strengthen project management, planning, risk management and release management; clarify responsibilities between different organisations involved in the delivery process; recruit new staff to fill vacancies at CSC and iSoft; enable earlier NHS involvement in software validation and testing; and break down the planned two releases of Lorenzo into four smaller releases, the first of which would comprise clinical functionality, with patient administrative functionality following in the second release.[125] Following these interventions, Connecting for Health remained optimistic about the prospects for Lorenzo, which was in the process of being demonstrated to the clinical community.[126] On the other hand, however, by the end of 2008, the application had still only been deployed at one of the three early adopter sites, South Birmingham Primary Care Trust, where it was supporting the podiatry service. It had been planned that Lorenzo would be implemented first at University Hospitals of Morecambe Bay NHS Trust at around the end of September 2008[127] – a date that was still being referred to in a written response to the committee dated mid September[128] (it ultimately first went live in just one ward, at one of the Trust's hospitals, in November).[129] The committee noted that 'Given the continuing delays and history of missed deadlines, there must be grounds for serious concern as to whether Lorenzo can be deployed in a reasonable timescale and in a form that brings demonstrable benefits to users and patients'.[130] They also pointed out that the revised roll-out approach which had been adopted, involving elements of the clinical functionality of Lorenzo being implemented ahead of the patient administration system, was untested and therefore posed a higher risk than previous deployments under the programme.[131]

At the same time, hospitals in London and the South which had deployed Millennium were also reported to have experienced considerable problems.[132] For example, in summer 2008 the Royal Free Hampstead NHS Trust identified issues associated with data entry, system processing, data management and reporting that were having a significant impact in relation to waiting list management and patient bookings, and on the finances of the Trust. Moreover, little clinical functionality was contained in the releases of Millenium implemented to date (this was scheduled to follow in later releases). Additionally, most Trusts decided not to switch on the limited clinical functionality that was available, since this would have required them to make onerous changes to their processes. Following the experiences at the Royal Free Hospital, the organisation of the implementation projects was revised to allow the trusts to interact directly with the application providers, rather than having to do this indirectly through the LSPs.[133]

No revised deployment timetable for the care records systems had been developed by the programme at the time of the review, but given the problems identified, combined with the termination of Fujitsu's contract, the committee doubted that the projected completion date of 2014-15, four years later than originally planned, would be achieved.[134] Moreover, they recommended that unless the position on deployments improved appreciably within the next six months, consideration should be given to allowing Trusts to put forward applications for central funding for alternative systems as long as these were compatible with the objectives of the programme[135] (the existing contracts with the LSPs assumed that Trusts would adopt the standard systems being provided, and the programme could direct all NHS Trusts to take these systems; this power did not apply to Foundation Trusts, but under Treasury rules they would have to provide a 'value for money' case for not taking the standard systems; also penalties were payable to the LSPs if Trusts did not take the core systems).[136]

The report also considered the implications of and the background to Fujitsu's departure from the programme, leaving only two LSPs remaining. The arrangements for the South had not been resolved at the time of the review, and because of the uncertainty new deployments in the region had ceased. Meanwhile, Fujitsu was continuing to provide systems support until May 2009 to those sites in the South where new care records systems were already operational. Negotiations were under way between the Department and BT to transfer responsibility for maintaining these sites (BT was considered best placed to take on this activity as it was also deploying Cerner's Millennium system in London).

In terms of the reasons for Fujitsu's withdrawal, while ultimately this appeared to be attributable to failure to agree revised price and commercial terms, the company advised that whereas the original assumption in the contract had been that there would be 'ruthless standardisation' across different Trusts, in practice there had been a constant need to make changes to suit the specific requirements of individual Trusts. This had resulted in a total of 650 change requests, which Fujitsu regarded as beyond the requirements of the contract. While the Department of Health acknowledged that the level of customisation that the suppliers were having to make for individual organisations was more extensive than had been anticipated at the start of the programme, they believed that most of what Fujitsu considered to be new requirements were in fact remedial and necessary to make the product fit-for-purpose for the NHS. The Department took the view therefore that Fujitsu had not met its contractual obligations.[137]

Other points emphasised in the report included:

- Overall leadership of the programme was still unclear in mid 2008, nearly a year after the announcement in summer 2007 that the then Director General of IT, Richard Granger, would be stepping down.[138] (The appointment of Christine Connelly, formerly CIO of Cadbury Schweppes, to the new position of Chief Information Officer for the NHS was ultimately made in September 2008. At the same time, Martin Bellamy, who had previously been CIO of the Pension Service, was appointed Director of Programme and System Delivery, with responsibility for running Connecting for Health).[139]

- The Programme was not providing value for money because of the slow implementation of care records systems.[140] There continued to be uncertainty around the estimate of £3.6 billion for the Programme's local costs, and there was a lack of transparency around progress against the timetables and revised projections.[141] While the Department had published the first benefits statement for the programme, for 2006-7, in March 2008, predicting total benefits over 10 years in excess of £1 billion, there remained much to do to measure and realise the benefits of the Programme.[142]

- It was hard for the programme to secure engagement and support from clinicians when little clinical functionality had been deployed to date, and given the difficulties being faced with the roll-out of the patient records systems. However, clinician support would be critical to the achievement of the long-term benefits of the programme.[143] Where systems had been implemented, they had required personnel to change the way they worked, without their seeing very much benefit and sometimes without consultation. [144]

- Patients and doctors continued to have concerns about data security.[145]

- In evidence to the committee, Mr David Nicholson, Chief Executive of the NHS, stated 'there is no doubt that this programme is incredibly ambitious and technically ambitious'. He also remarked (nearly six years into the programme) 'we are obviously learning to develop this programme at the moment'. [146]

In March 2009, deliberations concluded on how to deliver the programme in the South of England following Fujitsu's withdrawal. This involved firstly extension of BT's London contract to support the seven existing live Millennium sites, providing three new Millennium systems to Acute Trusts, and delivering 25 RiO systems to Community and Mental Health Trusts, at a total cost of £454m, and secondly the use of the framework of suppliers set up in 2008 to support the remaining Trusts (covering 28 Acute Trusts, 13 Community Trusts and 4 Ambulance Trusts), which it was estimated would cost £470m – which implied a somewhat lower average cost than under the BT contract. This decision to exclude a significant proportion of Trusts from the core systems set represented official acknowledgement by the programme of the challenges being faced by the LSPs in delivering and implementing the systems required on the scale required, and formal relaxation of the mandatory centrally-determined systems set.[147] This was followed by further relaxation in December 2009, where Trusts were given permission to build on their existing systems where this was possible, and/or take those elements of the new systems provided by the programme which they most required.[148]

Additionally, to ensure adequate integration was maintained between different systems across the NHS in support of joined up healthcare, the programme started developing what it called the 'Interoperability Toolkit', which was a set of national standards, frameworks and implementation guides which would provide a unified specification for system interoperability across the NHS.[149]

Separately, in March 2010 the Department reconfigured the contract with BT for London. This was partly a result of continuing problems with the delivery of Millennium, which at the time was found to have 84 defects against a contractual testing limit of 30, and concerns about BT's capacity to meet the scale of the contract. The revised contract also provided for more modular and tailored systems in the acute Trusts, and additional RiO functionality. The number of acute Trusts to which the programme would provide systems was reduced from 31 to 15, and the requirement for BT to deliver systems to the London Ambulance Service and to over 1,200 GP practices was removed from the contract. If they still required new systems, Ambulance Trusts and those acute trusts not being provided with systems under the programme would have to fund them themselves. GP systems in London would be provided at a cost of some £54 million under a separate contract called GP Systems of Choice, which was not part of NPfIT. The changes also enabled Trusts to choose within cost limits which core modules they wanted and in what order they would be delivered. Beyond these core modules, Trusts could choose to purchase additional modules, but would need to fund these themselves. The Department agreed to fund three releases of Millennium, with each release increasing the level of functionality provided by each module. The majority of the functionality provided through the programme would be contained in the third release. Similarly, the Department undertook to fund two releases of RiO. These changes resulted in a reduction in the total contract value of £73 million to £948 million.[150]

In September 2010, following the change of government from Labour to the Conservative/Liberal Democrat coalition arising from the May 2010 General Election, as well as a subsequent Cabinet Office assessment of the programme, the Department of Health issued a press release (see below)[151] which confirmed the changes being made in the programme's fundamental approach, and the move

THE FUTURE FOR THE NATIONAL PROGRAMME FOR IT[151]

A Department of Health review of the National Programme for IT has concluded that a centralise
national approach is no longer required, and that a more locally-led plural system of procureme
should operate, whilst continuing with national applications already procured.

A new approach to implementation will take a modular approach, allowing NHS organisations
to introduce smaller, more manageable change, in line with their business requirements and
capacity. NHS services will be the customers of a more plural system of IT embodying the core
assumption of 'connect all', rather than 'replace all' systems. This reflects the coalition
government's commitment to ending top-down government and enabling localised decision-
making.

The review of the National Programme for IT has also concluded that retaining a national
infrastructure will deliver best value for taxpayers. Applications such as Choose and Book,
Electronic Prescription Service and PACS have been delivered and are now integrated with the
running of current health services. Now there is a level of maturity in these applications they
no longer need to be managed as projects but as IT services under the control of the NHS.
Consequently, in line with the broader NHS reforms, the National Programme for IT will no
longer be run as a centralised national programme and decision making and responsibility will
be localised.

Health Minister, Simon Burns, said:
"Improving IT is essential to delivering a patient-centred NHS. But the nationally imposed
system is neither necessary nor appropriate to deliver this. We will allow hospitals to use and
develop the IT they already have and add to their environment either by integrating systems
purchased through the existing national contracts or elsewhere. This makes practical sense. It
also makes financial sense. Moving IT systems closer to the frontline will release £700 million
extra in savings. Every penny saved through productivity gains will be reinvested to improve
patient care."
Director General for Informatics, Christine Connelly, said:
"It is clear that the National Programme for IT has delivered important changes for the NHS
including an infrastructure which the NHS today depends on for providing safe and responsive
health care. Now the NHS is changing, we need to change the way IT supports those changes,
bringing decisions closer to the front line and ensuring that change is manageable and holds
less risk for NHS organisations."

away from wholesale replacement of trusts' systems to a more flexible arrangement where trusts would choose whether to adopt the new systems being offered by the programme or connect their existing systems to the infrastructure introduced through the programme.[151]

At the same time, despite the considerable difficulties the NPfIT continued to encounter, the Department of Health also announced that the programme's existing contracts, which required further payments of up to £2.9 billion for the delivery of care records systems, would still be honoured.[152] Together with the associated £1.4 billion of local implementation costs, this implied a further spend of £4.3 billion on this part of the programme (out of £5bn estimated still to be spent overall).[153]

A further review of the programme, with particular emphasis on the care records service, was undertaken by the National Audit Office in 2011.[154] This noted that although there were a number of parts of the programme that had either delivered or were well advanced, the problems with implementing local care records systems identified in previous reports had continued.[155]

Progress in delivering national systems to end March 2011 is shown below:

System	% of functionality delivered	% of NHS organisations with the system ready for use	Comment
N3 network	100	100	Fully delivered and routinely used
Spine	100	100	Fully delivered and routinely used
NHSmail	100	n/a	720,000 registered users of NHSmail, of which 440,000 are active users
Choose and Book	100	97 (Acute trusts) 95 (GP practices)	Around 52 per cent of first outpatient referrals were being processed through Choose and Book, compared to the 90 per cent originally expected.
Electronic Prescription Service Release 1 (paper) and 2 (electronic)	R1: 100 R2: 100	R1: 97 (GP practices) 95 (Pharmacies) R2: 56 (GP practices) 60 (Pharmacies)	Release 1 rolled out but most of the benefits depended on Release 2 which was not yet available for use in all pharmacies and GP practices. As at 31 March 2011, some 112,000 prescriptions had been transmitted using the service.

System	% of functionality delivered	% of NHS organisations with the system ready for use	Comment
Picture Archiving and Communications System (PACS)	100	100	Number of X-rays reported within 48 hours increased from 40 per cent to 75 per cent across England.
GP to GP transfer	60	59	Not possible to determine percentage of all patient record transfers made electronically through GP to GP transfer, because system did not capture transfers between GP practices using the same care records system.
Quality Management and Analysis System	100	100	Over 99 per cent of GP practices supplying data automatically through their practice systems
Summary Care Record	100	10 (GP practices)	As at 31 March 2011, 5.8 million summary care records had been created out of a potential 54 million.

Source: NAO 2011 p17[156]

In terms of the delivery of Detailed Care Records systems, progress as at 31 March 2011 was as follows:

	London		South		North, Midlands and East		Total	
	Delivered (%)	Total (Original)	Delivered (%)	Total (Original)	Delivered (%)	Total (Original)	Delivered (%)	Total (Original)
Acute trusts	8 (53)	15 (31)	7 (70)	10 (41)	4 (4)	97 (97)	19 (16)	122 (169)
Community health services	29 (100)	29 (31)	10 (83)	12 (31)	56 (59)	95 (90)	95 (70)	136 (152)
Mental health trusts	8 (100)	8 (10)	13 (100)	13 (14)	0 (0)	35 (35)	21 (37)	56 (59)

Source: NAO 2011, p9 and p11[157]

However, given the changes to the scope of the programme and the phasing of the various releases, the true picture was even less clear-cut. In particular:

In London:
- care records systems for 1,243 GP practices and the London Ambulance Service had been removed from the scope of the Programme in March 2010.[158]

- by 31st March 2011, three Acute Trusts had implemented the first release of Millennium and five had progressed to the second release. No Acute Trusts had at this point been upgraded to the third and final release of Millennium, which delivered the level of functionality anticipated at the programme's outset, although BT advised that this release was ready to be delivered. All further systems and upgrades of Millennium were expected to be delivered across the 15 Acute Trusts by October 2014.
- the first of the two new releases of RiO was due to be implemented at a trust in the summer of 2011. All subsequent contracted upgrades, releases, and enhancements were expected to be completed across all 37 NHS organisations using RiO in London by October 2014.[159]
- Notwithstanding this reduction in scope, the value of the contract had been reduced by only £73 million (7 per cent) from £1,021 million to £948 million. The NAO estimated that the revised figures implied an increase in the average cost of Millennium per Acute Trust of at least 18 per cent (although they stated that the Department had been unable to provide them with a full breakdown of the revised costs).[160]

In the South:
- GP practice systems were not included in the original contract for the South, and Ambulance systems were removed from the scope of the programme in March 2009.[158]
- BT took over support in March 2009 of the seven Acute Trusts which had already implemented Millenium. By March 2011 it had upgraded four trusts to the second release of Millenium, with two more sites due to follow by September 2011. No deliveries of Millenium had been completed at any of the three new sites by the time of the report, although the first deployment was scheduled for July 2011, with all three sites due to be completed by March 2012. Deployment of all releases across all 10 Acute Trusts covered by the BT contract was expected to be finished by October 2015.[161]
- The NAO reported that the costs of delivering the three new care records systems in Acute Trusts were some 47 per cent higher than the cost of delivering the same system in London, although BT advised that the systems were being delivered in a different way, and the Department disputed the figure quoted.[162]
- By 31 March 2011, BT had implemented version five of RiO at 23 Community and Mental Health Trusts in the South, and the two remaining RiO deployments

were expected to take place by May 2011. All subsequent contracted upgrades, releases, and enhancements were projected to be completed by October 2014.[161]

In the North, Midlands and East:
- While at the time of the report there had been no reductions in the number of systems to be delivered by CSC, negotiations had commenced in December 2008, and were still in progress, to reduce the total contract value by at least £500 million. To secure this cost reduction it was anticipated that the number of systems to be delivered and the capability of these systems would need to be reduced.[163]
- In November 2009, the Department of Health had concluded that CSC could not deliver Lorenzo within the timescales required in the contract as it was still not ready and had 3,128 identified defects against a contractual limit of 700.[164] As a result, they established a set of criteria by means of which to assess the progress being made in the development and deployment of the system. These covered whether the system existed, was robust and reliable, had been successfully delivered, could be delivered at scale by the supplier and was on track to be working smoothly at an acute trust by March 2010 (similar criteria were also applied to the Cerner Millenium application being deployed in London and the South).[165] In the event, the first full scale rollout of Lorenzo took place at all sites of Morecambe Bay University Hospitals Trust in June 2010.[166] By the end of March 2011 Release 1 of Lorenzo (containing mainly clinical functionality) had finally been implemented at 7 Trusts, while Lorenzo Release 1.9, which included the patient administration system upon which the majority of the additional modules were dependent, had been delivered at three sites, although this release had yet to be signed off by the receiving trusts.[167]
- Release 2 had not yet been delivered at any of the three early adopter sites, which included two Acute Trusts and a primary care trust, and this work was not now scheduled to be completed until June 2012.[168] No releases of Lorenzo had been delivered at a mental health trust despite work being undertaken at an early adopter site – Pennine Care Trust - with a view to mental health functionality being available for use by November 2009. Following a number of delays in development, the Trust announced in April 2011 that it no longer wished to remain in the Lorenzo early adopter programme and was now considering other systems.[169]

- The figures shown in the Table exclude interim systems. Due to the non-availability of Lorenzo, CSC had provided alternative or interim solutions in those trusts whose systems were in urgent need of replacement. In Acute Trusts and Mental Health Trusts, by March 2011, 40 interim systems offering a lower level of functionality had been deployed under the contract. An alternative system, TPP SystmOne, had been delivered to 50 of 90 community health services. As a result of these deployments, funds available for the implementation of Lorenzo across the cluster were lower than originally projected. Given this, and the pressure to reduce costs in the contract renegotiations, it was no longer expected that it would be possible to replace all the interim systems that had been installed.[170]
- By 31st March 2011, CSC had also delivered systems (Medusa Siren ePCR) to all six ambulance trusts in the cluster, all 54 systems they were contracted to provide to child community health service organisations, and all 136 systems that were required for prisons.[171] They had also delivered SystmOne systems at 1,377 GP practices, representing about 31 per cent of the contracted volume. The remaining 3,023 GP system implementations were scheduled to be completed by 2014-15, with almost all of these intended to be Release 4 of Lorenzo – although this version of the system had not yet been developed.[172]

Additionally, the report noted that even where systems had been implemented, further development would still be required to provide the contracted level of functionality. While the Department of Health advised that at the time of the review 91 per cent of the functionality for the acute system in London and the South had been proven to work, and 64 per cent of the acute system to be provided in the North, Midlands and East had been developed, the NAO expressed the view that these assessments presented an overly positive view of progress, since they failed to take account of the extent to which functionality had actually been implemented and was being used. Moreover, these estimates compared progress against the minimum specification level of functionality agreed with clinicians in 2008, rather than the full scope originally intended under the programme.[173]

The total cost of the reconfigured programme was now estimated at £11.4bn, of which £6.35bn had been spent by 31st March 2011.[174] The NAO also noted that there was still considerable uncertainty surrounding the successful delivery of the remainder of the programme within the budget of £5.05bn (of which £4.3bn related directly to the care records service).

In particular:

- Contract renegotiations with CSC were continuing. Given that these remained unresolved, the possibility of either termination of the contract or a substantial reduction in scope remained.
- The costs of the additional systems in the South to be acquired through the framework contracts were not yet known, while the level of funding available for these systems would be significantly lower (by about 50 per cent) than that which was available under the central contracts. The Department of Health advised that this was because these systems would have less functionality – although they would meet the minimum functional requirements previously established with clinicians.
- As payment was dependent on the successful delivery of systems by suppliers, any delays in implementation would mean that expenditure would slip into later years – but there was no guarantee that funding would be available at this time.
- Local costs could increase as a result of the need to make systems provided outside the programme compatible with those provided as part of the programme.[175]
- Despite the reductions in scope, there was still a considerable amount of outstanding work to be undertaken to meet the targets set for the programme. The report noted that the pace of delivery required to meet the timetable for implementation in Acute Trusts exceeded anything achieved anywhere in the programme hitherto.[176]
- By 2012, due to the reorganisation of the NHS, Strategic Health Authorities would be abolished and the existing governance structure for the delivery of the care records systems would disappear. Following this change, it was not clear who would be responsible for managing the existing contracts up to their expiry; who would measure and report on the benefits of the programme; or how the financial implications for the programme of the organisational changes to the NHS would be managed.
- Likewise, it was unclear how contractual responsibilities for the support of the systems implemented under the programme would be managed following the expiry of the existing contracts in 2015-2016.[177]

The NAO again raised concerns regarding the quality of information about the programme's costs, status and future plans which was available to them during their review. They also noted discrepancies between data provided to them by the Department of Health and that obtained from suppliers.[178]

Overall, the NAO concluded that the successful delivery of an electronic patient record for every NHS patient, which was a fundamental part of the programme's overall objective of improving services and the quality of patient care, would not now be achieved. Progress against plans had fallen far below expectations, and the Department had chosen to reduce the scope of the programme significantly, with substantial reductions in the number of acute trusts, ambulance trusts, and GP practices now planned to receive care records systems through the programme. No clear assessment of the implications of this reduction in scope for the expected benefits of the programme had been provided, but the report noted that the scope reductions had not been accompanied by a proportionate reduction in costs. The NAO therefore came to the conclusion that the £2.7 billion spent on care records systems to that point did not represent value for money, nor did it find grounds for confidence that the remaining planned expenditure of £4.3 billion would be any different.[179]

In contrast, the Department of Health responded that 'the money spent to date has not been wasted and will potentially deliver value for money. This is based on the fact that more than half of the Trusts in England have received systems under the programme and no supplier is paid for a system until that system has been verified by the Trust to have been deployed successfully. The Department believes that the flexibility provided by the future delivery model for the programme will deliver functionality that best fits the needs of the clinical and managerial community. The future architecture of the programme allows many sources of information to be connected together as opposed to assuming that all relevant information will be stored in a single system. This approach has been proven in other sectors and is fully consistent with the Government's recently published ICT strategy.'[180]

The NAO report was again followed shortly thereafter by one from the Public Accounts Committee, for which the hearing was held on 23rd May 2011.[181] This reiterated and reinforced much of what had been reported by the NAO. The report concluded in particular that:

- The Department had been unable to deliver its original vision of a standardised care records solution across the NHS. Many NHS organisations would not now receive a system through the programme, which would not therefore provide for transmission of information throughout the NHS.[182] In their evidence, however, the programme asserted that the vision remained valid, but they had adopted a different solution involving a 'networked architecture' which would still enable data to be shared across the systems.[183] They argued that this would give local NHS bodies greater flexibility by enabling them either to configure a series of available system modules offered under the programme to meet their specific needs, or to link to the core infrastructure using other systems not provided by the programme.[184] This new approach had been made possible by advances in technology since the programme had begun, and the Department believed it would still enable the programme's aims to be achieved.[185] However, it meant that individual Trusts now had the option to opt out of the programme (whereas one of the key original aims of the programme had been to avoid each NHS organisation procuring their own systems).[186]

- There were continuing uncertainties around future delivery, and around the costs and feasibility of connecting up the 'patchwork' of different applications that would result from the new approach. BT pointed out in evidence to the committee that 'from monolithic to modular is quite a challenge to do, and quite an extensive amount of work. The design is different, the deployment is different, the service is different, the number of domains is different, they bought different kit, the capability is different'.[187] There were also questions regarding the availability of sufficient funding for those Trusts that had decided to proceed outside the programme – although the Department pointed out that this was their choice. Given this, the Committee recommended the Department review urgently whether it was worth continuing with the care records system as proposed, to determine whether the remaining £4.3 billion could be used to better effect to buy systems that worked, were good value and delivered demonstrable benefits for the NHS.[188]

- There had been a substantial reduction in the number of NHS organisations which would receive new systems under the programme, but this reduction had not been marked by an equivalent reduction in costs. The committee felt this cast the Department's negotiating capability in a 'very poor light'.[189]

They noted that the Department was 'clearly overpaying' BT[190], since systems which were being provided for an average of £9m per site as part of the programme in the South had been purchased for under £2m by NHS organisations outside the programme (although the Department argued that this was attributable to differences in the sophistication of the solutions and the level of support being provided). Separately, whereas the NAO had been advised that the average cost of three new acute systems in the South would be 47 per cent more expensive than in London, new figures provided by the Department projected the cost of delivering an acute system in London at £31m, rather than the £19m reported by the NAO. This meant that the costs of these systems in the South would in fact be 24 per cent less expensive than for the London sites – which as well as failing to inspire confidence around the accuracy of the figures provided, still left the question of why these differences should exist.[191]

- The committee also expressed reservations about the ongoing contract renegotiations with CSC, which at the time of the review had been under way for over a year without resolution. While the Department advised that it could prove more expensive to terminate the contract than to complete it, the report noted that CSC had informed the United States Securities and Exchange Commission that it could receive materially less than the net asset value of its contract were the NHS to exercise its right of termination.[192] The committee also warned of the dangers of CSC acquiring a monopoly in the provision of care records systems in the North, Eastern and Midland clusters, particularly given its intended acquisition of iSoft. It argued that following the takeover, CSC could decide to cease development of Lorenzo, leaving many Trusts with little choice but to continue with out-dated interim systems that could be very expensive to maintain and to upgrade, or to accept a system of CSC's choice.[193]

- The Department was unable to show what benefits had been achieved from the £2.7 billion spent to date on care records systems (many of which were interim systems). This was in part because of its failure to provide up to date benefits statements, although they had committed to do so previously.[194] Despite the significant expenditure on programme management and the existence of a central team of 1300 people,[195] the Department had also been unable to provide timely and reliable information to make possible Parliamentary scrutiny of this project. Basic information provided by the Department to the NAO was late, inconsistent and contradictory. This was 'unacceptable'.[196]

- The Department needed to address possible compromises in security around health records; there were continuing concerns regarding the lack of evidence of risk management of security issues associated with medical records being held electronically.[197]

- Weak management and oversight of the programme had resulted in poor accountability for performance. In particular, the Senior Responsible Owner for the programme, Sir David Nicholson, the Chief Executive of the NHS, had not been able to fulfil his duties effectively, given the extent of his other responsibilities[198] (for example, Sir David acknowledged in evidence that he had delegated chairmanship of the Programme Board to his deputy, the NHS Director of Finance, Performance and Operations).[199] This had reduced accountability for the Programme's extensive delays and increasingly poor value for money. The Committee recommended that Sir David remained Senior Responsible Owner for the Programme to ensure a clear line of accountability and responsibility for performance as well as continuity in managing the substantial remaining risks, but this should be accompanied by much closer scrutiny and oversight of his actions by the Cabinet Office's Major Projects Authority.[200]

- Following the proposed NHS restructuring, responsibilities for care records systems would transfer to individual NHS Trusts in 2015-16. However, since the existing contracts were managed centrally, trusts had no understanding of the likely costs they would face in using and supporting the systems. The committee recommended the Department of Health make clear to every trust their future responsibilities for the systems, and the financial liabilities to which they would be exposed, including the exit costs from the LSP contracts, the future maintenance and running costs for those Trusts continuing inside the programme, and the support that the centre would provide to Trusts outside it.[201] It was noted that a body similar to Connecting for Health would probably be required to support the transition from the existing arrangements to the new ones put in place.[202]

Looking at the evolution of the programme in its entirety, the committee stated that it had been inherently risky from the outset and that when the Department signed the contracts for the delivery of care records systems in 2003-04 the suppliers did not have a product available that would meet the requirements.[203] The Department noted, however, that the programme had been subject to a number of third party reviews and risk assessments, and therefore that Ministers were aware of the risks[204], and that some of these risks were mitigated by the 'payment by results' structure of the contracts.[205] In hindsight, the Department accepted that the delivery of a one-size-fits-all system to the NHS had proved to be too difficult.[206] This was partly attributable to lack of support from clinicians. The committee asserted, and the Department agreed, that some of the pitfalls and waste could have been avoided if there had been greater consultation at the start of the programme with health professionals.[207] (This said, surveys suggested there remained disagreements among medical professionals as to whether the 'Clinical Five' represented the right areas of focus, so obtaining support and consensus among clinicians is likely always to have been a major challenge).[208]

In May 2011 the Prime Minister announced that further development of the patient record system would be frozen pending review of the reports from the NAO and the Public Accounts Committee, as well as from the government's Major Projects Authority.[209] In September the Department of Health issued a press release under the heading 'Dismantling the NHS National Programme for IT'.[210] This announced the restoration of local control over decision-making and greater choice for individual NHS organisations. A review would be undertaken by the new Managing Director of Informatics at the Department of Health, Katie Davis (who had taken over from Christine Connelly who had resigned)[211] of all applications and services to determine how best to take these forward. At the same time, the Department would work in partnership with Intellect, the Technology Trade Association, to develop proposals as to how they could stimulate the healthcare IT and technology marketplace in future, and offer greater choice of supplier to local NHS organisations, while still achieving value for money across the service.[210]

This announcement was presented by the government and widely reported by the media as marking the end of the programme.[212] However, none of the existing supplier contracts were cancelled, and in September 2012 negotiations with CSC resulted in an interim agreement on a new contract. This reduced the amount due to CSC by £1bn from the £2.9bn previously, and stripped CSC of exclusive rights to provide care records systems in the North, Midlands and East of England. As under the renegotiated BT contracts elsewhere, local health authorities in these regions would therefore no longer be compelled to use CSC's Lorenzo system; however central funding would be available from the Department of Health for any that decided to adopt the software.[213]

In reality, therefore, the change announced in September 2011 was probably less significant that it was made out to be (although presenting it in this way was no doubt politically expedient and advantageous). In effect, it represented formal acknowledgement of the more devolved delivery model for the care records systems that had been adopted since 2008/9. Moreover, part of what the programme had originally been created to deliver had been completed. This said, although the concept of a centrally mandated and driven systems solution for the NHS had clearly already been in retreat for a number of years, the announcement marked its formal death-knell. In a sense, things had come full circle, with responsibility for IT reverting substantially to individual health service entities. Of course, it was partly as a result of the problems associated with this that the NPfIT had originally been created.

Epilogue

In September 2013 the House of Commons Public Accounts Committee published a further review of what they described as the 'dismantled' National Programme for IT in the NHS.[214] The report noted 'Although the Department told us that the National Programme had been dismantled, the component programmes are all continuing, the existing contracts are being honoured and significant costs are still being incurred. The only change from the National Programme that the Department could tell us about was that new governance arrangements were now in place'[215] – although this should probably not have come as any real surprise. The report noted in particular that:

- CSC had still not delivered the necessary software and no trust had a fully functioning Lorenzo care records system (although the Lorenzo system was said to be working fully at the 'key site' of Morecambe Bay, albeit with the exception of the parts of the software that had not been fully delivered).
- Despite an interim agreement having been reached with CSC in August 2012, at the time of the committee's hearing, contract renegotiations were still continuing, partly because under the original contract, CSC had the

exclusive right to supply systems to 160 trusts in the North and the Midlands. However, following the restructuring of the programme, there were no longer 160 trusts willing to implement CSC's systems, so the Department of Health was now unable to fulfil its contractual obligation. As a result, it had paid £100m to CSC in compensation. Moreover, if the Department terminated the contract, it could potentially be required to pay the full value of the original contract (£3.1bn). Given this, the Department's negotiating position was acknowledged to be 'weak'.[216]

- In a benefits statement produced by the Department of Health in July 2012 (which had also been audited by the National Audit Office)[217], total costs of the programme were projected at £9.8bn (with £7.3bn spent by March 2012)[218], although this excluded the future costs associated with the supply of Lorenzo to a maximum of 22 trusts in the North, Midlands and East for which the Department would provide funding (estimated to cost £0.6bn).[219] In addition, the Department remained in arbitration with Fujitsu regarding the termination of their contract in the South in 2008, with both parties claiming compensation, which could also lead to additional costs being incurred.[220]

- The benefits statement estimated total benefits from the programme of £10.7bn to the end of life of the systems (which in the case of the care records systems in the North, Midlands and East would be 2024). Approximately two thirds of these were still to be realised at the time the benefits statement was produced. The Department acknowledged that, while it had provided guidance to trusts, there had been insufficient drive either from the centre or at local level to take ownership of the benefits from the various component programmes. They stressed that to drive benefits, local NHS staff needed to be convinced of the value of the transformation involved, and this required leadership from the top of the various organisations. However, it was not clear that this was happening. As a result, 'benefit leads' for each of the local care records programmes would be appointed, and more support provided to trusts to help in benefits realisation.[221]

- The report noted that the Secretary of State for Health had set the NHS a new goal of being 'paperless' by 2018. The committee concluded that 'After the sorry history of the National Programme, we are sceptical that the Department can deliver its vision of a paperless NHS by 2018. We have reported previously on the shortcomings of the National Programme, which included poor negotiating capability, resulting in deals which were poor value for money and weak programme management and oversight. There were also failures to understand the complexity of the tasks, to recognise the difficulties of persuading NHS trusts to take new systems that had been procured nationally, and to get people to operate the systems effectively even when they were adopted. Making the NHS paperless will involve further significant investment in IT and business transformation. However, the Department has not even set aside a specific budget for this purpose. As with the National Programme, it will be important to balance the need for standardisation across the NHS with the desire for local ownership and flexibility. The first 'milestone' towards the ambition of a paperless NHS is for GP referrals to be paperless by 2015'.[222]

During the hearing, Sir David Nicholson, the head of the NHS and the Senior Responsible Owner for the NPfIT made the following comments in response to questioning by Jackie Doyle-Price, one of the MPs on the committee:

'Before 2003—in 1998, as it happens—I was running a hospital...We had an extensive new system in the hospital that I was responsible for, but it had built up over many years, with many clinicians. It was a basic patient administration system, but many clinicians—gastroenterologists and so on—all created their own systems and connected it to the base system, so over the years, we built up this extraordinary conglomeration of systems. The National Programme for IT offered to take all that away and replace it with something standard, which will probably be less than you have now. In those circumstances, to me it is pretty obvious to work out that the reaction is difficult—people go, 'Why on earth would we do that?' The idea of ruthless standardisation—that you can enforce a set of things on the NHS— has proved illusory. It has proved to be something that you are not able to do... Because the NHS is not an organisation, but a set of organisations that have their own legal and statutory responsibilities, their own history and their own way of operating. You can get them to work together. You can bring things together and you can work co-operatively across it, but managing change of that nature from the top centrally is simply not possible in something as complex as this. The history of this programme over the past few years has been about trying to get the best out of what was there for the organisation as it is, as opposed to what you might hope it was'.[223]

CHAPTER 4: IT PROJECT SOURCES OF COMPLEXITY – THE THINGS THAT MAKE IT PROJECTS HARD

As noted, the point of the case study was not specifically to understand what occurred on the NPfIT project per se, and thus to seek to explain why it resulted in the outcomes it did; rather it was to provide a sort of 'laboratory' to help illuminate the broad suite of different complexities and difficulties that any IT project may potentially encounter – that is to say, the things that make IT projects 'hard'. Hence, the following sections seek to 'deconstruct' the NPfIT project and pull out the different sources of complexity that it experienced, and then to discuss why these particular aspects give rise to the difficulties that they do. This isn't intended to be an exhaustive list of all possible such sources of complexity, but one of the advantages of choosing the NPfIT as the subject of the case study is that as such a huge and demanding project, most of the common sources of complexity faced by many IT projects were evident within it somewhere at some point. In this analysis, I've therefore attempted to identify all the things that emerge from NPfIT which seem to have caused difficulty, either in and of themselves, or because they gave rise to choices which were problematic, where there were no panaceas, and where any course of action chosen would give rise to a further set of difficulties and challenges. As such, this provides a sort of 'Murphy's Law' – if it can go wrong, it will go wrong – lens through which to view IT projects.

This chapter breaks the sources of complexity down into the same three categories that emerged previously from the engineering and construction project 'mini studies' - namely contextual or situational complexities (ones that arise from the circumstances and situation the project is facing and in which it is being undertaken), inherent complexities (that is ones that come with the IT project territory and are likely to be 'part and parcel' of any IT project - although the way they manifest themselves will obviously vary depending on the situation and the choices made by the project), and events.

The table below seeks to list out the sources of complexity emerging from the case study. Each of these is then discussed in more detail in the sections that follow. For purposes of the argument, each of the different items will be considered in isolation. In reality, however, many of the different sources of complexity interact with each other, so choices made in response to one of the sources of complexity are likely to have implications in relation to other ones (much as in the case of the Brooklyn Bridge the width of the East River led to the decision to build a suspension bridge, which required the construction of bridge towers in mid-stream, which required the use of caissons, which required the selection of a supplier to manufacture the caissons and so on).

In parentheses, it is probably necessary to acknowledge at this point that despite my earlier comments about lists, this chapter represents a list. Hopefully, however, it is a list with a degree of logic to it (which therefore makes it acceptable).

SOURCE OF COMPLEXITY	HOW MANIFEST BY NPfIT	GENERAL COMMENTS
Situational Sources of Complexity		
Organisational context	NPfIT was a government initiated project taking place in the context of a fragmented and highly politicised NHS, all of which had a significant impact on the project and the way it unfolded	IT projects take place against the background of the structure, culture, and human dynamics of the organisation undertaking them, all of which have major implications for the nature and conduct of the project in question
IT legacy environment	One of the key challenges facing NPfIT was plotting and pursuing a sensible roadmap from the inherited mix of systems to the proposed end solution, especially given that due to the different systems in place in each different locality, the roadmap would be unique in each area	IT projects take place in the context of, and have to take account of, the existing IT environment and mix of systems in place in the organisation
Organisational activities and processes	NPfIT struggled to find and implement systems solutions capable of supporting fully the full suite of activities and processes that the programme was intended to address	The nature, breadth, depth and complexity of the activity set and organisational processes being addressed by the project is a critical contributory factor in the complexity of any IT project
Problem/ opportunity definition	NPfIT sought to address a number of profound issues: resolve existing shortcomings/ fragmentation of NHS records and IT systems; achieve greater integration/ standardisation; leverage IT to enable broader improvements in healthcare	IT projects are – or at least should be – in service of some broader organisational objective, ie to resolve an identified problem, or enable the organisation to take advantage of a new opportunity

SOURCE OF COMPLEXITY	HOW MANIFEST BY NPfIT	GENERAL COMMENTS
Inherent Sources of Complexity		
Project scope	The scope of NPfIT covered the full identified problem/opportunity space across all parts of the NHS in England	There are choices to be made about the extent of the 'problem/ opportunity' space that the project will cover
Disaggregation and Phasing	Delivery of NPfIT was broken down into a number of different component parts, the roll out of which was then planned to take place in a series of separate phases (which subsequently required modification)	There are choices to be made as to whether and how to divide up the project into component parts and/or phases for delivery
Requirements gathering	NPfIT was consistently criticised for its failure to engage sufficiently with medical professionals in identifying these requirements	IT projects need a means of identifying the full set of requirements that the organisation is seeking the system to be able to satisfy
Solution/ Software selection	NPfIT selected a small number of core third party packages, which ultimately required considerable enhancement to enable them to meet a critical minimum set of requirements; achievement of the full suite of requirements proved elusive	There are choices here as to whether to create a bespoke solution or to buy an off-the-shelf package, and if the latter, whether to modify this in some way
System configuration and architecture	NPfIT's basic architecture consisted of three main interlinked component parts, namely the National Spine, the National Network, and the Detailed Care Records systems	This covers an array of issues and choices regarding the configuration of the new system(s) and organisational processes, and the ways these will be combined with the legacy systems/processes
Organisational change	NPfIT was criticised for focusing too narrowly on the delivery of the IT systems, the contracting process and the ongoing management of the suppliers (all of course important) at the expense of the wider organisational change to which it would give rise; some specific issues also emerged from the Nuffield Orthopaedic Centre implementation	Many IT projects have significant implications for the operating processes in place in the organisation and the roles and responsibilities of affected employees; hence there is a significant organisational change aspect associated with these projects, which needs to be managed appropriately

SOURCE OF COMPLEXITY	HOW MANIFEST BY NPfIT	GENERAL COMMENTS
Inherent Sources of Complexity (continued)		
User involvement	NPfIT was consistently criticised for not engaging sufficiently with the users	IT projects need to interact with staff within the client organisation (particularly those who are users of existing systems which the new system is projected to replace, and potential users of the new system) – but there are choices as to how to undertake this engagement, and to what extent to involve the users
Stakeholder relationships	NPfIT was criticised for not engaging sufficiently with key stakeholders (eg medical professionals, patients, media)	IT projects require mechanisms which provide for engagement with key individuals and groups who are impacted by the project in some way (who may or may not be users of the system)
Supplier selection and relationships	Suppliers played a pivotal role in NPfIT; the initial choice of suppliers and the nature of the contracts entered into with them was critical in terms of the future evolution of the project, and relationships with all of the main suppliers proved problematic in a number of different respects	Where third party suppliers are engaged to participate in the project, the appropriate suppliers need to be selected, contractual arrangements need to be negotiated, and mechanisms put in place to manage their ongoing activities
IT technical issues	Various technical issues are referred to in the case study, eg system performance problems with Choose and Book, and problems emerging during the Nuffield Orthopaedic Centre implementation	Unsurprisingly, all IT projects need to address a myriad of IT technical issues
Testing	Problems with the Nuffield Orthopaedic Centre go-live point to shortcomings in the testing of the system ahead of its implementation	Appropriate testing of the solution needs to take place prior to implementation to ensure it is fit for purpose
Security and access	The adequacy of the mechanisms to protect and control access to sensitive medical information held within the systems was an ongoing source of concern throughout the lifetime of NPfIT	Means need to be in place to safeguard the information contained within the system from unauthorised access, modification and corruption

SOURCE OF COMPLEXITY	HOW MANIFEST BY NPfIT	GENERAL COMMENTS
Inherent Sources of Complexity (continued)		
Organisational readiness and implementat-ion	The Nuffield Orthopaedic Centre example illustrates many of the difficulties that may be encountered here, especially if there are weaknesses in the preparations for go-live	This covers a number of different activities, including data migration, training, cutover, and the establishment of ongoing operational support arrangements, all of which need to be addressed with appropriate rigour
Financial aspects	There were uncertainties around projected NPfIT costs, and some of the programme's benefits were difficult to evaluate financially; there were also ongoing problems with the consolidation of costs and the measurement of benefits	IT projects are likely to encounter a number of financial issues, particularly in relation to ensuring that there is a positive value proposition associated with the project, the ongoing management of costs, and the delivery of the financial benefits arising from the project
Delivery model	NPfIT adopted a centrally-co-ordinated model with contracts let to service providers for provision and subsequent operation of an agreed suite of systems obtained from identified vendors; with local NHS entities also having some responsibilities for systems implementation	There are choices to be made as to how the project will be structured and organised to enable the suite of activities entailed to be undertaken
Project management/ methodology	NPfIT adopted PRINCE2 methodology; however, certain parts of the project were criticised for poor project management (eg Lorenzo development activity)	IT projects are complex and multi-faceted undertakings, and need to be managed professionally and with the necessary rigour and discipline; a project management methodology is a necessary part of this – although only a part
Governance and sponsorship	Some difficulties were experienced in relation to NPfIT governance – eg turnover of Senior Responsible Owners during the early years of the project, criticism of the final SRO for his insufficient involvement	IT projects require mechanisms which provide for the client organisation (through its senior representatives) to exercise appropriate oversight and control over the project, in pursuit of the achievement of the intended organisational objectives arising from the project

SOURCE OF COMPLEXITY	HOW MANIFEST BY NPfIT	GENERAL COMMENTS
Inherent Sources of Complexity (continued)		
Resourcing, expertise and capability	The scale of NPfIT, along with the reliance on a small (and decreasing) number of providers, resulted in some significant resource gaps	IT projects need to be sufficiently well resourced with individuals with the necessary expertise and experience
Progress measurement and monitoring	NPfIT was criticised for failing to provide a definitive view of project progress and costs incurred	Mechanisms are required to measure project progress, so as to be able to identify and correct problems and issues arising as the project proceeds
Managing changes	NPfIT established mechanisms to prevent scope creep – although some of this nevertheless did occur	IT projects are prone to requests for modifications (eg to incorporate additional features) as they progress – so mechanisms are required to manage this
Benefits	NPfIT was criticised for failing to demonstrate the benefits arising from the project	Since IT projects are enablers of a particular end, mechanisms are required to ensure the benefits intended to arise from the project are realised in practice
Independent Review	NPfIT was subject to considerable independent review – although the impact and value of some of this is perhaps open to question	Informed independent advice and input is valuable throughout the life of a project to guard against subjectivity and self interest on the part of those directly involved in the project
Events		
Events	Among the significant events impacting NPfIT during its life were: a change in government, reorganisation of the NHS, changes in key personnel, and changes in suppliers	All IT projects will be subject to events and changing circumstances which are outside their full control, unexpected and/or predictable, which will impact on the project, and to which the project will need to respond, either directly or via risk management activities

The following sections seek to discuss each of the sources of complexity identified above in greater detail.

SITUATIONAL SOURCES OF COMPLEXITY

ORGANISATIONAL CONTEXT

For IT projects, it is the organisational context in which the project takes place which serves as the equivalent of the geological, geographical and environmental context which provides the backdrop to construction projects like the Bell Rock Lighthouse or the Brooklyn Bridge, and is the source of much of the complexity which such projects encounter.

As NPfIT illustrates, this organisational context manifests itself in a number of different ways, in particular:

- the size and geographical extent of the organisation: the NHS is the world's largest public healthcare organisation – in September 2010 it employed over 1.4 million people in England, making it one of the world's top ten largest employers.[1] The scale and reach of NPfIT was such that it had potential implications for a sizeable part of this organisation across the whole of the country – although unlike some projects, it did not encounter the challenges associated with activities which extend beyond a single country, and potentially into many different countries.
- the structure of the organisation in question: in the case of NPfIT, the devolved and fragmented nature of the NHS had profound implications for the project. In particular, the project was to some extent configured as a direct response to this fragmentation, both as a means of imposing greater standardisation, and as a reaction to the delivery challenges that the devolved structure was perceived to have caused previously. But this meant that the resulting delivery model was substantially at odds with the organisation structure in existence in the NHS, which inevitably resulted in some of the tensions that the project encountered.
- the internal power dynamics of the organisation: some of the dynamics of the NHS which had significant implications for NPfIT included the following:
  - o reflecting the organisational structure, significant power within the NHS resides within the individual component parts (local NHS Trusts, GPs), rather than at the centre;
  - o significant power also rests with medical professionals, particularly consultants and other senior doctors, often leading to tensions between this group and managers and administrators;

o the organisation employs large numbers of lower paid administrative and support staff; there is a sizeable union presence among these groups, which may often be resistant to change, especially if this is perceived as likely to have an adverse impact on the immediate situation of the membership;

o combined with the organisational fragmentation, these power dynamics further constrained the ability of ministers, officials and administrators to effect material control and direction over the wider NHS.

Such dynamics are of course not unique to the NHS; most organisations exhibit some dominant groups or individuals, some of whom may be supportive of a particular project and the changes it is expected to bring, and others who may be resistant. Another common feature of organisations is inter-departmental and inter-managerial tensions and rivalries. All of these again form part of the backdrop to a project, and are likely to prove something to which the project has to respond as it progresses.

• the capability, capacity and culture of the organisation to undertake the project in question; this includes such factors as the access to resources required, but also considerations like the degree of previous exposure to IT projects, the ability of the organisation to put in place and then to operate with the necessary rigour and discipline the structures and processes required to steward the project through to delivery; and the patience and tenacity to overcome the difficulties likely to be encountered.

• the degree of organisational support for and alignment behind the project, the extent to which it is seen as a genuine priority, and hence an organisational imperative, in which case there is more likely to be a broader and enduring commitment across the entity to do whatever is necessary to drive the successful delivery of the project, rather than being regarded as somewhat lower down the pecking order of priorities, in which case it is likely to prove more difficult to energise the organisation behind it. The NPfIT experience also shows that the level of organisational support is likely to change over time: in particular, support will tend to wane in the absence of visible progress (although this is again less likely if the project is perceived as a genuine organisational imperative).

This tends to imply that the structure, culture and internal dynamics of some organisations will prove to be more amenable to the successful delivery of IT projects than others. In particular, organisations in which there is greater alignment both between management and other staff, and across different sub-teams, tend to be better placed to progress such undertakings than those which are more fragmented – not least because this tends to give rise to broader collective support for the initiative across all quarters of the organisation, and increased preparedness to engage positively in the project, especially in the event of the project running into difficulties (which is of course not unusual). In contrast, where there are major fault lines in the relationships between leadership and staff, or between different departments, there is likely to be less widespread initial support throughout the organisation for the undertaking, and if the project runs into difficulties, a greater likelihood of inter-departmental blame and recrimination. Hence, in much the same way as a river will erode along a geologic fault, the project will find and lay bare the weak points and tensions within the organisation.

IT LEGACY ENVIRONMENT

One of the key challenges encountered by NPfIT involved managing the transition from the inherited mix of systems to the proposed end solution, especially given that due to the different systems in place in each different locality, the transition path would be unique in each area. The intention was where possible firstly to integrate the existing systems with the wider programme, at this stage only replacing those that could not be integrated; the roll out of the new systems would subsequently be extended to eliminate all the remaining legacy systems. As well as integrating and replacing systems, this would also entail converting data from the old systems to the new ones.

In practice it appears that the scale of this challenge was underestimated by the programme. For example, the 2006 National Audit Office report noted that: 'One key factor affecting the Local Service Providers' rate of deployment of systems has been the heterogeneous nature of the NHS... each NHS organisation may employ different systems, different numbers of systems, and in some instances a number of systems to do the same thing...This has meant that Local Service Providers' solutions need to be tailored to each organisation's requirements. These differences in requirements have meant that even after a Local Service Provider has ensured that its solution meets the requirements of one organisation, new work is needed to roll-out that solution to each organisation within its Cluster, making the task of rolling out systems considerably harder than in more homogeneous organisations'.[2] This is a common situation with which many IT projects have to contend wherever there is an established configuration of systems (ie a 'brownfield' as opposed to a 'greenfield' site). If at least some of the existing systems are being retained as part of the new end solution, this is likely to entail some measure of integration of the new system or systems with the old ones; likewise, where old systems are being replaced, various steps will be required to transition from the old solution to the new one being rolled out. Very often the new solution will involve both the replacement of some old systems and the retention of others, and hence there will be a need for both integration and migration activities. Moreover, the more highly integrated and complicated the set of existing systems and the spaghetti of interfaces between them, the more complex the task of implementing the new system or systems is likely to be. Some of the difficulties encountered here will be discussed further below (see the section on System Configuration and Architecture).

ORGANISATIONAL ACTIVITIES AND PROCESSES

Another 'situational' source of complexity encountered by many IT projects concerns the nature of the activities or processes that the organisation is seeking to support by means of the system in question. It probably goes without saying that the more extensive and complex these are, the more complex the solution that is likely to be needed to support them, and hence in all probability the more challenging the project to implement the solution.

There is a sense that in the same way that the complexity related to IT projects is sometimes not well understood by those who commission them, the complexity associated with particular organisational activities and processes is also not fully appreciated by those who are not closely connected to them. Hence, the full extent of the complexity of the activities and processes within the scope of the NPfIT is not really readily apparent to the lay person. On one level, the computerisation of medical records does not seem particularly remarkable. Of course, in reality the system sought to do much more than this, as shown in Figure 2, which seeks to provide an overview of the coverage of the system.

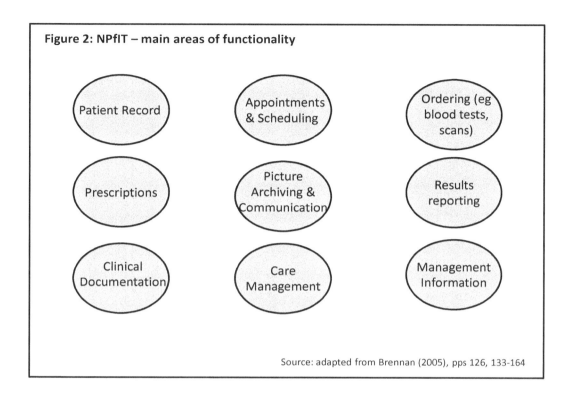

Figure 2: NPfIT – main areas of functionality

Patient Record

Appointments & Scheduling

Ordering (eg blood tests, scans)

Prescriptions

Picture Archiving & Communication

Results reporting

Clinical Documentation

Care Management

Management Information

Source: adapted from Brennan (2005), pps 126, 133-164

It should be emphasised that this provides only a very high level, summarised view of the activity sets in question, and hence underneath this there would have been multiple layers of additional complexity. To illustrate this, Figure 3 shows a high level process description for the Choose and Book component of the programme (corresponding to Appointments and Scheduling in the above diagram); while Figure 4 shows a more detailed outline of the process flow for just one aspect of Choose and Book, called Clinical Assessment. The level of detail in Figure 4 is closer to – but still does not reach down fully to - the level at which the system would need to operate. For each of these sub-activities and processes, a set of rules and procedures would need to be established to ensure the system could accommodate and respond to each and every possible situation encountered. Moreover, these would also need to take account of any interaction between the sub-activity in question and the other sub-activities covered by the system(s) – in the way that an appointment made through the Choose and Book module would need to be reflected in the Patient Record. The greater the variety of different situations and

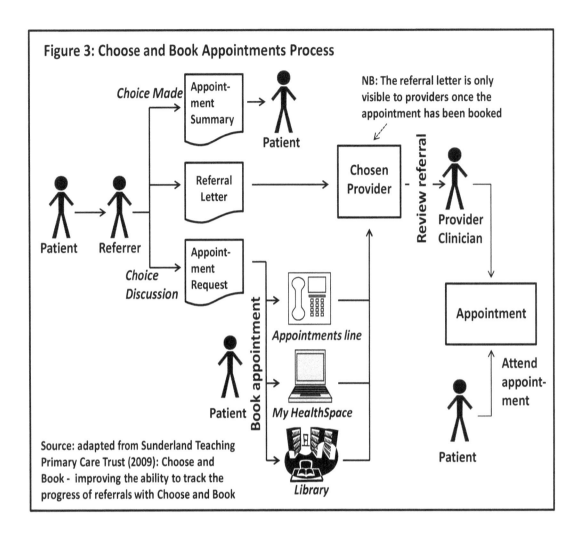

Figure 3: Choose and Book Appointments Process

Choice Made → Appointment Summary → Patient

NB: The referral letter is only visible to providers once the appointment has been booked

Patient → Referrer → Referral Letter → Chosen Provider ← Review referral — Provider Clinician

Choice Discussion → Appointment Request

Book appointment → Appointments line

Patient → My HealthSpace

Library

Appointment

Attend appointment

Patient

Source: adapted from Sunderland Teaching Primary Care Trust (2009): Choose and Book - improving the ability to track the progress of referrals with Choose and Book

interactions, and the greater the flexibility required in dealing with these, the more complex the solution will need to be. Hence, for example, a sales capture and invoicing solution will necessarily be more complex in an organisation which offers a wide diversity of different terms and conditions to its different customers than in one which deals with its customers on a standardised basis. As a result, it may be beneficial for an organisation to look to simplify and streamline its activities and processes prior to the implementation of a new system, since this is likely to reduce the cost and risk of the subsequent IT project. This said, such an approach does not

Figure 4: Choose and Book Clinical Assessment Process

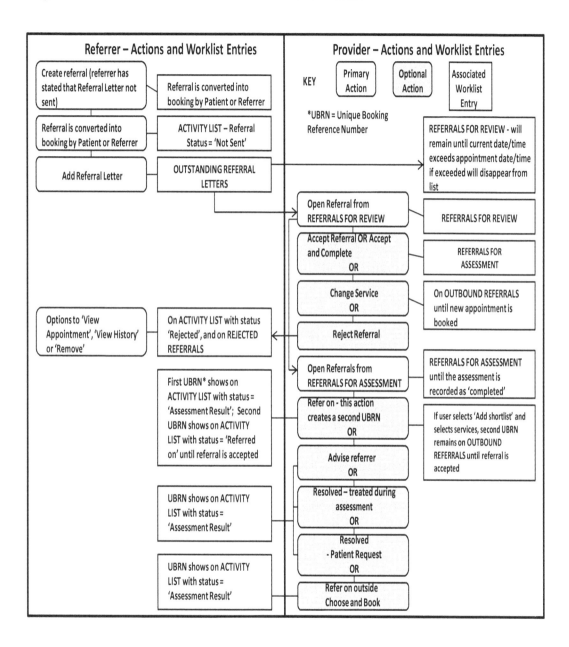

Source: National Health Service (2009): Choose and Book: Clinical Assessment Services – Best practice guidance for using Clinical Assessment Services functionality within Choose and Book

offer a panacea, because the organisation exchanges one set of challenges and difficulties associated with implementing a system able to accommodate considerable process flexibility for another set arising from the simplification of its process and activity set, and all that this entails, not least in terms of user engagement and overcoming user resistance. Moreover, for some organisations, the greater preparedness to be flexible in the way they conduct business with individual customers may form an important part of their offer and a source of competitive advantage, and so not something that can easily be foregone. In light of all this, the more unique the organisation in terms of its activities and/or the way it manages them, or wishes to manage them, the less likely it is that it will be able to implement a standard, readily-available, off the shelf application solution to meet its needs, and so the greater the probability that it will need either to tailor (or perhaps configure) the package to meet its particular requirements, or design and build its own bespoke solution. Hence such process complexity is an important determinant of the solution selection complexity discussed below.

PROBLEM/OPPORTUNITY DEFINITION

All projects, regardless of type, are undertaken in pursuit of a particular end. In fact, a definition of a project is 'a temporary endeavour with a defined beginning and end (usually time-constrained, and often constrained by funding or deliverables), undertaken to meet unique goals and objectives' (Noles and Kelly, 2007).[3] As such, the completion of the project is not – or at least shouldn't be – the end, it is the enablement of the end. Therefore, it is important in the case of any IT project to be able to articulate what the project is intended to achieve, what organisational problem(s) it will resolve, and/or what opportunities is will enable the organisation to pursue.

The problem or opportunity clearly derives from the situation in which the organisation in question finds itself – just as with the justification for the construction of the Brooklyn Bridge or Heathrow Terminal 5 (hence why it can be considered a 'Situational' source of complexity). In the case of NPfIT, the logic for the project appears to have derived from the following problems and opportunities:

1. Poor information quality in many parts of the NHS, with many of the records being kept on paper, leading to additional costs, delays, inconvenience and

potentially incorrect care and treatment of patients, which could in the worst case result in needless loss of life.

2. A lack of integration of information across different parts of the NHS, resulting in difficulties in accessing patient records at different sites.

3. Deficiencies in the quality of IT systems in place in large parts of the NHS, in terms of differences between what was in place in many Trusts and what was regarded as best - or sometimes even good - practice.

4. A wide variety of different systems in place across the NHS, contributing to 1. and 2. above, and potentially leading to inefficiency and added cost due to duplication.

5. Deficiencies (real or perceived) in the capability of individual NHS organisational entities to undertake the necessary IT projects required to address the shortcomings.

6. Deficiencies in the quality of information provided by the existing systems in use in the NHS, therefore making it difficult to make informed decisions eg about resource allocation.

7. The opportunity to make fuller use of IT and implement leading edge health care systems to provide enhanced and more efficient care throughout the NHS – as was being done elsewhere in the world, notably the US.

8. The opportunity to reduce the cost of purchase of IT in the NHS by centralising procurement rather than devolving it to individual Trusts.

On one level, this is all fine. Clearly, there were (and are) significant deficiencies in the NHS IT infrastructure, and likewise opportunities to make more use of IT to improve the overall quality of the healthcare available. However, this does not necessarily mean that this was 'the right problem' for the project to pursue. This can only be determined with confidence if firstly there was a feasible solution to address the problems/opportunities defined, and secondly there was genuine value in seeking to do so, given the benefits projected relative to the costs, complexities and risks involved. To these one might also add a third consideration, namely the relative merits of this particular project compared to any other activities the organisation in question could have chosen to pursue instead with the money and resources available. For any potential project, none of these questions can be addressed fully without a thorough understanding of the solution options available and their respective feasibility, viability, advantages and disadvantages. This in turn requires an appreciation of the complexities each option is likely to encounter. This is of course no different from engineering projects, although the laws of physics may provide a clearer sense of what is and what isn't feasible here. In the case of the Brooklyn Bridge, for example, having identified the need for – or at least the opportunity provided by – some form of fixed crossing between Brooklyn and New York, then the question remained as to whether there was a technically feasible way of doing this given the technology available at the time, and whether this could be done for an acceptable cost relative to the rewards anticipated to arise from doing so. In practice, the options available for achieving this were probably quite limited, especially given the prevailing technology (although there were still choices to be made, eg around location, detailed design and delivery model). Moreover, the ability to modify the problem definition, so as to provide for different – and potentially less complex – solutions, was likewise quite restricted (reducing the width of the East River was after all not an option).

In contrast, however, in the case of IT projects there is often considerable freedom to refine or revise the problem definition and therefore to amend the form of the project required to increase the likelihood of a successful outcome. A bridge clearly needs to span the whole divide, otherwise it has no value as a bridge: while if it spans more than the divide, it incurs unnecessary redundancy. However, an IT project can vary in the degree of coverage of the activities in question which it addresses. It can still have value if it does not span the full divide – that is, it does not address fully all the problems or opportunities identified - with manual processes or existing systems filling any gaps arising; likewise, it may have greater value if its reach is extended to address other activities beyond those at its core – so for example it may be worthwhile to broaden the scope of a proposed accounting system to cover also order capture and processing, warehousing and distribution, or management reporting.

What this implies, of course, is that the problem/opportunity definition is not independent from the solution. To some extent therefore it may be helpful in the case of IT projects to think less about the definition of the problem or opportunity per se, but about the definition of the broader 'problem (or opportunity) space' into which different solutions may play, and which may provide a different mix of benefits, complexities, costs and risks. It's clear that had this been defined more narrowly for NPfIT, while the potential benefits would have been reduced, so too would the complexities, costs and risks, and the chance of successful delivery would have been increased accordingly.

Obviously, the reach of the NPfIT was much greater than is the norm for IT projects, but the issue of defining the problem or opportunity correctly, and understanding the full implications of this in terms of potential solutions still applies. Ideally, the objective should be to find the optimal fit between problem/ opportunity and solution, taking into account all relevant criteria.

All of this means that the definition of 'the right problem' (or opportunity) is very often a source of considerable complexity for IT projects. We will return to this issue below as part of the discussion regarding Project Scope.

The combination of these four factors – the nature of the organisation in question, the IT legacy environment, the activities and processes which will be impacted by the system, and the problem or opportunity which the system is intended to address provide the backdrop against which the project will be undertaken. With the possible exception of the problem/opportunity definition – where as we have seen, there is potential for flexibility, this context is of course largely fixed, much in the same way that in the case of the Brooklyn Bridge the width of the East River was likewise fixed. The challenge for the project in this regard is therefore to ensure that the complexities inherent in the context are understood and addressed as effectively as possible.

This brings us on to consideration of those sources of complexity which are inherent in any IT project.

INHERENT SOURCES OF COMPLEXITY

PROJECT SCOPE

As discussed above, the identification of the problem to be addressed or opportunity to be pursued is only the first stage in the definition of an IT project; following this there are a number of further vital steps to be undertaken before the 'right project' can be defined and its scope determined.   This is a multi-faceted and complex undertaking in itself. As noted, in many respects, it may be more complex for IT projects than for many engineering and construction projects, given the range of options available.   In the case of an IT project, there is significant choice both in terms of the definition of the problem/opportunity to be addressed, since one can choose to define this more narrowly or more broadly (unlike the width of the East River), and then in relation to the different potential solutions available. Different problem/opportunity definitions will imply a different range of potential solutions, and vice versa. Of course, all other things being equal, the more broadly the problem/opportunity space is defined, the more complex the solution entailed; therefore, given that there is the flexibility to do so, it may be preferable to reduce the scope of the problem space so as to reduce the complexity (and thus the cost, the risk, the likely time to complete and so on). But in so doing the benefits are also likely to reduce. And any decision to reduce the scope of the immediate project may have implications if the intention is to address other parts of the broader problem-space in the longer term.

I believe that this flexibility around the problem/opportunity definition and the scope of the project, and the interdependency of these and the trade-offs between them, is part of the reason why IT projects prove as difficult as they do. In particular, they mean that the process of determining 'the right project' is inevitably a somewhat non-linear one, whereas our normal inclination is to look at projects as linear activities, where the definition of the problem leads logically on to the identification of the solution. In the case of IT projects, there is a need to iterate around the problem/opportunity and the solution, until the best combination of both is reached. (Note also that this non-linearity means that the ordering of the different topics which are addressed in this chapter should not be taken to imply the sequence in which they come into play – although their relative significance may vary over time as a project unfolds, they all have some relevance throughout its life cycle; and moreover, understanding all of them as comprehensively as possible at the start of the project is of vital importance in ensuring that the project is best positioned to succeed).

The NPfIT provides a good illustration of this. Clearly there was a valid and defensible underlying logic for the project, as set out previously. Based on this, it is perhaps therefore understandable why such a large and ambitious project should have been attempted, because it offered the closest fit with the problem/opportunity as defined. It therefore represented the all-encompassing solution. However, even without the benefit of hindsight, there is no question that this choice implied a hugely ambitious, complex and risky undertaking. Under these circumstances (in fact under any circumstances, but under these circumstances in particular), it would seem to have been prudent to consider what alternative options might have been available; while the alternatives would inevitably have offered less benefit, they would also have been accompanied by less complexity and risk. The extent to which this was done for the NPfIT is not fully apparent from the information about the project made publicly available. The fact that a pre-project risk assessment described the project as extremely high risk was however revealed during one of the Public Accounts Committee hearings.[4] Certainly, one is left with the impression that faced with the list of problems and opportunities in relation to IT in the NHS referred to above, and in light of the difficulties encountered in the more devolved approach to improving the quality of IT systems in use in the NHS previously, a decision was taken to press ahead with the project in the form adopted almost regardless of anything else. But most observers (and taxpayers) – informed or uninformed – would probably argue that a less ambitious and complex solution which offered some reduction in the overall benefit but at a lower cost and risk, and therefore a greater likelihood of delivery, might well have been preferable (and certainly worthy at least of consideration).

Any such exercise designed to establish the range of available options and choices also forces the organisation to consider the criticality of the different elements of the problem/opportunity space that have been identified. This is extremely valuable, since it's only through an appreciation of the potential benefits of resolving or pursuing these that one can gain a real sense of what scale of effort will be justified to achieve the ends desired, and equally the organisational impact of adopting a solution which does not fulfil a particular identified requirement. For example, in the case of the NPfIT, whilst one can see the attraction of being able to have access to a patient's information anywhere in the country, it's perhaps worth reflecting on how vital this really was or is. In the absence of this (which was of course the status quo), in most cases the solution would seem to be as simple as requiring the patient to fill in a form or asking them a few questions. If so, it could therefore be argued that the number of situations where national access to such information would really make a difference in terms of the quality of care is in the overall scheme of things probably quite small. However, this requirement appears to have been an important driver of the solution proposed under NPfIT, and therefore of the cost and complexity arising. It is at least worth asking whether the benefits associated with this were sufficient to justify the extra costs and complexities involved – and equally importantly, whether solutions which did not provide this were considered and properly evaluated.

Moreover, without the requirement for an integrated, national approach, it would also have been easier to pilot the proposed solution in a more circumscribed geography. And in fact, this would not necessarily have ruled out subsequent integration of the regional systems at a later date. This illustrates another point about IT systems which is again different from many (but by no means all) construction projects - namely that one option available to meet the full suite of objectives that the project is seeking to achieve is to break up the solution into a series of separate phases delivered in a logical sequence. This would not have been a viable approach for projects like the Brooklyn Bridge or the Great Eastern, which rely on the totality of their design for their integrity, but would be practical in the case of, say, a new motorway or rail route, or a project like the Boston Big Dig[5], where parts of the solution can be built and put into service before others, as long as they can be connected to the existing networks. Such an approach again brings new complexities, particularly in terms of integration of the different phases so that at each stage there still exists a working solution, but it reduces the complexity and risk associated with each individual phase. After all, the suggestion that 'When eating an elephant take one bite at a time' (General Creighton Abrams)[6] is generally good advice - although in fact the NPfIT was probably more of a blue whale than an elephant! Again, in retrospect, the NPfIT might well have benefited from adopting a more sequenced approach – whereas in fact, as we have seen, while the project was split up into a number of component parts, many of these were pursued in parallel rather than in sequence, at least initially.

One also wonders whether those who initiated the project were too quick to dismiss the more devolved approaches taken previously, or at least to overstate the disadvantages of these at the same time as they overstated the advantages and understated the challenges and risks of the centralised NPfIT approach. At least

144

from the public record, the impression is that a centralised approach was perceived to be the only means of achieving the intended objectives, and that based on past experience, devolved approaches were doomed to failure. However, while clearly these previous approaches had not yielded the results sought, this did not necessarily imply that there were no possible ways of structuring a devolved project that could prove successful. Likewise, there may also have been hybrid approaches that combined some degree of central co-ordination with varying levels of local involvement. Such approaches may have been preferable in the context of the fragmented structure of the NHS. This said, all of these would have brought their own mix of complexities and risks – which of course would also need to be considered and understood prior to any decision to proceed.

What this all shows is that ultimately IT projects put themselves in a stronger position to succeed the more thorough their efforts to identify and evaluate the different options available, to understand the implications of these in terms of the problem/opportunity space, to identify the benefits and costs and timescales of each, the risks and the rewards and the complexities involved, the potential for descoping the project or for sequencing its delivery, and so on. To do this properly is of course likely to be far from straightforward. A large part of the challenge here is to build an appreciation of the difficulties different configurations of the project will be likely to encounter prior to the project commencing. To do this effectively requires a profound understanding of IT projects and all that they entail, and is likely to be a complex and time-consuming exercise – which may partly explain why it is often not done, or not done with sufficient rigour: even in the case of NPfIT, the 'world's largest computer project' it is not altogether clear that the level of rigour and pre-analysis that went into the project definition and scoping phase was sufficiently comprehensive.

Moreover, one additional aspect of IT projects which further complicates this is that at least in some senses they can be described as 'fractal'[7] (which is not a word I was familiar with until it was explained to me in this context). This refers to a geometric pattern which looks the same whatever level of detail you look at it (see Figure 5). There are lots of examples of fractal (or near fractal) structures in nature - such as a fern leaf, or coastlines, so if you look at the earth from space, the coastline is a wiggly line - just as it is on any map on any scale; and then if you actually go and stand on a cliff and look down on the coastline below, it still looks decidedly wiggly. In the same way, IT projects remain equally complex and problematic throughout all stages of their life cycles and at whatever level of detail you approach them. As

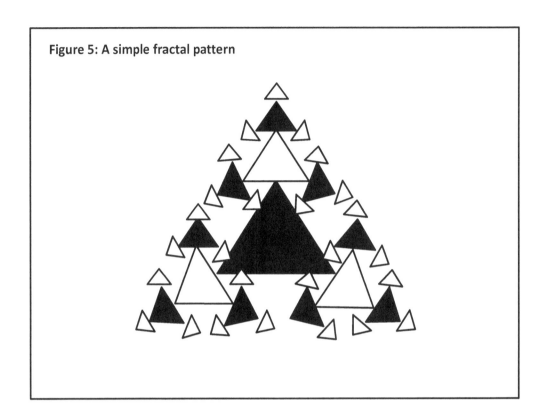

Figure 5: A simple fractal pattern

we have been discussing, there is considerable complexity in determining what constitutes 'the right project' before it commences, but new and more detailed complexities then emerge progressively as part of project delivery, and the sheer unadulterated grind of working through the myriad of issues and problems and challenges to achieve success (or perhaps failure, since success is rarely if ever guaranteed with such undertakings). The challenge therefore is to understand and appreciate the complexities the project is likely to experience at subsequent stages in its life cycle before it has commenced.

Given this, IT projects lend themselves particularly well to a staged or 'gated' decision making process[8], where there are a number of pre-determined 'stop/go' points where a conscious decision is taken to allow the project to progress through the stage gate into the next stage (or not), based on a considered evaluation of the information about the project available at that point in time. Done properly, this is a very powerful way of helping to structure the pre-project preparation phase. Typical phases would consist of:

- 'Initiation' – which focuses on the identification, definition and evaluation of the problem to be addressed or opportunity to be pursued, consideration of the feasibility of addressing/pursuing it, and assessment of the relative merits of this particular project compared to other alternative projects the organisation could choose to pursue, with a view to informing a decision as to whether or not to progress to more detailed project definition.

- 'Selection' – having successfully passed through the stage gate at the end of Initiation, the next step is to consider in more detail the options available for addressing the problem/opportunity identified in the way described above, and ultimately to narrow these options down to the preferred choice. The end of stage decision is therefore to review this recommendation, and the logic for its selection – which necessitates consideration of its merits relative to those of the alternatives. Of course, there is also the option of not proceeding with the project at this stage, if none of the potential options are considered sufficiently attractive, or of modifying the requirements, or repeating the Selection phase with some different options not previously considered. If the decision is taken to cancel the project at this juncture, the costs incurred should still have been quite small.

- 'Definition' – this stage involves the detailed design of the chosen solution, and of the structures required to deliver it. Key outputs during this phase would include the intended IT and functional architecture, the proposed organisational process model, identification of all the changes required to the existing systems and processes to achieve these, project plans (at increasing levels of detail), the project delivery model, organisation structure and resourcing requirements, the proposed governance model, and the full project financial case. Ideally, all of the documentation produced should be subject to informed independent scrutiny before any decision is taken to proceed with the project into the Delivery phase. Clearly, if this stage is performed properly, it requires a sizeable commitment of effort and time, so it is at this point that project costs start to mount significantly – although not by as much as during Delivery. However, if a thorough job has been performed during the preceding phases to ensure that 'the Right Project' is being undertaken, then the risk of these costs being incurred wastefully is hugely reduced. And of course, given the decision points built in to the process, there remains the opportunity to cancel the project or to revert to an earlier stage if the information emerging from the ever-deepening analysis calls the decisions taken previously seriously into question.

- 'Delivery' – on one level, this stage might be considered as simple as implementing the plan developed during the previous phase by means of the delivery model, project organisation, resources, governance model and so on, all of which would also have been identified during the Definition phase. In practice, however, 'no plan survives contact with the enemy' (generally attributed to the German General Helmuth von Moltke)[9], and so a large part of the project management task during this phase is to obtain a clear understanding of the progress of the project, the challenges it is facing, and the complexities that are emerging, and make any required course corrections as necessary. Again, ideally the project should be subject to periodic informed independent scrutiny, and there should be regular progress reviews with stakeholders.

This book is not however really intended as a 'how to do' IT projects guide, and there are plenty of other sources available that can provide more comprehensive descriptions of the different project phases (probably using different terminology – other labels for the different stages are available) and the associated decision gates. The key point I want to make here, though, comes back to this question of complexity, and the fact that this is likely to reveal itself in different guises as the project unfolds. Hence the better the understanding of the difficulties the project is likely to encounter in advance, the better the chance of making a good decision about 'the Right Project'. Of course, this still does not guarantee success. But in the case of IT projects, there is no question that 'Time spent in reconnaissance is seldom wasted' (British Army Field Service Regulations, 1912; also variously attributed to Sun Tzu, Wellington, Montgomery and others)[10]; and likewise that 'Fools rush in where angels fear to tread' (Alexander Pope).[11]

One final example to illustrate this from my own experience: I was asked to assist a medium-sized Swiss-based commodity trading organisation define a replacement for its core Management Information (MI) system, which was considered to be unfit for purpose. We identified two options for doing this, one of which relied on capturing additional information into the existing accounting system and then downloading this into a new MI database, from which the desired reports could be produced; and another which involved investment in a new tool to record all the transactions engaged in by the business and their evolution over time (ie from their initial commitment to the movement of cash). This would provide for additional information not included in the current systems to be captured and made available for reporting. However, both of these solutions would give rise to considerable complexity and cost in relation to the modification of the existing system or the implementation of the new one, and a significant burden in terms of ongoing data capture and recording. The business concluded that neither of these was really justified in terms of the benefits that would be provided, and decided instead to make some small-scale improvements to the existing system to address the most serious shortcomings. It was acknowledged that this would not provide a perfect solution, but it would be sufficient to meet the real needs of the organisation. While on one level this was a disappointing outcome from a personal perspective, as it meant that any future income stream deriving from a more material project was no longer on offer, on the other hand I believed that the organisation had arrived at the right conclusion, and that the analysis we had undertaken to identify the various more radical options and their implications had put them in a position to make this decision in an informed way.

DISAGGREGATION AND PHASING

Linked to this question of project scope, and how best to 'eat the elephant'[12], as noted above it's not unusual for IT projects, including relatively small ones, to be broken down into a number of different component parts or phases, each to be rolled out separately, as was the case with the NPfIT. As we have seen, this was split into eight main pieces, each then subdivided into separate phases where software of increasing sophistication was to be implemented. This in part reflected the timing of the availability of the software being developed. Overlain on this at the Cluster level was a sequencing of the roll-out of the applications in a series of separate initiatives at individual Trust level. Even within individual Trusts the roll-outs were phased - for example, at the Morecambe Bay University Hospitals Trust where one of the earliest implementations of Lorenzo took place, this was implemented in a series of steps to the five different hospitals within the trust, and to different wards within each of these.[13] This illustrates that even at the more manageable and typical scale of the individual Trusts, a degree of implementation phasing was considered appropriate.

There are obvious advantages to breaking up a large and complicated undertaking into a number of component parts. In particular it makes the project more manageable and reduces the delivery risk, in that each sub-component can be treated as a separate initiative. It also reduces the implementation risk, as rather than deploy the new system in one 'big bang' roll-out, with potential implications across large parts of the organisation if things go wrong, any potential problems will be limited to a narrower area. Disaggregation also provides the opportunity to make at least some functionality available to the users sooner than if they had to wait for the system in its entirety to be available, which can be very important in terms of maintaining stakeholder support for and engagement with the project (the reduction in user support for NPfIT over time appears in part to have been attributable to the delays in any tangible deliveries[14]; also it is noteworthy that some rephasing of Lorenzo took place to prioritise functionality of benefit to clinicians ahead of some of the purely administrative functionality as a means of helping to maintain the interest and engagement of medical professionals).[15]

This said, however, the subdivision of a project in this way may also cause complications, not least because it gives rise to a number of interim steps which the organisation will need to go through prior to achieving the ultimate intended end state. This brings with it cost and complexity. While the size of the bangs may be smaller, each of these interim phases involves a separate implementation, and hence everything involved in this - planning, testing, training, data migration, cutover, early life support and so on. Moreover, each phase involves a different and unique system and process configuration, which has to be viable, and each of these may require new interfaces to be built with other legacy systems (some of which may subsequently become redundant as later parts of the project are rolled out) and new organisational processes to be put in place to support it. This is also likely to increase the amount of organisational change that users have to endure, as each different phase brings with it a different process model and potentially a different mix of systems with which they have to interact. In some cases, the segmentation of an integrated organisational process into a number of different sub-elements can create significant operational problems, complexities and risks, which may make the disaggregation of the project impractical - or at least give rise to a situation where the perceived risks of disaggregation exceed those associated with a 'bigger bang'.

As a result, identifying the optimal segmentation and phasing of any project may again be a matter of judgement reflecting a number of different considerations, including the timescale for the delivery of different pieces of software, the practicalities and additional costs associated with disaggregation relative to the risks of not doing so, and the potential impact on the users and other stakeholders of more and earlier deliveries compared to fewer and later ones. Once again, these are wider organisational decisions rather than solely technical IT ones.

REQUIREMENTS GATHERING

The identification and crystallisation of at least the broad problem/ opportunity to be addressed and the scope that the system needs to cover leads on to the description of all the things that the system needs to be able to do - often referred to as the requirements of the system. That this can prove far from straightforward is again illustrated by the NPfIT, where a recurrent criticism throughout the lifespan of the project was that there had been insufficient input from medical professionals in the preparation and specification of the requirements that the systems would need to meet. While the 2006 National Audit Office report found that the programme had taken adequate steps to ensure the systems met the users' needs[16], and noted that an independent review by Qinetiq had found that the specification had been developed 'after engagement with a broad spectrum of NHS stakeholders'[17], a number of the key medical professionals involved in the activity questioned whether in reality the process had been as thorough or effective as it was portrayed. Moreover, the 2011 Public Accounts Committee report identified the lack of user input to the requirements as one of the critical points of failure for the programme.[18]

Some of the complexity here is perhaps best illustrated by analogy. Rather than eating an elephant, having decided that an elephant (or something like it) is either needed or will enable an opportunity to be exploited, the challenge we would then face is to describe the elephant in such a way that we could start to build one – or, at least make an informed decision as to whether we needed to build one, or could alternatively buy one off the shelf (obviously it would have to be quite a strong shelf) which would meet most of our needs. At this stage, this is less a case of developing detailed plans, and more one of providing a clear sense of what our elephant needs to do, how it should do it, and broadly what it would look like in its entirety. But this said, providing a viable description of the elephant at this point is still likely to require quite detailed knowledge. 'Large grey animal with four legs and a trunk' is unlikely to be of much assistance to the designers (or the buyers). We would need to be able to provide a description – at an appropriate level of detail (whatever that is) – of all the important attributes and subsystems that we want – or need (see below) - to go into our elephant, and potentially a perspective of how these are intended to work, both individually and collectively. We'd also need to provide an understanding of how the elephant should fit in with its wider surroundings. Moreover, to ensure our description is appropriate, we would need to have confidence that we hadn't left anything important out – what if our elephant can't see or hear or reproduce? (for those who are interested/inclined, I recommend an attempt at specifying an elephant as a worthwhile exercise in providing insights into the complexities of the requirements identification process).

Likewise, in the case of IT projects, the challenge is to provide a thorough description – at an appropriate level of detail (which increases as the project progresses) – of all of the different activities that are required to take place within the identified problem/ opportunity space and scope of the undertaking. In most cases, this involves quite a detailed level of understanding of the organisation's affairs and processes, which is very often beyond that held by those who have been party to any decision to commission the project, and instead resides in the operational staff responsible for the activities in question – that is, the users. Hence, it is often at this point that the users, or at least some of them, first become exposed to the project. However, there is something of a conundrum here, in that while user involvement is almost always necessary, there is a danger that this will lead to the list of requirements being extended to include non-essential and cosmetic requests (so that one might end up with a pink elephant – or even a white one).

This in turn raises the question as to the mechanisms and processes by means of which the full suite of requirements is best developed and assembled, and about the right level and form of user participation in the process – which is normally achieved through interviews and workshops, and perhaps secondment of key users into the project team (see the section on user involvement below). Various different methodologies are available to support this activity. In the case of the NPfIT, the primary emphasis was on the development of an 'Output Based Specification', which sought to identify everything that the system needed to provide in terms of outputs (ie things like reports, documents and forms – either on-screen or on paper - produced by the system to support the organisation's activities), but not necessarily how it should provide them - the point being that at least in some cases organisations can be largely ambivalent about the processes by which the various outputs are achieved, because there is no particular advantage or disadvantage for the organisation in the use of one process compared with any other. This approach helps to avoid one common tendency with user input, which is to conflate requirements with process – that is to view the requirement not only in terms of the end or output to be achieved, but also in terms of the ways of working and organisational processes entailed in achieving it. This can sometimes manifest itself in a desire to re-engineer the previously prevailing processes into the new system, regardless of whether this is truly advantageous or not.

On the other hand, however, there are many situations where it may be necessary or at least helpful to set out the processes by means of which the organisation wishes to perform its activities and which the system is required to support. Ultimately, this is likely to be needed if the organisation chooses to build the new solution rather than buying it, so that the build can incorporate its preferred processes. Moreover, even if the organisation chooses to purchase an off the shelf package, the degree of fit between its preferred process model and that which is offered by the system is likely to be important information in terms of evaluating packages and choosing between them, and also in managing any subsequent organisational changes arising from the implementation of the new system (it is apparent that the mismatch between the appointments booking process in use at the Nuffield Orthopaedic Centre and that implicit in the new system gave rise to considerable operational difficulties). Under these circumstances, the requirements gathering process may also entail an attempt not only to identify the organisational activities and process areas that the system is required to support, but also to specify - at an appropriate level of detail – the way in which they should operate. This is often done by means of some form of 'process mapping' activity – which is again likely to necessitate considerable input from the users. In practice, it is quite difficult to conceptualise a coherent set of optimal organisational processes in isolation, and hence the simplest way of doing this is normally to map the organisation's existing ways of working (the 'As is' process model) and to use this as the basis for development of the possible future processes (the 'To be' process map – sometimes also referred to as the 'Target Operating Model', although this is perhaps more widely used to describe a higher, organisational level construct showing the interactions, relationships and interdependencies between different organisational entities – see also the section on System configuration below). Of course, while making use of the 'As is' model as a starting point for the preferred future processes helps ensure completeness and realism, adopting such an approach again runs the risk of re-incorporating the existing processes into the new model. A related approach which may avoid this risk to some extent involves the development of 'use cases', which start with the various outputs or goals that the system is seeking to deliver, and then seek to document the various steps required to deliver each of these.

As noted above, the level of detail at which the requirements need to be identified is likely to increase as the project unfolds. This may also vary depending on the solution adopted – for example, the level of specificity needed will generally be greater in the case of a bespoke development than if an off the shelf package is selected. Different development methodologies also imply different approaches to the identification of the detailed requirements – whereas a classical 'waterfall' approach will necessitate them being specified comprehensively prior to the commencement of any development taking place, where an 'agile' approach is adopted, involving the evolutionary development of the solution through a series of iterations, with developers working in close collaboration with users, the full suite of requirements effectively emerge as the development process progresses. This again serves to emphasise the non-linearity of IT projects (being iterative, agile development itself is of course a non-linear process – more a spiral than a line).

Regardless however of the approach adopted, a key challenge during the requirements gathering process is to distinguish between those requirements emerging which are genuine and necessary and those which are merely desirable (it is usually easier to identify those which are cosmetic or superficial), given the likelihood of a lack of detailed knowledge and understanding of the process areas in question by anyone other than the users. To come to an authoritative determination here may again take a significant investment of time and effort in analysis, and then in gaining agreement. Moreover, there tends to be a trade-off between permitting or preventing what may in reality constitute non-essential refinement and gaining or losing user buy-in to the solution. Ultimately this becomes a matter of judgement.

A further consideration here is that different users may identify conflicting requirements, which may ultimately prove difficult or impossible to reconcile. In the case of NPfIT, Frank Burns, the former head of IT for the NHS, speaking in an interview in 2002, stated that 'My great concern is that any national solution would have to be watered down to make it nationally acceptable...so my worry would be the higher the level of centralization the lower the spec. So it would be a complete shell, a national e-mail system instead of what was intended' (quoted in Brennan (2005)). Likewise, surveys suggested that when the focus of the programme was narrowed down from 2008 onwards there was no clear consensus among medical professionals as to the appropriate priority areas of functionality to be included in the 'Clinical Five'.[19] Recognition of the potential difficulties here may have contributed to the desire on the part of the NPfIT to limit the level of direct user engagement in the project's requirements gathering process, and the reliance on the existing materials already available that had been prepared in support of previous initiatives in parts of the NHS.

We will return to the question of the 'right' level and nature of user involvement below. However, in terms of the requirements gathering process, there is a clear potential tension here. As with NPfIT, many projects are likely to have a high reliance on user input; on the other hand, this brings with it a risk of non-essential and unnecessary requirements being identified, which may prove difficult to identify, given that the detailed knowledge of the subject areas resides with the user community, and difficult to resist, given that this may alienate the users who are a critical group in terms of the achievement of the organisational changes taking place in association with the project.

SOLUTION/SOFTWARE SELECTION

One of the most significant problems faced by NPfIT concerned the functionality and capability of the care records systems selected for the programme to meet the requirements. This was most starkly evident in the case of iSoft's Lorenzo system (but in addition the IDX solution was rejected in the South, and difficulties were also experienced with Cerner's Millenium product). This necessitated significant effort over a number of years to develop the products to the point where they provided sufficient functionality and reliability to meet a minimum set of needs, even if this was not the full suite of functionality originally identified as being required. The difficulties encountered here point to another set of challenges faced by IT projects concerning the selection of the best software solution to meet the requirements identified and hence achieve the organisation's objectives from the project. In practice, this is rarely straightforward. The decision-tree to arrive at a particular choice is often a convoluted one. In the first instance, there is of course a question as to whether to buy an off-the-shelf package or whether to develop a new bespoke application. This decision in turn depends on there being off-the-shelf packages available which will meet the requirements identified, and sometimes there are not. Also, while some packages may offer considerable flexibility by providing solutions which are highly configurable – and which prima facie can appear quite an attractive route - the more configurable the system, the more demanding the activity to configure it, to the point where some 'configuration' efforts start in practice to resemble development projects. Very often, there are packages available which will address some, or even most, of the organisation's requirements, but not all of them. In this situation, the options are to adopt the available solution in its entirety, and accept the consequences of this (changing the organisation's processes and working around any shortcomings); seeking to tailor the package so that it meets at least the bulk of the needs identified; selecting additional packages, or building new bespoke functionality to address the gaps; or building a new system in its entirety from scratch.

None of these options are likely to be simple. Adapting the organisation's activities and processes to align more closely with the available application may entail a significant degree of organisational change, which is in itself problematic (see below). Tailoring an existing off-the-shelf package can prove highly complex, since the changes being sought may not be compatible with the way the system was originally designed, and moreover whenever a system is modified there is a strong likelihood of introducing new defects. In addition, it can give rise to longer term issues in relation to the upgrade path of the modified system post implementation, because unless the changes made become part of the standard package offered by the supplier, whenever the supplier upgrades the core package (as they tend to do quite frequently), additional development work may be required to upgrade these non-standard elements, resulting in additional cost. Under these circumstances, it is not unusual for upgrades to be deferred and the version of the system being used to become outdated and ultimately unsupported by the vendor.

Integrating different systems, especially from different vendors, may also prove problematic. This was in reality the approach adopted by NPfIT. Various technologies exist to support the integration and interfacing of different systems from different suppliers, and tend to convey the impression that systems can be linked up at will ('plug and play'), but despite the availability of these tools, such integration has a tendency often to prove considerably more problematic than anticipated: in particular, there are a set of issues associated with data, which necessitates some form of mapping and translation between systems to overcome different naming conventions. Integration is also more challenging if updates in one system are required to be immediately reflected in other systems forming part of the integrated solution (see below).

And finally of course developing new bespoke software is a complex undertaking - even in a relatively simple organisational context. For many organisations, this may not be something they would be in a position seriously to contemplate, given everything involved, and they would probably choose to adopt or adapt a package unless there was a substantial gap between their identified requirements and what the available packages had to offer. This said, given the difficulties that may be entailed in tailoring a package, it is also sometimes suggested that unless an off the shelf solution can be found offering at least a 60 per cent fit – and perhaps even as high as an 80 per cent fit – with the requirements, an organisation may be better served by developing bespoke software. Another lens I've seen used is if an organisation genuinely believes and can demonstrate it has a real competitive advantage in its internal processes and modus operandum in a particular sector of its operations, then there is a clear justification to build rather than to buy. Otherwise, there is no reason not to make use of the 'commodity' processes embedded in one or other of the packages available on the market, even if there are aspects of these which are considered sub-optimal. However, if this is ultimately considered to be the preferred approach, the next set of questions relate to how to progress such a development - whether to undertake this in-house, or whether to engage a third party to undertake this on the organisation's behalf. If the former, then there is the question of how to resource and manage this effort (for example through existing employees, or contractors, or some mix of both); if the latter, there is the question of which supplier (or suppliers) to select. Moreover, the choice of any supplier is likely to involve a number of criteria (see below), including reputation and track record, capacity and capability, experience in the field in question, anticipated responsiveness, size, financial situation, location (onshore or offshore) and of course price. Some of the further complexities implicit in the decision to pursue a new system development are likewise considerable, not least in relation to development methodology, IT technical issues, testing, and project management – as the problems experienced by the Lorenzo development illustrate. Detailed consideration of these is beyond the scope of this book.[20] Suffice to say, however, that the choice of a bespoke development solution is not something to be entered into lightly (and probably only after other alternatives have been eliminated), nor are there any panaceas (so, for example, an 'agile' development approach – where the software solution evolves through a series of incremental iterations with developers working in close collaboration with users - may overcome some of the difficulties encountered in a classic 'waterfall' one – where development takes place through a logical sequence of stages, beginning with requirements gathering, followed by design (at increasing levels of detail), construction, testing and implementation, but it is itself accompanied by significant challenges).

Of course, the software selection decision is not simply a question of finding the solution which offers the best fit with the set of functional requirements identified. Cost is likely always to come into the equation. There may additionally be technical considerations associated with different packages that influence the decision, eg in terms of the amount and sophistication of the IT hardware and communications infrastructure required. Likewise, there may be other differences in the relative difficulty of the implementation of different solutions, especially if significant configuration is required.

It's probably also worth noting here that any software selection decision has longer term implications in terms of ongoing support – since by and large the only organisation able to support the system is the one which sold it or developed it. Hence, rather like a dog at Christmas, a system is for life (or at least for several years), and what is being entered into here is really an extended partnering arrangement. This emphasises the need to undertake appropriate due diligence on the vendor to ensure it is in a position to meet its commitments. The NPfIT experience with iSoft indicates some of the challenges that may be encountered in this regard (see the Supplier Relationships section below for further consideration of this issue).

All of these different factors therefore need to be considered as part of any evaluation. This in turn means that the process of choosing between the different options available to identify the best course of action is itself likely to be complex and time-consuming – if it is to be done with any confidence.

Such a process normally starts with the identification of a 'long list' of third party packages on offer in the particular sector of activity, and then – using the information that is reasonably readily accessible, perhaps involving the use of consultants with expertise in the field - narrowing this down to a smaller number of the apparently more attractive offerings, the vendors of which are then engaged in a conventional bidding process, possibly culminating in a small number of suppliers being invited to tender to meet a specified set of requirements. This may also include requests for details of other organisations where the systems can be viewed in live operation, and for the vendor to undertake a demonstration of their system to indicate its capabilities, possibly using a set of representative scenarios prepared by the buying organisation as the basis of the demonstration. Based on all the information accumulated, some form of assessment and scoring process is ultimately undertaken to determine a preferred way forward.

While organisations which conduct regular acquisitions of IT systems or similar products or services may have established processes available which they can use – or at least easily adapt - to undertake this activity, for organisations which are not in this position then an appropriate process will need to be designed. Either way, the operation of the process with any degree of rigour is likely to take time and expertise; and further engagement with the user community may be required to develop the set of representative scenarios for use during the demonstrations.

In addition, regardless of the quality of the process used and the expertise of those involved in it, arriving at a definitive conclusion as to the best course of action remains problematic. Firstly, as the NPfIT experience would seem to demonstrate, it can be difficult to determine whether a particular software solution will in practice meet the full suite or even the majority of an organisation's requirements. To reach a point where there can be confidence in any decision here requires significant investment in analysis and evaluation; however, given the costs involved, and the time such analysis can potentially take, this is not something which organisations – buyers or sellers – are always keen to enter into prior to a contract being signed. As a result, it is not unusual for the evaluation of the various alternative options to be circumscribed. However, as NPfIT illustrates, this is risky, as vendors are inevitably in pursuit of sales, and hence there is an inclination on their part to assert that their offerings will meet the bulk of the requirements, at least at the high level at which they are described in most specifications, and perhaps to overstate their capabilities (as in the case of iSoft's description of

Lorenzo as 'on the market' when significant further development was still necessary). It is therefore prudent to treat the claims made by suppliers about their systems, as well as those regarding the ease with which they can be reconfigured or modified to address any gaps identified, with a degree of circumspection. Moreover, suppliers are also likely to ensure that their wares are displayed to best effect in any demonstrations that are undertaken, while as Collins notes, seeing a system in operation at one of the reference sites provided by the vendor, even if this outwardly may appear to be quite a similar organisation operating in the same sector, does not mean it will necessarily be a good fit in any other organisation.[21] At the same time, the potential for overstatement of the capability of supplier offerings is combined with a likelihood of some misrepresentation of the requirements that the system needs to satisfy, given the difficulties in capturing and identifying these comprehensively and accurately, as discussed above, and the fact that the discussion about requirements and system capabilities at this stage of a project's evolution tends to take place at quite a high level of abstraction, and hence much of the detail and nuance of the organisation's activities and processes is unlikely to emerge at this stage. Additionally, the description of the requirements to be satisfied represents those prevailing at the particular point in time at which they were assembled, and are likely to be subject to change over time.

The indications are that NPfIT overestimated the capability and readiness of some of the available packages – not just Lorenzo - and that this did not emerge fully from the validation process that was undertaken (which involved the various suppliers demonstrating how their solutions would support a number of representative process scenarios). This points to the difficulties in making good initial supplier selection choices, and the value of ensuring that a structured and thorough procurement process is followed (whereas despite the scale of the programme, the process employed by NPfIT was criticised at the time for having been conducted too quickly and for having failed to involve clinical professionals).

Another source of uncertainty is the fact that any scoring system for evaluating competing options requires some degree of weighting to be assigned to different variables. For example, at its simplest, there is very likely to be a trade-off between cost and functionality; all other things being equal, the most functionally rich option is likely to be the most expensive. The question then emerges about the relative weightings to be allocated to cost and to functionality – and to all the other variables that may form part of the equation. Ultimately, this is likely to be as much a matter of judgement as it is of science.

All of this goes to show that in reality there are no panaceas here, only a series of trade-offs. Different options are likely to have different advantages and disadvantages. Choosing a ready-made solution reduces development risk (but only if there is no or minimal tailoring), and may simplify the longer-term upgrade path, but it may increase implementation risk, for example if it necessitates significant organisational change to adapt processes to a new way of working; choosing a bespoke development route may reduce the level of process change required, but is accompanied by all the complexities of undertaking a new-build project. Clearly while these selections are being made in the context of uncertainty around the future evolution of any initiative, the challenge for any organisation faced with such a decision is to ensure that it is approached with appropriate rigour, is well-informed, and is taken with an appreciation of the relative risks and rewards implicit in the choice made and the other options that are rejected. What constitutes 'appropriate rigour' in any situation is dependent on the degree of risk involved, and the potential consequences if it is not employed. We shall return to this issue below, but given subsequent events it would seem reasonable to assert that the process followed by NPfIT may have lacked the rigour required in certain respects, especially given the scale of the undertaking. This said, as NPfIT also demonstrates, there are often considerable time and cost pressures on organisations which may impinge upon them doing this well.

SYSTEMS CONFIGURATION/ARCHITECTURE

Closely connected to the software/solution selection decision – and in fact potentially intertwined with it – is the need to determine a feasible, and ideally the optimal, configuration of the new system (or systems). There are both technical and functional aspects to this. From a technical perspective, the solution of course needs to meet the organisation's requirements, and it needs to work effectively and efficiently, not just in isolation, but also in most cases in the context of the organisation's IT legacy environment to form a functioning whole. Hence, a key aspect of this activity is to determine how best to integrate the new system with the organisation's existing systems. Likewise, if the new solution is to be composed of a number of separate components, it will be necessary to decide how these should best fit together. This may also extend to consideration of interfaces to third party systems, eg in terms of the provision of data feeds, or for information exchange.

From a functional perspective, there is a need to make sure that the proposed configuration will be capable of effectively supporting without any material gaps or inefficiencies the full suite of organisational processes covered by or impacted by the solution. For example, this may involve the effective transfer of data from one system to another within a prescribed timeframe; ultimately, the configuration needs to be such that all the activities which the organisation needs to perform on any given day can be accommodated within a day's operation – whilst allowing time also for any routine daily systems housekeeping activities.

Ensuring both the technical and functional integrity of the overall systems configuration may be further complicated if the roll-out of the new solution is intended to be phased over time, as this means that there are likely to be a series of interim stages prior to achievement of the intended end-state, each of which must be functionally and technically viable solutions in their own right.

The degree of complexity in this area will therefore vary considerably; in some cases, for example where the project concerns a single new system which is fully stand-alone, with no connections required to other systems, determining the systems architecture will normally be quite straightforward. However, at the other extreme, where the solution involves a number of different systems which need to work together, and/or where the new solution is introducing significant change into an already tangled and messy IT legacy environment – which may in turn be supporting a convoluted set of organisational processes and activities spanning a number of existing IT systems, and perhaps via a number of different rollout phases, then it is likely to prove considerably more problematic. This is illustrated by NPfIT, where the basic systems configuration adopted consisted of three main components, namely the National Spine, the National Network, and the Detailed Care Records systems, along with the infrastructure required to link and support these. This represented a significant addition to the existing infrastructure in place throughout the NHS, with some of which it needed to integrate, and which as we have seen in practice proved a very challenging undertaking, given particularly the diversity of the IT legacy environment and process models in operation across the estate prior to the project. It is possible that there were alternative architectures and configurations which would have reduced the extent of these difficulties; however, to a considerable degree the configuration selected followed logically from the problem/opportunity definition, as discussed above, and the prevailing technology (note that in evidence to the 2011 Public Accounts Committee, it was argued that the less centralised architecture the project had more recently started to implement was only possible because the technology had evolved during the period since the project had been initiated).[22] Hence, although different and perhaps less radical architectural solutions may have been possible, they would not necessarily have been able to address the full set of problems and opportunities upon which the project was focused. The adoption of such an approach would therefore probably have necessitated some modification to the problem/opportunity definition and the scope of the project (which of course in retrospect might well have been desirable). What is also apparent is that in practice knitting the new systems together with the existing infrastructure proved to be more difficult than anticipated, in large part because the full diversity of the legacy environment may not have been fully appreciated. There seems little excuse for this, since the legacy environment is – by definition – something which already exists, and therefore the nature of this should be relatively simple to establish. Once this is done, the implications of this for the project can then be factored into the thinking and the approach. Had this been done rigorously in advance, it is possible that it may have resulted in a different approach being chosen. This again points to the importance of understanding as thoroughly as possible the full suite of complexities facing a project before such key decisions are taken. That the decision regarding the system architecture was indeed a critical one for NPfIT is clear from the fact that it was in turn fundamental to the design of the project delivery model and likewise to the scope of the contracts put in place for provision of the systems and services.

In this connection, it is probably also worth touching on some of the challenges and issues associated with the integration of systems. In fact, Collins identifies integration as another of the potential traps into which many an IT project can fall (in fact he describes it as 'the most dangerous word in the computing vocabulary'). He suggests that integration is not overridingly important, but merely desirable, and makes the point that it is better that all the systems work individually and not in harmony with each other rather than none of the systems work at all.[23] Certainly integration brings with it considerable complexity, for example to ensure the accurate and complete transfer of data from one system to another, to translate the data from one system into a form that can be understood by another one, and to establish mechanisms for identifying and dealing with problems and errors. All of these are likely to involve some degree of organisational overhead. In the case of one major project with which I was involved, where an ageing bespoke system was replaced with a new third party application, albeit a highly configurable one, the integration activities took 18 months longer than the configuration of the new system we were seeking to implement (for those who find analogies helpful, we likened the activity required to cutting out a slice of pizza where there are lots of strands of stringy cheese, and then replacing this slice with a new one – of a slightly different size - and having to join up all the strings of cheese with the new slice). And although the IT technology and approaches in support of integration continue to advance, this remains a non-trivial activity.

On the other hand, from an organisational process perspective, there are of course considerable advantages to integration, since it is likely to reduce the need for employees to extract information from one system and then rekey it into another one, which is both inefficient and prone to error. Again, the right course of action here can only be determined by a thorough appreciation of the balance of the costs, benefits and complexities arising.

This also serves to illustrate that this area is likely to be an iterative and evolving activity that continues throughout the course of the project's life, beginning with a high level Target Operating Model (describing the key interactions, relationships and interdependencies between different organisational entities, and the way in which the systems and processes will support these) and associated architectural design, and becoming increasingly detailed as the project unfolds. A key challenge here is to ensure that the high level design is appropriately cognisant of and informed by the complexity lurking in the detail, and does not lock the organisation into a solution which subsequently proves to have serious negative consequences. Linked to this is a need to have access to the necessary expertise to inform the choices made.

ORGANISATIONAL CHANGE

A key point here is that given the importance of many IT systems in supporting and enabling a set of organisation activities and processes, any significant changes to these systems are likely to have implications for these activities and processes. Wherever this is the case, this immediately takes the IT project in question into the realm of broader organisational change, and the human dynamics associated with this. Hence it is often argued that there is really no such thing as an 'IT' project per se: what these projects are is in fact 'IT-enabled organisational change' projects.

This same point was made in relation to NPfIT in the Parliamentary Office of Science and Technology briefing paper, and repeated in a number of the National Audit Office and Public Accounts Committee reports, which expressed concern about the insufficient focus being placed upon this aspect of the project by NPfIT.[24] Certainly initially, the emphasis appears to have been very much on the IT aspects of the programme, on the speedy conclusion of the procurement process and the negotiation of the contracts for the provision of the systems and services, rather than positioning these as part of a wider programme of organisational change. While there may be situations and projects where such an approach may be appropriate, for example where the emphasis is more technical (such as IT infrastructure projects) with negligible impact on the users, or where there are no powerful user groups, it seems less suitable in the context of NPfIT. Moreover, while the programme was initiated at least in part as a means of achieving a material change in the operation and effectiveness of the NHS[25], there is very little mention of this in any of the published reports. Nor does the link between the programme and the wider direction for the NHS appear to have been made particularly explicit in a way that could be understood by NHS personnel, patients and the public at large. In the absence of such a connection, it was inevitably harder for such groups to understand the logic for the programme and the level of investment being made in it. It was just another IT project. The weaknesses in the reporting on the achievement of the benefits from the programme may also have contributed to the difficulties in establishing such a connection(although perhaps there would have been more enthusiasm for better benefits reporting if there had been greater progress and more benefits were being delivered). In addition, where benefits were identified in association with the programme, they tended to refer to savings in the costs of procuring systems and services, not in terms of achieving the improvements in the operation of the NHS being sought (this may partly reflect a desire to focus on the tangible and more easily measurable rather than something which is more qualitative – see below).

Again, a tendency to regard IT projects as largely technical undertakings and to downplay the wider organisational change aspects of them (sometimes referred to as 'adaptive' challenges – see for example Heifetz and Linsky, 2002[26]) would appear to be quite a common feature of many such initiatives. However, all the evidence suggests that organisational change is itself a challenging and difficult thing to achieve, regardless of whether there are IT elements to this or not, and therefore wherever a project enters this territory, it needs to be cognisant of the complexities involved. There is an extensive literature on the challenges of organisational change[27], which it would clearly be impossible even to attempt to summarise this here. However, the following key points seem worth emphasising in relation to IT projects:

- wherever there are users who are likely to be affected by an IT initiative, the project needs to take account of and address the complexities of organisational change.
- it seems to be a common human reaction when confronted by change for at least some of those affected by it to seek to resist it (while research suggests not everyone will react in this way, at least some will). Related to this, another typical response is that of 'not invented here' - so that any change which originates from elsewhere in an organisation (or beyond) is often dismissed (rightly or wrongly) as inappropriate in the context of any particular organisational sub-entity.
- under these circumstances, while in some highly hierarchical, command/control-type organisational cultures it may be possible for management to impose a solution on a user population without some form of considered engagement with them, in most situations to ensure its success it is likely to be necessary, and certainly preferable, to find ways of reducing and overcoming this resistance, and building support for the project. This is likely to involve firstly ensuring there is understanding of the logic for the project, and secondly finding ways to involve those who are affected by the project in it in some way, so that they feel they have a degree of control over it.
- the nature of this engagement needs to be sensitive to the culture of the organisation and its internal dynamics. For example, as shown by the NPfIT, the more devolved the decision making in an organisation, and the greater the power that is disseminated to local units and to individuals, the more difficult it

is likely to be to impose a centrally mandated solution. Likewise, the significant share of organisational power vested in doctors and other medical staff in the NHS meant that mechanisms were required to ensure they remained at least sufficiently supportive of the initiative so as not to obstruct it.

- this pattern is often visible in relation to much smaller projects than NPfIT, and much smaller organisations than the NHS. As discussed previously, all organisations have their own internal dynamics, their pattern of internal relationships, and their unique distribution of power among different individuals and departments, and the reaction of each of these to the changes associated with the project is very likely to differ accordingly. Hence a key challenge for the project is to devise and then implement appropriate strategies for managing all of these.

USER INVOLVEMENT

While there are IT projects which will have no or only a negligible impact on users (at least directly) – such as those which are focused on replacement or upgrading of hardware or communications infrastructure - and therefore take place 'in the background', for a large proportion of IT projects some degree of user involvement will be essential (and even technical infrastructure projects may have implications for users in the event that anything goes wrong with them, and users are unable to do the things they need to do or access the information they need to access). We have already discussed the key role to be played by the user community in relation to the requirements gathering process, and we have also touched on their importance in connection with the wider organisational change elements of IT projects. Given that so much of the detailed understanding of organisational activity - at what might be termed the 'transactional' level –very often resides with the users, this involvement is likely to extend also to numerous other aspects of IT projects, including for example the development of detailed scenarios for use in demonstrations or in testing, the identification of material gaps between a possible system solution and the organisation's requirements, the assembly and validation of reference data, or the assessment of the acceptability and readiness of the system to go live.

Despite this, the NPfIT was criticised throughout its existence for its failure to engage adequately with users, and in particular medical professionals. This is again a consistent theme for many IT projects, and perhaps points to some of the challenges encountered in involving the users effectively:

- firstly, as discussed previously, there is a propensity for users to identify requirements for the new system which may not be truly essential. This is not just an issue at the initial requirements gathering stage; it can be an ongoing challenge for the project, as more users gain exposure to the new system for example through testing and training, and the system becomes more tangible and visible, and the users start to be able to see what is really being provided. Hence, as the project unfolds, there are likely to be further requests for enhancements and refinements. This places a major onus on the robustness of the change control process to determine the necessity of the proposed changes (see below) – which again is likely to prove challenging, given that the detailed process-level knowledge required to make such a determination is normally largely concentrated among the users. Ultimately, there is something of a tightrope to be walked here, since clearly there is a desire to avoid the cost of unnecessary changes, but on the other hand if such requests are consistently rejected then this is likely to bring about a reduction in user support for the undertaking.

- moreover, meaningful user involvement is likely to bring with it some practical difficulties. None of the obvious mechanisms available to provide for this - such as the secondment of key users to participate in project teams, conducting user workshops to provide input, actual user participation in acceptance testing, etc – is without some degree of challenge.

- in terms of the secondment of users to project teams, more often than not the users who are best placed to contribute most to the project are those who are most critical to the day-to-day operation of the organisation, and therefore the ones that the organisation is most reluctant to release, given the likelihood of some loss of operational efficiency in their absence. These are obviously also the individuals for whom it is most difficult to provide cover or to backfill – and there may of course be costs incurred in doing this. As a result of the potential impact on ongoing operations, if they have choices, organisations often choose to second those who are regarded as less pivotal from an operational perspective – which tends to mean they have less comprehensive knowledge of the activities and all their nuances and subtleties, and less standing, authority, credibility and influence with the wider user community. The latter is important, as one of the roles of the users seconded to the project is to act as the representative of the wider constituency of users from which they are drawn, so that this broader community feels at least some degree of ownership over the project and the decisions taken that may have implications for it. The ongoing maintenance of this ownership is likely to require regular interactions between the user representatives and the communities they come from – which in turn may involve the establishment of another set of mechanisms. In practice, it is easy for user secondees to become distanced and detached from the constituencies from which they come, especially over time, and especially if they were relatively junior staff with less credibility with these communities in the first place; hence this may give rise to declining user support for and involvement in the project, especially where project timescales are lengthy.

- the secondment of users to project teams tends to be particularly problematic for smaller organisations where there is considerable reliance on a small number of key personnel, and few other staff available and with the capacity/capability to provide the cover needed (this said, large organisations will of course likewise be made up of a number of separate smaller departments and units, so are far from immune from this issue). On the other hand, maintaining an ongoing sense of user ownership is likely to be more difficult the larger the project, because even if there are user representatives of some sort, the extent to which they are known to, or able to interact with all the different user communities they at least nominally represent, is likely to be minimal. In such situations, there is likely to be a heavy reliance on a lively and robust communications process to keep the various user groups informed of progress, and provide them with at least some opportunity to input – which was an approach adopted by NPfIT, albeit with mixed results. Again, of course, setting up and operating such a process is likely to require resource, effort and of course cost.

- part-time user participation in projects provides one possible alternative to the full-time secondment of staff. However, this tends not to be particularly effective, as operational requirements have a habit of interfering and taking precedence, while equally many of the user-related tasks to be performed are likely to be demanding and time-consuming. Neither is it desirable if this responsibility is shared among a group of individuals, as this may result in inconsistent input and places additional demands on the core project team to maintain a broader set of effective working relationships with the different participants.

- equally, involving a wider group of users in events like workshops or acceptance testing is again likely to raise practical issues associated with the need to accommodate these activities alongside the ongoing operation of the organisation, which makes it difficult to release a larger proportion of operational personnel to participate.

- users are also likely to require considerable support to assist them in some of the other activities where their participation is needed; most users will have only a limited appreciation of what may be required of them in terms of project input – much as the majority of IT staff will have little understanding of the minutiae of organisational operational activity and processes. This gives rise to a need for 'translators' who are able to bridge this particular gap. This function is often provided by a cadre of people known variously as 'systems analysts', 'business analysts' or 'functional analysts', who have both an appreciation of what is needed from an IT perspective, and a range of skills and techniques they can access to engage effectively with the user community. High calibre systems analysts, able to establish good interactions with users, can be of enormous value in these sorts of initiatives – as can the presence of users who have an appreciation of what is entailed in systemising complex organisational activities and processes (although this can sometimes be something of a double-edged sword, as sometimes users who have a high level of IT expertise can prove challenging to manage in these sorts of undertakings, as they may tend to be dismissive of the decisions taken by and the efforts of the projects team, believing they could do things better themselves).

Clearly therefore there are again a number of dynamics and tensions at play in this arena. What this all points to is that there is no simple answer to finding the right level of user involvement in an IT project, and ultimately the determination of the 'Goldilocks point' – not too much, not too little, just right – is a matter for judgement and experience. It also varies depending on the nature of the organisation and the nature of the initiative. Likewise, structuring the right mechanisms for providing this involvement, and ensuring that this is managed and controlled, is also something which requires thought and consideration.

STAKEHOLDER RELATIONSHIPS

Another set of relationships that IT projects need to consider are those with a broader group of interested parties who may be affected by the project in some way, albeit less directly than the users of the system per se, and who may therefore seek to exert influence on the undertaking. In the case of the NPfIT the list of such interested parties was probably longer than for virtually any other project imaginable, and covered a wide diversity of individuals and groups, for example medical professionals – and particularly the bodies that existed to represent their interests – who whilst not necessarily users of the system, nevertheless would be affected by it and had views about it; NHS managers, administrators, and staff, and likewise their representative bodies; and of course patients. In addition, there were other groups and individuals with a particular perspective or interest in the project, such as politicians of all hues and the media. All of these different constituencies interacted in some way with the project, and hence the project needed to respond accordingly. Different responses were employed in relation to different interest groups, albeit with mixed results: for example various formal engagement mechanisms were established to provide the connection with the medical profession, surveys of NHS staff were conducted to enable them to input their views, and the Connecting for Health website was set up as a means of providing information to the public at large – all of whom were of course potential NHS patients. As the project unfolded, and its struggles became increasingly evident, criticism from these groups inevitably increased, and there appears to have been a reduction in the extent to which NPfIT sought to maintain their support for and involvement with the project – and clearly it is hard to stifle the voices of opposition in the absence of demonstrable progress. On the other hand, it is probably under these circumstances that it is most critical that the underlying logic for the project is communicated and reiterated, and attempts are made to build as broad an understanding as possible of the difficulties and challenges being encountered and the intended strategies for dealing with these.

Of course, few if any projects are likely to encounter quite the scale and extent of interest and input from different stakeholders experienced by NPfIT, but equally most projects face some degree of comment, and perhaps critique (however well informed), from different individuals and groups who may not be direct participants in the project, but are nevertheless connected to it in some way. Given this, even in quite small projects it is desirable that a communications strategy is put in place to ensure there is at least some understanding of the project on the part of these different constituencies, and of the logic for it, the progress being made, and the issues which confront it – not least because people tend to be more supportive the more they comprehend the reasons underlying what is happening.

Another common pattern which may confront any project is where an influential manager of, or members of staff from, a department within the organisation which is not directly or only marginally affected by the new system expresses a view on the conduct of the project (or on IT projects in general). Often, such views may not be particularly helpful to the project: clearly the project then faces a choice as to how best to respond, whether for example to ignore them – which may however just give rise to further and more vocal criticism in future – or whether to engage more actively with the manager or group involved, perhaps by requesting their participation in the project governance board, which can be an effective way of increasing the understanding of the project and the complexities it is facing among its critics - or whether to find ways to exert pressure on those in question so that any unhelpful input is silenced. Any course of action pursued here is likely to have further consequences for the project.

SUPPLIER SELECTION AND RELATIONSHIPS

The way the NPfIT was approached meant that it was highly dependent on the suppliers who were engaged to deliver it. Notwithstanding the fact that the contracts may have been structured in such a way as to transfer the financial risk associated with poor or non-delivery to the providers, this did not mitigate the risk of non-delivery per se, and its implications for the achievement of the broad transformation of the NHS being pursued. Thus, the selection of the suppliers, the nature of the relationships with them (contractual and otherwise), and the ongoing management of them, were critical elements in the success or failure of the NPfIT.

Again, these issues are likely to be of significance for many IT projects. This said, the degree of importance will vary, depending on the choices made around the delivery model. In the case of NPfIT, substantial responsibility for project delivery sat with the suppliers, and this will be the case wherever a project involves the purchase (and perhaps configuration and modification) of third party software applications, which require supplier support both to implement them and then for ongoing maintenance and potentially enhancement of the systems, bespoke development by a third party, which again has implications for ongoing support and system improvement, and/or the engagement of consultants or contractors to supplement the in-house resources available to work on a project. Clearly there are other delivery models which are likely to be less reliant on suppliers – for example in the case of a bespoke development project undertaken by in-house personnel, although these will still need to run on hardware acquired from a vendor or vendors, are still likely to involve the use of some third party software products and tools, and may involve the use of contract personnel to supplement the in-house team - so even in this situation there will probably be some involvement with suppliers.

The process of choosing a supplier or suppliers, and some of the criteria that may need to be considered as part of this, were addressed in some detail previously as part of the discussion regarding software selection. Very similar considerations are likely to apply in connection with the engagement of the selection of third parties to provide other services or products to the project, so it is not proposed to repeat the discussion here.

A second area of supplier-related complexity highlighted by NPfIT concerns the nature of the contracts agreed with the suppliers. In the case of NPfIT, these were fixed price contracts covering both the provision of the solution and its ongoing operation for a number of years. The contracts also linked payments to the progress made in delivering systems, contained significant penalty clauses in the event of supplier withdrawal, and provided for the payment of sums in advance to suppliers – which could subsequently be recovered if the projected deliveries were not achieved. Additional costs would be charged by suppliers in the event of changes to the solution arising from modifications to the requirements.

Although the way and the speed with which the NPfIT procurement was conducted and the nature of the contracts entered into was viewed positively by the National Audit Office in their 2006 report (in fact going so far as to recommend it to other organisations)[28], the approach adopted remains open to question. In particular, the scale of the programme, and the uncertainties implicit within it meant that pricing of the contracts inevitably involved a considerable leap of faith on the part of the suppliers (exacerbated by the length of time the contracts were required to cover). It was therefore very difficult at the outset to determine what a 'good' price would be for the contracts. The prices established were ultimately those arrived at under the competitive bidding process, but even in retrospect it is unclear whether these represented a fair price for both the taxpayer and the supplier. There are indications that the commercial balance of the initial contracts was skewed to some degree towards the government and against the suppliers. Some of the contractual conditions imposed by the government were considered quite onerous by some potential suppliers, who chose to withdraw from the bidding process. The withdrawal of Accenture suggests that they had come to the conclusion that the costs and risks they were facing did not justify the benefits and rewards. This was probably sub-optimal in that it was not necessarily in the interests of the programme that some prominent suppliers chose not to compete for the business, nor was it desirable that some suppliers withdrew part way through the project. Likewise, the revised prices agreed subsequently under the renegotiated contracts suggests that in light of the experiences hitherto there was general acknowledgement that the original prices agreed were too low. Of course, if suppliers do not consider they are being appropriately remunerated for their efforts, there is every likelihood that they will look for ways both to reduce their costs and increase their revenues, for example by reducing the quality of their outputs, and seeking to maximise the opportunity for changes, for which they can then charge extra fees.

This was however not the only way in which the contractual arrangements could have been structured. For example, as we saw earlier, a different model was adopted in the case of Heathrow Terminal 5 through the Terminal 5 Agreement, which provided for payments to be made to suppliers on the basis of costs incurred and work completed, and left a greater degree of the financial risk of the project in the event of overruns with the customer. Similar models can of course be adopted in the case of IT projects. As the Terminal 5 experience demonstrates, these bring their own set of challenges and complexities: not least because they may give rise to greater uncertainty over the cost of the project. Clearly, this could ultimately give rise to a higher price being paid. On the other hand, it is possible that where there is considerable uncertainty around the precise definition and scope of the project (as in the case of NPfIT) such an approach could equally result in a lower cost, since the supplier does not need to include such a high level of contingency in the price quoted to cover all the potential unforeseen circumstances, and the cost of changes is also likely to be lower. Moreover, in the case of NPfIT, it would probably also have been preferable if the project had ultimately delivered a greater proportion of its intended outcomes, even if this came at a higher price. At the very least, it is apparent that any contracting approach adopted will have both advantages and disadvantages.

Of course, it tends only to be larger organisations which are in a position to dictate contractual terms and conditions to their vendors, and many smaller organisations may instead end up being presented with a set of standard contractual terms offered by the supplier, which – unremarkably – often tend to favour the supplier. This said, no organisation is compelled to sign something which is disadvantageous to them, and hence the onus in any situation is firstly to understand the implications of what is being proposed, and secondly to be prepared to negotiate with the supplier if there are aspects of the contract that are considered unreasonable. If the supplier refuses to make what are felt to be justifiable modifications, then this probably says something about the future relationship that the two parties are likely to enjoy. Ultimately, all organisations have the option of walking away. The challenge however is to ensure that the organisation enters into any arrangement with its eyes open and aware of the potential issues associated with the contract. This said, in practice it is not unusual for organisations to sign contracts presented to them by IT vendors with very little consideration.

The signing of the contract is only one stage in the ongoing interactions with a supplier, and just as in the case of Brunel's relationship with Russell during the construction of the Great Eastern, the relationship will evolve over time and require management and attention. The 2008 National Audit Office Report alluded to the importance of 'Managing Suppliers Effectively' as a key element of the programme.[29] The report noted that relationships were 'maturing', and increasingly collaborative and based on partnership (which was of course one of the key objectives of the Terminal 5 Agreement). This said, it is clear – not least from some of its public pronouncements (eg 'we will subject the suppliers to radical surgery'; 'if suppliers cannot do the job, they will be replaced')[30] - that at least during the earlier part of the programme, NPfIT had adopted quite an assertive stance with its suppliers. Again, such an approach has advantages and disadvantages. On the one hand, it helps ensure that there is clarity on the part of the supplier as to what is expected, and a clear focus on delivery. On the other it may give rise to a somewhat adversarial pattern of interactions, mutual point scoring and a resistance to find compromises and collectively beneficial solutions to points of issue. It is perhaps significant that as the project evolved it sought to strengthen co-operation and partnering with its suppliers.

Another issue which the NPfIT appears to have encountered in this regard is the way that users in a particular Trust interacted with the system providers. Initially, it seems that user contact was primarily with the relevant Local Service Provider, who would then undertake any discussions with the software suppliers. While this may have been in accordance with the formal delivery model established for the programme, it was perhaps not the most efficient means of managing the interactions, and also gave rise to considerable potential for 'chinese whispers' and misinterpretation. Subsequently, this engagement model was modified to enable personnel within the Trusts to interact directly with personnel from the software providers.

An important element in successfully managing the ongoing relationship with supplier organisations concerns the formal structures put in place in support of these, providing a means for issues of concern on both sides to be aired and potentially resolved. Where suppliers are key participants in the delivery model, it is quite common for them to be represented on project Governance and Steering Boards, and to form part of the project management team. Additionally, regular meetings may also be scheduled with key suppliers to ensure the relationship proceeds as smoothly as possible. Again, the Terminal 5 experience may provide a useful blueprint here.

Clearly, none of this happens automatically, so once again some commitment of organisational resources, time and energy is required in this arena if these relationships are to be managed successfully. Moreover, in many cases, rather than devolving responsibility for this to the project team per se, or to the IT department, it may be desirable for there to be some degree of wider organisational ownership of the relationships at a senior executive level – especially where the supplier in question is critical to the success of a project with considerable organisational significance.

Finally, as both Brunel's experiences with John Scott Russell and the NPfIT case study illustrate, there nevertheless remains significant potential for relationships with suppliers to become difficult and acrimonious. What is also clear is that rectifying such a situation once it has been reached is extremely problematic. In the example of the NPfIT, despite the effort that had been invested in the contracting process, the contracts themselves did not prove a particularly effective vehicle in ensuring supplier delivery. Moreover, even given all the delivery problems, there was a clear reluctance on the part of the government to pursue any legal action against the contractors for breach of contract, or likewise to enforce the penalty clauses incorporated in the contracts in relation to those suppliers who withdrew from the programme. Again, this is not an uncommon pattern in relation to IT projects. In the first instance, despite all the difficulties being experienced, it may still be deemed preferable to continue with the existing supplier than to sever the relationship, commence legal proceedings, and meanwhile seek to continue the project or start it again with another partner. In fact continuing it with a new partner may not be feasible (for example if the original supplier was implementing its own proprietary software package), so under such circumstances, the only alternative – other than abandonment (which may of course be an option, depending on the motivation and degree of imperative underlying the project), will be to start again. But there is no guarantee that by starting again with a different supplier the project will be any less problematic than the original attempt. Moreover, the existing supplier is likely over the course of the project to date to have built up an appreciation of the problem space and the client organisation that ought to be of benefit in the future progress of the project, whereas it would take time for any new supplier to establish this. Secondly, the contract may not lend itself to successful pursuit of legal action – especially if it was the standard contract presented by the supplier at the conclusion of the initial selection process, which was signed by the customer without any great scrutiny. And thirdly, it may be difficult for the customer to establish that the supplier was responsible for the problems experienced to the extent required under law – given that it is quite likely that at least some of these stemmed from the actions taken by the customer itself (an obvious example of this would be changes to requirements made by the customer as the project progressed).

What this points to is the critical importance of selecting the right supplier in the first place, structuring the contract so that it aligns the interests of both customer and supplier to their mutual advantage, and ensuring that effective arrangements are in place to promote successful relationships between the parties as the project unfolds. Which is of course easy to say, and much harder to achieve in practice. But clearly, for many IT projects, as with NPfIT, this area is one of the most important in determining the project's ultimate success.

IT TECHNICAL ISSUES

Many of the concerns raised in the first of the two letters sent by the group of leading academics to the Health Select Committee in 2006 related to technical concerns with the solution being proposed for NPfIT, and there is of course no avoiding the fact that IT technical matters form a significant part of all IT projects. In particular, the academics expressed reservations about the technical architecture and the detailed design of the system, its performance and responsiveness especially given the quantity of data it would need to accommodate, the reliability and robustness of the system in continuous 24/7 operation, and the recovery arrangements in the event of problems being experienced.

Some such issues are likely to be of relevance in respect all IT projects, large or small. Ultimately, all systems have to work at least adequately. This requires them to meet a number of criteria – notably, they need to perform consistently and reliably the activities intended in the way intended, and they need to be able to perform these within certain time constraints; in addition, in the event of problems occurring, mechanisms need to be in place to ensure that no important information is lost.

In terms of performance, at a macro level, this may involve being able to ensure that the system will be able to support the organisation carrying out all the activities it needs to undertake on any given day. This will also need to take account of the fact that the level of activity and the number of users may increase (or decrease) over time, but the system will still need to accommodate such changes; and that the nature of activity may vary from day to day and month to month - so for example the organisation and the system may be performing different activities, which still need to be undertaken within the time windows available, at month and quarter ends, for example to run monthly management information reports or produce the accounting results.

Linked to this, at a micro-level, as part of the requirements identification process, performance targets are normally established for typical tasks that users need to perform on and with the system - such as for being able to input data and the system to be able to save it, or to retrieve information previously input. Another aspect of this question is that not only does the new system need to work in isolation, it is quite likely that it will also need to work in association with other systems already in place in the organisation, and possibly also with external systems (ie if it is in receipt of data and information sourced externally, or provides feeds of information to third parties). This will entail the design and development of the integration and interfacing required - which again will need to be viable within the available time windows and efficient.

There are also likely to be another set of requirements associated with system reliability and ensuring that the information held on the system is not lost in the event of a breakdown. This plays into the question of the level or resilience and redundancy to build into the solution. Obviously, the more sophisticated these arrangements, the more continuity of operations is safeguarded against a range of different events (which can ultimately extend beyond just failure of the IT infrastructure to preventing against a range of more extreme eventualities, such as for example fire and flooding, in what is referred to as Disaster Recovery and Business Continuity planning, which may entail the need to establish alternative facilities and locations for use in such emergencies), the greater the cost involved. This again points to the importance of wider organisational involvement in the decisions taken here, to ensure that the expenditures proposed are justified on the basis of the organisational risks being mitigated.

Note that this was one of the principal factors to which the difference in cost for the systems provided through NPfIT compared to those purchased directly by Trusts from suppliers was ascribed as part of the 2011 deliberations with the Public Accounts Committee.[31] This is worth noting, because it does point to a difference of view around the right level of resilience and redundancy required for the sorts of systems in question. In practice, the appropriate level of such protection for any system in any organisation is ultimately a question of judgement. This in turn relates to the criticality of the availability of the system in the context of the organisation and its activities. The fact that the NPfIT and individual NHS Trusts appear to have come to different conclusions here does not necessarily imply that one or other of them was wrong in their assessment - it may be that both were right, given the particular context they were dealing with, since the Trusts that had signed up to participate in the NPfIT tended to be some of the larger and therefore arguably more critical Trusts, where continuity of service may genuinely have been more important than in at least some of those who chose to proceed independently.

Associated with these various requirements are a set of activities including the detailed design of the technical architecture on which the system will operate, the acquisition and installation of any hardware required (which may be leased as well as purchased, or involve the use of third party facilities and equipment), testing of the configuration proposed, and development of ongoing systems operational processes (such as scheduling of batch runs and back-ups).

The achievement of these various technical activities is of course very heavily dependent on the contribution of the technical IT personnel engaged on the project. These may be in-house personnel, supplier personnel, other contract staff, or some combination of all three. Inevitably, if the software selection decision involves the use of a third party package, there will be a heavy reliance on the supplier to provide input and guidance on the technical requirements, capabilities and set-up of the system in question, as the supplier is likely to have something of a monopoly on this information. This said, it there is in-house technical IT expertise available to the client organisation, then at least this puts them in a position to ask the right questions of the supplier and therefore provide a degree of scrutiny and validation of what is being proposed. Failing this, the organisation may choose to engage another third party to perform this role.

Notwithstanding such arrangements, the technical implementation area is normally one of the most difficult aspects of any IT project for the commissioning organisation to understand and oversee, since few of the executives who commission IT projects and then perhaps act as their sponsors have profound expertise in this area (see McDonagh and Coghlan, 2001, for an interesting analysis of the relationship dynamics between corporate leadership and the IT Department).[32] Under these circumstances, there is always a possibility that the solution proposed and adopted may be suboptimal. There are a number of different forces at play here: for example, it is not unusual for IT professionals – be they in-house or external – to seek to make use of the latest and most exciting technology, regardless of whether this is best suited to the situation, and even though this may bring with it a number of risks and complexities; equally, there is a possibility that solutions may be over-engineered, as this increases the role and contribution of the IT department and the revenue stream for the supplier, and moreover reduces the risk of problems arising once the system is operational that may be considered reputationally damaging; likewise, sometimes there may be a possibility of the solution being under-engineered, perhaps because the supplier recommends its standard solution, without fully appreciating all the nuances of the client's operation, and in the expectation that once this is implemented, there will be little option but to accept it, 'warts and all'.

Given these risks, at no point should the commissioning organisation choose to divorce itself from all involvement in these issues and sub-contract them entirely to the supplier, or perhaps even to the in-house IT department. Ultimately, all the technical decisions taken in association with the project remain ones which need to align with the identified organisational objectives and ends. This extends also to IT infrastructure projects where there may be little direct impact on the user fraternity, but where there still needs to be an organisational value proposition, which goes beyond simply increasing the elegance of the solution and utilising the latest available technology. All such initiatives require some degree of organisational scrutiny – and moreover, in any situation where there are scarce resources, there is also the question of the relative merits of any proposed IT investment compared to those of any alternative projects that the organisation could choose to pursue.

It is perhaps worth noting here that in those situations where they provide a practical option for the organisation, the advent of Cloud Computing and the availability of 'Software as a Service' solutions[33] has provided the opportunity to simplify many of the technical complexities to be encountered with the implementation of a new system, since these approaches rely on the technical infrastructure required by the system being provided by the vendor. This avoids the necessity of the organisation setting up its own dedicated infrastructure to support the system, and then needing to operate this on an ongoing basis. Also the burden of providing continuity of service under a range of different emergency scenarios transfers to the supplier.

Whilst this may be an attractive proposition, the ability to adopt such a solution depends on there being such offerings available on the market that meet the functional and other requirements of the organisation in question – which takes us back to the solution selection question discussed previously. Further, whilst they may eliminate the vast majority of the technical implementation tasks entailed, they still require all the other set-up tasks such as data loading, establishment of user profiles, testing and training to be performed. At least as things stand currently (although this may change as the market evolves), Cloud Computing and Software as a Service solutions lend themselves better to self-contained situations where there is less need for significant integration with a wider web of interconnected systems. And of course while such solutions may eliminate many of the costs and complexities incurred in a conventional implementation, there will equally be a price tag associated with achieving this, which would also need to be factored into any decision. So once again, whilst there are clearly advantages with such approaches, they do not represent a universal panacea, nor do they eliminate the need for the commissioning organisation to access some degree of technical IT expertise in support of the activity. Meanwhile, of course, at the other extreme, the technical aspects associated with a bespoke development project will be considerable. Again, even if the development is outsourced to a third party, appropriate internal expertise within the commissioning organisation is essential if it is to exercise effective scrutiny and oversight of the development work.

TESTING

There are a number of references to difficulties with testing in the NPfIT story, which serves to illustrate that testing of IT systems is often more complex than might initially be imagined. This is again despite the existence of sophisticated testing methodological frameworks which have been developed for use in connection with IT projects. Ultimately however the challenge for any testing approach is to ensure that the solution adopted will work at least adequately once it goes live in the organisation in question.[34]

Some of the particular complexities faced in this connection include:
- Design of an appropriate test approach in the context of the particular project in question. If a system is an established application and is used 'out of the box' with no modifications, and no interfaces to other systems, then the testing burden for the implementing organisation is likely to be quite small. However, where a system has been modified or configured to meet specific requirements, interfaced to or integrated with other systems, or is a bespoke development, there is likely to be a need for a considerable investment of time, effort and resources in testing on the part of the user organisation.
- Development of an appropriate set of test scenarios and provision of the necessary test data, so as to provide a sufficiently thorough basis on which to assess the effectiveness of the solution in meeting the needs of the organisation. As well as establishing whether the solution is able adequately to perform all

the various functions as intended, there is also the requirement to ensure this can be done sufficiently quickly to meet the organisation's needs, especially during busy periods when the heaviest demands are placed on the system. Clearly, the greater the number of potential scenarios that are subject to testing, the greater the confidence in the suitability of the system – equally however, the greater the costs and time involved, so there is likely to be a trade-off here. A decision also needs to be taken about the level of detail at which the tests will be performed – in particular, will the individual key strokes required to enter the information be specified, along with the expected outputs at every stage of the activity, or will the tests be based on ensuring a particular set of end results arise following a series of inputs. The former relies on greater initial effort in preparation, whereas the latter is likely to require greater expertise of and familiarity with the organisation's activities. Ideally some form of simulation of real operation is desirable, because this will inevitably provide for situations and eventualities which are not covered by the more scripted testing – including those for example where users do not behave as intended or expected, or where bad data is input or fed from another system, as in practice often proves to be the case. An extreme form of this is the Parallel Run, where the new solution is run alongside the one that it is replacing in live operation, to ensure that the same results are generated by both. This obviously has advantages in that it provides clear confirmation of the efficacy of the new system in live operation, and can be a way of providing a contingency in the event of significant problems with the new solution. On the other hand, this is usually complex to set up, places significant demands on the organisation to run both solutions at the same time, and outputs may differ for good reasons, or because of problems with the old system rather than the new one. Again, such an approach does not provide a panacea.

- Creating a sufficiently realistic test environment that will provide an appropriate facsimile of the systems configuration that will exist in the organisation post the implementation of the new solution. This is especially problematic if the new system is to be integrated into a complex existing IT infrastructure, as the test environment will need to replicate, or at least find ways to represent, the integration with and interfaces to and from these systems – certainly the most important ones. Clearly the more closely and extensively the test environment reflects the actual production environment the greater the costs involved in setting it up and operating it.

- Establishing an appropriate set of criteria to determine whether the solution has passed the tests. Superficially, this might seem straightforward – surely if any outcome is different from what was expected, this constitutes a failure. However, some of the problems which tend to emerge from testing may simply be cosmetic, while others may be attributable to problems with the test data being used. Some may be addressed by a change in process rather than modification to the system per se. This therefore necessitates an exercise to evaluate the failures experienced, establish their severity, and then prioritise those which need to be fixed most urgently. In terms of the testing of system performance, there may be some leeway in relation to the targets set, since the target performance criteria established are often somewhat subjective – so for instance if a target of 3 seconds is established for the system to perform a particular function, and tests show this as taking 4 seconds, is this a cause for concern? Again, this is a matter of judgement, and requires an understanding of the organisation's internal operations and processes to make an informed assessment.
- Linked to all this are a series of resourcing and logistics challenges. As well as demands on IT personnel to set up the IT infrastructure and environments required, there are likely to be demands on users – particularly what might be termed 'expert users', that is those with the most understanding of the organisation's processes in the particular area or areas of activity covered by the new systems to assist with the development of test scenarios and the design of the tests, and then to take part in the testing itself (most testing normally concludes with a round of 'User Acceptance Testing'). This may involve users being taken away from their routine day to day activities in order to participate in testing, which can place operational pressures on the rest of the staff. Hence the scheduling of testing activities is likely to need to take account of the potential demands on staff during different periods. It may also be desirable to establish a dedicated room where the testing can take place away from the distraction of the normal daily activities.
- Given all of the above, it is not unusual for testing to be significantly less comprehensive in practice than might be ideal. Moreover, for the user organisation to be able to undertake any meaningful testing requires the availability of a system which is an accurate representation of the one that is to be implemented, and which is substantially operational. In the event of delays in the delivery of this, if an implementation date has been fixed and there is a reluctance to postpone this (which is again a common pattern), the time

available for comprehensive testing is inevitably constrained – as was the case with the Nuffield Orthopaedic Centre. Ultimately, this leaves the organisation in a position of having to make a judgement regarding the relative risks and rewards of proceeding without having undertaken adequate testing, or delaying the go-live. Again, this is an organisational decision, not an IT one, or a project one.

SYSTEM SECURITY AND ACCESS CONTROL

An area of complexity which proved particularly difficult and contentious for the NPfIT – given particularly the sensitivity of the personal medical records to be held on the system - was that around the security of the system, the control of access to different parts of the system and the protection of the data held on the system. This area was again identified as one which presented significant challenge in the Parliamentary Office of Science and Technology briefing paper at the start of the project.[35] Nevertheless, it continued to generate concern and disquiet throughout the programme's existence.

Whilst there were perhaps some unique challenges facing a system which would store and provide access to medical records, a significant proportion of systems are likely to contain some information which will be considered confidential to some degree. For example, banking, payroll and personnel systems will all face at least some of the same sorts of security concerns as those faced by NPfIT (in fact some of the unique pressures faced by a project as visible as NPfIT are illustrated by the contrast between the degree of controversy engendered by the issue of security and information access here and the comparative lack of concern we all seem to display in relation to on-line banking). Meanwhile, the transaction and accounting systems used by even quite small enterprises normally hold banking details of various third parties; most commercial systems are likely to hold proprietary information which the organisation would wish to protect from competitors. In the UK, the Data Protection Act also places responsibilities on organisations to ensure appropriate mechanisms are in place to control access to certain types of information held in IT systems, and similar legislation is in place in many other countries. At the same time, systems face threats from computer viruses and hackers – the latter motivated as much by the desire to make mischief and cause disruption rather than specifically to gain access to sensitive or confidential information.

Hence, most IT projects need to confront this issue of how best to protect and control access to the information to be contained within the system. This is accomplished principally by determining a set of access privileges and permissions within the system; these are allocated on an as needed basis, and protected by means of passwords. NPfIT also employed smart cards to restrict access to information, and the use of biometric identifiers was also contemplated.[36] Encryption routines may also be employed to increase the security of data. There is clearly a significant technical component to this, but a key question for the organisation concerns who should be able to access what information, and under what circumstances, and in what way - for example, can they just read this information, or can they update it. A classic example of this is around the payments process, where the process is often segmented into a number of separate stages - such as order entry, receipt of goods, approval of invoice, entry of payment details, and approval of payment - for each of which the ability to update the system is given to different individuals, as a means of reducing the risk of fraud. Obviously, the level of segregation of responsibilities is dependent on the size of the organisation in question, and the way the different roles performed by people within it are configured. It is not unusual however for the implementation of a new system to require some reconfiguration of the roles within an organisation to ensure consistency between these and the workflow and security permissions implicit in the system. In some cases, it may be considered necessary to revise the system so that it supports a different distribution of roles and responsibilities - as in the example of the Nuffield Orthopaedic Centre referred to in the case study, where the system worked on the basis of clinicians being involved in the booking of appointments, whereas at the Nuffield Orthopaedic Centre this task was performed only by administrative staff. Presumably it was felt to be easier in this case to change the system rather than to change the organisational processes, roles and responsibilities.

Ultimately, any IT project where there are users has to map the different users and their roles against the different functions and permissions within the system. This is always likely to be a complex undertaking. This also gives rise to an ongoing administrative activity to set up new users and delete old ones as employees join and leave the organisation, change permissions as individuals change roles, and so on – since clearly somebody has to do this, and it needs to be properly controlled.

ORGANISATIONAL READINESS AND IMPLEMENTATION

There are a number of complexities and difficulties associated with the preparations for the introduction of any new system, and with its actual implementation. These are well illustrated by the NPfIT case study (see in particular the results of site visits to 15 Trusts which had implemented new Care Records Systems referred to in the National Audit Office 2008 report, and the experiences at the Nuffield Orthopaedic Centre[37]) as well as – in a slightly different context - by the problems arising on the opening of Heathrow Terminal 5 discussed earlier. Particular areas that require attention in this regard include: Go-live timing; User Training; Data migration; Technical Implementation; Contingency Planning; Post Go-Live Support; and Go-live decision-making. Each of these activities has its own set of associated challenges, which the following sections will seek to review.

Go-Live Timing:
Prima facie, the timing of the Go-Live is determined by the time taken to undertake the project. Once all the tasks entailed have been completed satisfactorily, then, and only then, the system can go-live. The project plan provides the projection of this, and one of the tasks of project planners is to optimise the plan so that the project is completed as quickly as possible (within any constraints imposed, such as around costs or resources), for example by ensuring that those activities that can be undertaken in parallel are done so, rather than in sequence. Nevertheless, the plan is only a means of organising the activity, and ultimately it is the actual length of time taken to perform all the various tasks that determines the implementation timing.

In practice, however, as the Nuffield Orthopaedic Centre example illustrates, other considerations may influence the decision as to when to go-live with a new system – which in this case was driven particularly by the fact that the existing system was considered to have reached the end of its life, and organisations have a degree of flexibility around a number of variables that may enable the go-live to be accelerated (or deferred) if deemed desirable. This is of particular significance if there are limited windows of opportunity where organisations feel able to take new systems live, for example due to the need to avoid particular busy periods - such as associated with annual price changes or accounting period ends. For example, it may be possible to reduce the amount of functionality to be incorporated in the implementation so as to shorten system development times, and rely on other means of meeting these requirements either temporarily (in which case the functionality can be deferred to another later software release) or permanently; similarly a decision can be taken not to resolve some of the defects arising from testing, and cover these gaps by means of alternative 'workarounds'. Such changes may impose an increased operational burden on the organisation post go-live, which may in turn have implications for the project's financial case, but this may be offset by the earlier go-live than otherwise. Likewise, the amount of testing or training can be reduced from that which was originally intended. Such a course of action inevitably results in an organisation taking on additional risk in association with the implementation - although this said, there is a view that taking a system live may prove to be a quicker and more effective way both of resolving any outstanding functionality problems and of getting users up to speed with its operation than any amount of structured and formal testing and training. This also plays into questions around the extent and quality of contingency planning, support for users during the immediate post-implementation period, and the availability of development resources to fix any system defects encountered (see below). Ultimately, the decision on go-live timing is therefore a question of reward and risk; again, as the Nuffield Orthopaedic Centre case shows, the short-cuts taken enabled the organisation to achieve the earlier implementation it was seeking, but this came at a cost of quite considerable initial disruption.

Training:

Training was identified in the Parliamentary Office of Science and Technology briefing document as a key challenge for NPfIT[38], while the Nuffield Orthopaedic Centre experience pointed to some of the difficulties that may be encountered here. Clearly, to be of greatest benefit, training needs to involve hands on interaction with the new system – which did not prove possible in the Nuffield Orthopaedic Centre case. The National Audit Office case studies also refer to problems associated with the use of a 'generic' training environment rather than one incorporating all the local modifications. To be able to provide a training system which closely resembles the one which is being implemented by the organisation in question however requires completion of most of the required development activity, for this to be packaged into a software release, installed on the hardware to be used for the training (at least some of which may be newly acquired for this purpose), appropriately configured (eg with the necessary user accesses and security permissions), loaded with realistic data relevant to the organisation in question, tested and working. To arrive at such a position requires the project to be well advanced, and the majority of project tasks to be complete or nearing completion.

At the same time there are a number of logistical issues associated with training that need to be overcome. Special training rooms may need to be set up with all the necessary hardware. And in particular there is the question of the scheduling of the training. This needs to be done in a way that does not compromise the ongoing operation of the organisation. This sets an upper limit on the number of users able to attend each session, which in turn dictates the number of sessions that will be required, and the period of time needed in order for all these to be undertaken. Additional sessions may also have to be scheduled to pick up non-attendees. This may mean that training has to commence some time ahead of the intended go-live date (for example, the report into the Nuffield Orthopaedic Centre go-live concluded that 10 to 12 weeks were needed to train their staff on the new system to be implemented). On the other hand, to ensure users retain the maximum information that has been imparted to them, it is desirable if training takes place as closely as possible to go-live (in practice, users are unlikely to remember very much of the training they were given 10 or 12 weeks previously). Moreover, as the Nuffield Orthopaedic Centre case again demonstrates, delays in the availability of a close to completion system coupled with fixed implementation deadlines may restrict the time window within which training can take place. Again, under these circumstances, there is an organisational judgement call to be made as to the relative risks and rewards of taking the system live as scheduled without the users having been properly trained compared with delaying the roll-out to enable this to take place.

Another significant training-related task is the development of the content of the training to be provided. Again, to be most effective, this needs to be tailored to the different types of users so that it focuses on the system functions relevant to them (note that this also requires clarity on which users are going to be performing which role following the introduction of the new system – which of course may be different from under the existing system and processes). The content may consist of a suite of relevant scenarios to be demonstrated and followed in the classroom, along with user manuals and other guidance (such as on-line help) - all of which of course needs to be developed. Following the training some form of testing may be beneficial as a means of ensuring user competence - especially in situations where the absence of such competence could have serious adverse consequences.

Training or education may also need to extend to staff who are employed by third party organisations where they may interact with the new system. For example, I was involved in a project which required lorry drivers from third parties who were picking up loads to enter a different number from the one they were used to entering when they made the collections; although they had been notified of the need for this change, this did not extend beyond providing written instructions, and very few drivers observed the change required. This caused considerable problems with the operation of the new system, as well as to the operation of the business concerned, which took a number of months to resolve.

Data Migration:

As with many IT projects, the National Audit Office review found that migrating data from the NHS Trusts' old systems to the new ones also proved to be a challenging activity, and this is again an area where the degree of complexity is often underestimated. Many systems require a body of data to be in place in order to operate – for example, in the case of the NPfIT, this included information such as names, addresses and the NHS numbers of patients, details of their GPs, existing medical conditions, allergies and so on. Such information – often referred to as 'static' or 'reference' data, since it tends to be less subject to change over time, and the system may 'refer' to it to validate that information being entered is correct - needs to be pre-loaded into the new system before it can start working. However, this exercise is often in practice more difficult than anticipated – for example the existing data available to provide this information (which may be paper records, or may be data from existing systems) often contains inaccuracies, duplications and omissions. However, to correct for these problems tends to be a time-consuming and onerous process. In addition, no two systems ever require the same information in the same format, so wherever a project involves a replacement of one system by another, a laborious process has to be undertaken of identifying and collecting any new information required, and reformatting the old data into the style required by the new system. While automatic routines can often be developed to facilitate the reformatting process and the identification of duplicate or missing records, filling in any gaps tends to place significant demands on a small core of users from inside the organisation who are most familiar with the types of information involved; this can be challenging for the organisation as this group are likely also to have important ongoing operational responsibilities. Whilst it may be possible to engage some external resource either to assist with the data 'clean-up' exercise, or to provide backfill for users in their operational roles so they can be released to work on the data, both of these approaches give rise to additional cost, and both tend to result in inefficiencies of one sort or another. Another option is prior to go-live to load only the minimum amount of data required for the system to operate, and then to rely on the mechanisms in place to manage the ongoing additions and amendments to the data to augment this information subsequently as usage evolves. This can reduce the burden on the organisation during the project phase, but inevitably increases it once the system is in production, and may therefore require additional resources to support this activity. Of course, if they don't already exist, these ongoing maintenance mechanisms will need to be put in place. As part of this, controls may need to be established to ensure the accuracy and integrity of new information, to prevent duplication or the introduction of errors, and to restrict the ability to update the records only to those who are authorised to do so – especially where the information involved is sensitive.

A second data migration question relates to what may be referred to as 'dynamic' or 'transaction' data. These are the records of particular activities or transactions entered onto the system. In the case of NPfIT, they could relate for example to a particular course of treatment already in progress – perhaps beginning with a visit by the patient to a GP, and tracking all the subsequent interactions between the patient and the NHS relating to this condition. When a new system is implemented, there are again various strategies that organisations can employ in relation to the migration of such transactional data (and in fact the National Audit Office review pointed to different Trusts having employed different approaches). Probably the most common approach is to load only those activities which are 'live' at the point at which the new system is implemented, at their existing state of evolution, so that the record contained in the new system is current at the time of go-live, thus making it straightforward to use the new system to update and manage any subsequent developments in relation to that particular activity. This may sound simple, but in practice it requires an accurate, comprehensive, up to date, point in time 'snapshot' to be obtained of the status of all the relevant activities or transactions that are in progress at the time of the go-live; moreover, since the new system is more likely than not to record these activities in a different format and manner than the previous system (which may of course have been a manual, paper-based process), a means of translating and mapping the old information to the new, and if necessary filling in any information gaps, is again likely to be required.

An alternative approach, which can be adopted if the old system is still accessible and available to the users, is rather than to migrate any of the live transactions or activities, to use the old system to continue to process these, and only enter new transactions into the new system. This way, over time, the amount of activity in the old system decreases while that in the new system steadily ramps up. This obviously reduces some of the complexity associated with the sort of instant cutover referred to above, but clearly it requires duplicate systems to be retained in place for a period of time, which could be quite lengthy, involving additional costs and logistics complexities, and it places additional demands on the users during this period who have to work with two different systems, which will in all likelihood operate differently, and can therefore prove confusing.

At the other extreme, organisations may choose to migrate additional transactions or activities across to the new system beyond just those that are live at the go-live date. This increases the volume of information to be transferred, although because such transactions are complete, the particular complexities around tracking their status at the point of cutover will not arise. This approach may confer advantages in terms of providing a comprehensive record of information in the new system – which would seem to be quite important when maintaining something such as a definitive healthcare record, or where a new accounting system is implemented part way through a financial year, in terms of ensuring that a full year's worth of accounting information is contained in the new system (this relates back to the point made earlier in relation to go-live timing, in that organisations are often reluctant to implement new accounting systems at the end of an accounting period, as this tends to be a very busy period for them operationally, when they are least well-placed to handle the additional burdens and potential disruption associated with implementing a new accounts system).

This raises another question around access to historic information where this is not transferred across to the new system. There are regulations in place around the length of time that many types of records must be kept and remain accessible in most jurisdictions, so a project may need to find ways to comply with these. Some of the information contained in the old system(s) may also be valuable for dealing with queries or to aid in analysis. Options here include maintaining access – perhaps in a restricted way – to the old system for this purpose, or transferring relevant information to some form of historical archive (in which case, the historical archive will need to be created).

Development of Reports (and other output formats):
The Nuffield Orthopaedic Centre experience again points to some of the difficulties that are often encountered in this area, with problems arising with the printing of appointment letters, and with the generation of the performance and activity reports required for the Trust to manage its operation effectively and to report externally.

This is not necessarily an operational readiness activity as such – it could equally be regarded as part of solution specification and development - but it is often left until quite late in the life of the project since it is desirable to have a substantially working system available, thus making it easier to ensure the correct information is feeding into the different outputs – which as well as reports of various types may include things like invoices and statements and other documents produced by the system – such as appointment letters in the case of NPfIT (although on the other hand the availability of a subset of these is valuable during testing, to ensure that the system is performing the right calculations and producing the reports and outputs expected). Moreover, the degree of difficulty in ensuring that the right information is shown in the right way on the various outputs is often underestimated, or perceived as something that can be rectified once the system is in operation (which of course it can be, as the Nuffield Orthopaedic Centre example again demonstrates).

This area is normally again one where there is a need for co-operation between the users, who have an appreciation of the reports/output formats that are required, and the format they would like to see them in, and IT personnel, who understand the data within the system which is needed to feed the reports and what is necessitated to extract and present this. Users often have a set of outputs from their existing systems with which they are familiar and comfortable, and there is frequently pressure to recreate these exactly as part of the new solution - even if the new system can readily provide the same or similar information albeit in a slightly different format, perhaps via a standard or 'canned' report or layout. There is also a tendency for users to regard the introduction of a new system as an opportunity to request substantial numbers of additional reports that they believe would be useful, in order to enable them to deal with particular ad hoc queries, rather than to support the core operation of the organisation. One way of providing a means to support such ad hoc reporting - and potentially also delivering some of the core reporting needs - is through the use of third party reporting tools which extract data from the core system and then enable this to be re-presented in a format determined by the users. Again, however, while these tools can be very powerful, they require a degree of technical expertise and understanding of the organisational requirements to set them up in the first place, so that the correct data can be extracted. Moreover, the selection of any single tool from the alternative options available may repeat some of the complexities discussed previously in the solution selection section (although often the vendor of the core application will have an arrangement with a reporting tool provider, or will seek to recommend a particular reporting tool).

Technical Implementation:
There are a myriad of technical and technically-related activities which also need to be undertaken in association with any new system go-live.

For example, these may include the following:
- set-up of users with the required hardware and software to access the system - this may include such things as new servers and PCs with additional capability, extra screens, the loading of new software onto servers and user desktops, provision of new printers and changes to printer access on user PCs, and so on. In the case of NPfIT this included also the distribution of smart cards to users as part of the controls on user access, which proved logistically quite challenging – of course, associated with this was the need to install all the required card readers, and the software to make them work; other projects may likewise have to install similar ancillary equipment – for example bar code scanners for point of sale retail systems, or credit/debit card readers. Linked to this is a requirement for at least a measure of testing to ensure all the items installed work properly in an operational setting (note that one of the most significant problems experienced by Nuffield Orthopaedic Centre was caused by a power failure shortly after go-live at Fujitsu's primary data centre, following which the in-built resilience for the power supply failed to operate as intended; while this should have been tested prior to go-live, the compressed timetable meant that this testing had been deferred until later).
- removal (or limitation) of user access to the old system.
- switching on of interfaces, data feeds etc to and from the new system, and switching off of those to and from the old system.
- technical activities required in support of data migration and loading.

- establishing arrangements for archiving of old data.

Many of these tasks need to be performed in a tight time window, since the new system needs to be operational as soon as the old one is turned off (or access to it shut down). Clearly this is likely to be more difficult for organisations like the NHS that operate 24 hours a day, 7 days a week, compared to those which work a 5 day working week.

Contingency Planning:

Given the possibility of things going wrong when the new system goes live – as was the case at Nuffield Orthopaedic Centre, and in much the same way that the commencement of operations at Heathrow Terminal 5 was beset by severe difficulties – it is prudent for an organisation to put in place appropriate contingency plans so that it is as well prepared as possible to respond in the event of problems occurring. However, while contingency plans for a range of different situations had been established for Nuffield Orthopaedic Centre, the particular circumstances that actually occurred were not provided for in the plans that had been put in place. This is not unusual, since in reality it often proves very difficult to anticipate the full range of scenarios that may occur during the implementation. Moreover, prior to go-live, people tend to be heavily focused on and invested in delivering 'Plan A', and believe that there is only a very low probability of major problems occurring, so this activity is often neglected. However, even if the precise nature of the circumstances arising may be difficult to anticipate, there is certainly value in thinking through the sorts of problems that could be experienced, and putting in place the decision-making and crisis management processes and structures that may be required to respond to any severe issues in the event they do come to pass, and identifying who will be part of these.

A subset of contingency plans are what are sometimes called 'roll-back plans' which cover the actions to be taken during the course of the implementation to abort the go-live and revert to the previous system and mode of operation in the event of major problems being experienced. More often than not, there is only a short time window when such an approach is feasible, since as soon as data is being input or fed into the new solution, rather than the old one, to revert to the old system will require this to be extracted and re-input to the old system, which is likely to be a very difficult undertaking. It may also require interfaces and data feeds which are now linking to the new system to be re-reconfigured to point once again to the old system. Often problems with the new solution only come to light after a period of time has elapsed, by which time it is impractical to go back. Given the time pressures, if a roll-back is being contemplated, there is a need for any such decision to be taken promptly, and given the potential complexities, for this to be executed effectively. This in turn implies the need for the provision of timely and accurate information to the decision makers, clarity around the decision making processes and lines of authority, and robust roll-back plans to be established in case these are needed.

Post Go-Live Support:

Even in the case of the best managed projects in organisations with the most experience of implementing them, some difficulties are almost inevitable in the aftermath of the go-live, and clearly the risk of these occurring is significantly increased if there were gaps and deficiencies in the project's activities prior to this point. Hence the experiences referred to at the Nuffield Orthopaedic Centre during this period were in no way especially remarkable. Given this, arrangements need to be in place to address any such immediate issues arising. In addition, in the longer term, there will also be a requirement to provide ongoing support for the new system, so that any new problems arising can be resolved, and system modifications and software upgrades accommodated as and when required.

In the immediate post go-live period, there are perhaps two different types of issues that projects are likely to face. The first of these are relatively minor initial set-up and familiarisation issues, often associated with things like users being unable to log on to the new system (as was the case at Nuffield Orthopaedic Centre), or print to a particular printer, or remember certain aspects of their training. These sorts of 'housekeeping' problems are probably unavoidable. As the 2008 National Audit Office report noted, good practice is to have expert help on hand to provide immediate assistance to users whenever any such minor problems occurred, for example by means of 'floorwalkers' (sometimes called 'expert users'). Such arrangements can also help supplement the core training activities by providing reminders and addressing any gaps. The floorwalkers are also able to ensure that any more serious problems are properly captured and properly referred to the support teams.

This brings us to the second type of problem experienced in the aftermath of the new system going live, which concerns defects in the solution or in the supporting processes, which mean that it does not perform as intended. These may not necessarily be apparent immediately, but may only come to light at a later time, when particular processes are undertaken or particular pieces of functionality used for the first time. Likewise, certain hardware or technical issues may only become evident over time, such as a steady deterioration in performance. Sometimes these issues are of such severity as to have a profound impact on the organisation's activities and ability to operate effectively. The National Audit Office case studies noted the widespread incidence of a variety of such problems arising in the aftermath of the various implementations.

These sorts of problems require a structured set of support arrangements to be in place, firstly to receive notification of the problem, prioritise it, diagnose it, determine how to resolve it (potentially both in the short term with an immediate workaround, and in the longer term with a permanent modification to the system), undertake the necessary changes - ideally not in the operational system, but rather in a controlled development environment where operations are unaffected if this causes problems, test the solution developed to ensure it works - again in a secure setting separate from the live system, and finally implement the agreed changes into the operational system, as well as providing instructions and perhaps training to the users on the changes made. Obviously this requires significant investment in time and resources prior to go-live to set up all the necessary structures, processes and infrastructure required, and then post go-live to operate them and provide the support needed. Such arrangements are likely to be more complex if there are a number of different parties involved in the provision and support of different parts of the system, for example if responsibility for the software application (or applications) resides with one or more vendors, and responsibility for the technical infrastructure lies elsewhere, for example with the in-house IT department. This requires once any problem has been reported a mechanism to be in place to determine the nature of the problem and hence the responsibility for addressing it. Large organisations may institute 'help desks' as the first point of contact for any problems, which can then serve as a sort of clearing house to allocate these to the appropriate support team - although determining who is really responsible may not always be straightforward, and requires a thorough understanding of the system and the supporting infrastructure by the support desk personnel (the National Audit Office review reported significant criticism of the NPfIT central service desk). Once the new system is considered reasonably stable (although sometimes before this point, given budgetary pressures) the intensive support processes operated in the immediate aftermath of the go-live will give way to the ongoing operational support model – which again is something that the project will need to design and agree with the different parties involved (likely to include suppliers, users and the in-house IT department), ideally prior to the system's deployment.

Go-Live Decision Making:
The decision as to whether or not to go live with the new system should again, prima facie, be pretty straightforward. If the system is ready to be implemented, then it can go live. Otherwise, it can't. In the same vein, the Nuffield Orthopaedic Centre review concluded that the introduction of a new system should not proceed if critical tasks have not been completed.

But in practice, as with much else relating to IT projects, as by now hopefully is becoming apparent, things are rarely this simple.

The primary difficulty here relates to the determination of 'ready' and 'complete'. This can prove problematic. In the first instance, there are a number of different things that need to be ready/completed. These include: the software; the hardware and IT infrastructure; the data; the users; the support and help arrangements; the final go-live implementation plans; and contingency and roll-back plans in the event of serious problems being encountered. Readiness therefore needs to be assessed for each of these. Good practice here would normally involve the establishment of a set of criteria (sometimes called 'Go/No Go criteria'), and the evaluation of actual progress against these. Both of these are likely to involve some degree of complexity and effort. In terms of the establishment of the go-live criteria, the question is how good does the solution need to be to be able to go live successfully. Most operational systems have defects and data problems, and users are not always fully familiar with all of the system's features. While obviously the go-live criteria can be pitched at a level at or close to perfection, this may therefore result in unnecessary prolongation of the project while many less important issues are resolved which would not have a significant impact on the system in production, or could be quickly addressed once the system was operational. As a result, the criteria may be set at a level which seeks to ensure that there are no critical problems with the solution being implemented, even if some - or many - non-critical problems remain. This is in turn quite difficult and potentially arbitrary, as it requires an assessment to be made as to what is and what is not critical. In order to make such an assessment is likely to require some user input. This may in turn give rise to tension because the project team may seek to reduce the scope of what is considered critical, in order to complete the project as quickly as possible, minimise costs, move on to the next project and so on, whereas the users may tend to want to increase the range of issues considered critical so as to reduce the potential for problems to arise post go-live, leading to extra work. Some form of process which balances the various different perspectives is therefore required to establish the appropriate criteria.

Having agreed on an appropriate set of criteria, there may also be challenges in determining the actual status of the project relative to the criteria established. This obviously requires a set of activities to be put in place to assess this in a reasonably objective way. For those elements of the system covered by a moderately structured testing process, this should yield the necessary information required (even if, as noted, testing is only as informative and as comprehensive as the scenarios that have been developed and the tests that have been undertaken). Even so, it may not be quite as simple as ensuring that no critical defects remain - since taken together a number of separate non-critical problems which will need to be met by 'workarounds' once the system is live may in sum prove too much for the users to accommodate, and therefore add up to a critical problem (again, the determination of this is likely to involve a measure of judgement). Hence, the actual status of the solution needs to be considered in the round, in addition to relying solely on the data. The status of other aspects of the solution may be harder to assess. For example, although all the users may have been trained, this does not mean that they are all certain to have retained the information that the training sought to convey; and while contingency plans may have been developed, there is no guarantee that they are sufficient to meet the precise nuances or the full range of situations that may be encountered.

Ultimately, therefore, the decision to take a system live is again a somewhat inexact and subjective one, and more of an art than a pure science. While the decision can be informed and supported by good data and good process, this cannot fully eliminate uncertainty and risk. Linked to this, there is always a balance to be struck between risk and reward in any such decision, with the risks of serious problems arising having to be set alongside the potential benefits of earlier rather than later implementation of the system. This is again inevitably a matter of judgement – albeit one that should be as well informed as possible. While the Nuffield Orthopaedic Centre review makes clear that a number of significant short-cuts were consciously taken in the lead up to the implementation of the new system, the extent to which the risks arising from these decisions were fully understood by those ultimately responsible for the organisation's activities is uncertain – again pointing to the importance of an appropriate set of structures and mechanisms being established to provide those responsible with the necessary information and inputs to enable them to make an informed determination. Ultimately, the decision to implement the new system is an organisational decision, that is one to be viewed from the perspective of the organisation as a whole - not just that of the project team, or that of the users. Hence, it is preferable if the sponsor and the governance board are responsible for taking this decision.

FINANCIAL ASPECTS

Not unlike many IT projects, the NPfIT project wrestled with a number of different financial issues over the course of its existence. In fact, some degree of exposure to financial considerations is probably unavoidable in the conduct of any IT project, if not in any project. Such issues include:

- Articulation of a definitive financial value proposition: in the case of NPfIT much of the difficulty experienced here was probably attributable to the challenges encountered in putting a financial value against some of the benefits projected to arise from the project. Some of the complications here are discussed in more detail below in the Benefits section. Clearly this is again not an issue unique to NPfIT. In addition, however, some problems appear also to have been experienced in projecting the anticipated costs of the project. Some of the issues here, certainly from a client perspective, were – at least in theory - avoided by the nature of the key third party contracts entered into, which it was intended would serve to lock in the price payable to the suppliers. This said, considerable uncertainty remained around the actual costs to be borne by the various suppliers in delivering the agreed solutions. In practice, given the difficulties experienced, the decision of some suppliers to withdraw from the project, and the increased costs that arose from the subsequent contract renegotiations, it seems probable that the actual costs they incurred were rather higher than anticipated. Ultimately, any cost estimate is obviously only as good as the understanding of the complexities prevailing and perceived as likely to be encountered at the time the estimate is made, along with any contingency to allow for the unexpected. Once again, this points to the importance of understanding the potential sources of complexity as comprehensively as possible before proceeding with the project.

- Separately, there appears to have been uncertainty and ambiguity throughout the lifetime of NPfIT around some of the other costs associated with the project, in particular those incurred by local NHS entities in the implementation of the solutions provided under the third party contracts. This points to the importance – and perhaps also the difficulty – of ensuring that all costs associated with a particular initiative are properly identified, estimated and monitored.

- Hence, although it is unquestionably good practice for a comprehensive financial case to be prepared as input to the decision to proceed, given the uncertainties relating to both benefits and costs, this is unlikely ever to provide definitive justification for any decision to proceed – or not to proceed – with the project. In reality, given the uncertainties, it is preferable to consider a range of different cost and benefit scenarios when making such decisions, rather than base this on a single 'most likely' case; and then to view these different potential scenarios with appropriate circumspection and caution.

- NPfIT clearly also experienced difficulties with the ongoing measurement of both costs and benefits. These are discussed further under the measurement and monitoring heading below.

DELIVERY MODEL

Another task facing all IT projects – which is no different for any other project - is to put in place a set of structures and arrangements by means of which the project will be undertaken. This is more than just creating an organisation chart for the project team, although this will ultimately form part of the activity; initially it concerns the establishment of the over-arching configuration of all the key elements and participants in the project, and identifying which activities will be undertaken in-house and which by third parties, and how the different activities will be co-ordinated. Again, the right delivery model is a matter of choice and judgement. Some of the dilemmas here are once more nicely illustrated by NPfIT.

As we have seen, the delivery model initially adopted by NPfIT involved a centrally co-ordinated and financed programme made up of a number of separate but interlinked elements, each covered by its own long term contract, comprising both provision of an agreed set of systems – which would be delivered by subcontractors to the main contractors - and their subsequent operation. Local implementation of the systems would be principally the responsibility of the Local Service Providers working alongside the NHS entities involved. As such, the model stemmed in large part from the problem/opportunity and scope definition, and in particular the desire to drive standardisation across the country, and the proposed system configuration made up of three main components, namely the National Spine, the National Network, and the Detailed Care Records systems. Obviously such alignment is highly desirable. The division of the country into the five regional clusters each with its own Local Service Provider was done to make the scale of activity with which any one provider had to contend more manageable, and at the same time to reduce reliance on one set of suppliers. While not unique, the structuring of the contracts was however somewhat unusual; by prescribing the software solutions to be used (and hence the subcontractors) in the contracts, NPfIT retained control over the selections, but much of the responsibility for project delivery was transferred to the service providers as the main contractors; likewise, by extending the contracts to cover the operation of the systems, this also transferred responsibility for ongoing system support and improvement to the main contractors.

Nevertheless, and unavoidably, the model adopted also brought with it a number of issues. In particular:

- the centrally co-ordinated delivery model was superimposed on a highly devolved NHS organisational structure. This inevitably led to difficulties and tensions (see the comments by Sir David Nicholson quoted at the end of the case study[39]).
- successful delivery of such a complex and lengthy undertaking was highly dependent on the key long-term contracts put in place right at the start of the programme. This served to concentrate the delivery risk. By tying the programme into these long term contracts it also reduced the degrees of freedom available to the programme from the very start, since the opportunities for modifying the programme as it evolved and as more was learnt from experience were inevitably constrained by the contracts that had been agreed.
- under the model, a large part of the implementation effort still fell on the local Trusts and GPs. However, they were being asked to implement systems with which they were often unfamiliar, and which they would not necessarily have selected if given the option – especially since the emphasis on standardisation

meant that particular requirements of individual Trusts were not necessarily fully catered for by the solutions.

- the structure adopted reduced the direct involvement of the software providers in any local implementation, as they were expected to work through the Local Service Providers – in practice however the LSPs often appeared to lack the detailed understanding of the software tools to address all the issues arising, and in fact the model was subsequently modified to enable a greater on-site presence by the software providers during local implementations.

This said, any alternative delivery model that had been adopted would similarly have had its own advantages and disadvantages. For example, a consistent strand of criticism faced by the programme was that there needed to be more 'local ownership'. As a result, the model was progressively adjusted to provide for this. With this however came a number of new pressures, for example a loss of standardisation due to increased local modification, more complexity in relation to the integration of different local solutions into the national infrastructure, and additional demands on local NHS entities in terms of procurement and financing.

This illustrates that there was again no definitive 'right answer' here. And in situations which are much less complex than NPfIT there are still likely to be some matters to be resolved in relation to the precise form of the delivery model adopted. For example, even where the organisation in question has chosen to engage a third party to undertake the project on its behalf, there will invariably be some areas where user and in-house IT staff involvement is still likely to be necessary – for example the development of test scenarios, the assembly of reference data, participation in acceptance testing, and some technical implementation activities – since these require a level of knowledge of the activities of the organisation in question, which will not otherwise be available to a third party, or are tasks that simply cannot (or at least should not) be outsourced – for example, by definition, a vendor is not really in a position to undertake user acceptance testing. Hence, provision for such involvement needs to be made as part of the delivery model adopted. Another delivery model option available in such situations is for the organisation to engage an independent consultant with appropriate IT project expertise as an adviser, who may also help manage the interface with the supplier. Obviously, for bigger and more complex projects, there is likely to be greater choice – and hence greater uncertainty - around the definition of the preferred delivery model.

PROJECT MANAGEMENT/METHODOLOGY

There is obviously a substantial literature on project management in general, and that on IT project management forms a not insignificant sub-section of this. Moreover, there are a number of established project management frameworks and methodologies available which are widely used in the IT project sphere, some of which also entail the opportunity for practitioners to become accredited - PRINCE2 (PRINCE stands for 'Projects in Controlled Environments') perhaps being the most well-known of these.[40] As noted in the 2006 National Audit Office report, NPfIT had 'put in place sound project management', including 'using the PRINCE2 tool to manage the projects within the programme'.[41] In addition, a National Programme Office had been established to provide central services to support the planning, control and reporting of activities within the programme. An independent appraisal undertaken by QinetiQ of the management processes in place within NHS Connecting for Health, comparing them against an internationally recognised systems engineering standard, commissioned by the National Audit Office as part of its review, concluded that project control processes and project planning processes were in place.[42]

And yet...despite this, the programme still struggled. What this indicates, I believe, is that while the establishment of a sound project (and where appropriate, programme) management framework and methodology may be a necessary condition for project (or programme) success, it is by no means sufficient to ensure this. Too many of the issues encountered in the course of a major IT project are too complex and profound to be resolved simply by the application of a prescribed set of practices. Ultimately what is needed is quite a subtle mix of expertise, understanding and judgement – which extends into areas such as relationship management, conflict resolution, building constituencies of support, overcoming resistance and changing behaviour every bit as much as the technical aspects of information technology per se or the formal elements of project management.

For example, the last project of any significance that I managed involved me in:
- seeking to maintain the business leadership's support for and interest in the project, which was proving rather more than they may have bargained for, not all of them having been convinced of the necessity for the project in the first place, or that the right solution had been selected (in my defence, my own

involvement only started some time after these decisions had been taken), but no-one wanting to go so far as to abandon it;

- seeking to maintain some degree of user interest in the project, despite this likewise placing unexpected demands on them, especially given the ongoing need to perform their respective day jobs (exacerbated when other staff members were on holiday or off sick) - this proved particularly problematic in relation to the assembly of the full panoply of reference data, testing and training;
- on top of this, seeking to get the users from different sub-teams from within the organisation to work together - not least to provide a single coherent set of reference data - when they were more used to working independently, and all had hitherto maintained separate and somewhat different records and datasets;
- seeking to deal with the resistance of the in-house IT team, who in particular appeared to have resented the supplier's proposal that the operation of the new system be outsourced to them on a 'software as a service' basis (though in the event it had been decided not to pursue this offer); this had resulted in a breakdown in relations and a lack of co-operation on technical matters between the client and the supplier (which proved particularly problematic in addressing any performance issues arising in the run-up to go-live – and beyond);
- seeking to maintain at least moderately harmonious relationships with the supplier, who - on top of the tension with the IT team - was felt by some client staff to have failed to provide a clear sense of the extent to which the implementation of the new system would a) meet the business's requirements without the need for modifications (notwithstanding the fact that at least some of these requirements were quite specific and detailed) and b) place demands on them in terms of things like assembling reference data, testing and training, the extent of these activities appearing to come as a considerable surprise to many. This was compounded by a degree of intolerance on the part of some supplier personnel to the sensitivities at play in the client. As the relationship deteriorated, it became increasingly easy for all concerned to blame the other party for any difficulties or problems experienced, and even less was achieved in the way of progress.

Whilst this may have been a particularly problematic project and situation, the sorts of issues and complexities with which I was wrestling – perhaps not always terribly successfully, admittedly - were not the sorts of things that PRINCE 2 really helps with (certainly in terms of the skills and subtleties involved in dealing with these sorts of issues), and this is probably true to some extent of most projects. (In parentheses, I'm pleased to be able to say that ultimately we did succeed in getting the system implemented and working more or less as intended, albeit after a very difficult initial period of operation, somewhat reminiscent – though on a smaller scale, and without the media coverage - of the Heathrow Terminal 5 experience).

Hence, based on my own experiences, and having also worked with some excellent IT project managers as well as some not so good ones, I would contend that IT project management is more of an art than a science. It may also be helpful to distinguish between IT project management, as a collection of prescribed activities that can be described and documented in a check-list, and the management of IT projects, which is a much broader and more 'organic' set of activities, involving the 'stewardship' and 'shepherding' of the project to a successful conclusion. This is not something which can solely be the responsibility of project managers; it requires wider organisational involvement and commitment, and points to the critical role of the sponsor and other stakeholders.

In much the same vein, McManus and Wood-Harper (2008) in a British Computer Society study of 214 IT projects, concluded that:
'One of the major weaknesses uncovered during the analysis was the total reliance placed on project and development methodologies. One explanation for the reliance on methodology is the absence of leadership within the delivery process. Processes alone are far from enough to cover the complexity and human aspects of many large projects subject to multiple stakeholders, resource and ethical constraints'.[43]
Hence, it may be that too much emphasis is placed on the adoption of a proper project management methodology as a core ingredient for project success. This cannot and should not be seen as a panacea. Truly successful IT project management extends well beyond the application of a methodology, regardless of how robust this is and how effectively it is applied (see also The Royal Academy of Engineering and the British Computer Society, 2004[44]).

PROJECT GOVERNANCE AND SPONSORSHIP

Given that IT projects should only ever be conducted in pursuit of some broader organisational end, then by definition there is a need to ensure the wider organisation maintains appropriate ownership and control of any projects it undertakes. This is provided by means of governance and sponsorship.

Governance refers to the mechanisms established to ensure the project aligns with the organisation's objectives and delivers the outcomes intended in an efficient manner. As such, it is a means of both providing oversight of and support to the project team undertaking the project on behalf of the wider organisation. By involving them in the governance structures, this also provides a means of maintaining the connection between a project and its critical stakeholders, keeping them informed, and potentially helping to manage opposition. Effective project governance is generally viewed as playing a vital role in the successful delivery of all projects. Sponsorship provides one of the key governance mechanisms available, and involves the nomination of a senior individual from within the commissioning organisation to 'own' the project on its behalf, oversee its successful completion and ultimately be accountable for the delivery of the identified outcomes.

Hence, the governance arrangements and the sponsor play a critical role in representing the organisation that has commissioned the project, which in the case of NPfIT was the NHS and the government. As the case study shows, various mechanisms were established to provide Governance and Sponsorship of NPfIT, although it is at least questionable how effective some of these were in practice. For example, some particular issues appear to have been experienced in terms of sponsorship, as follows:

- the then Prime Minister appears to have been involved in discussions around the initiation of the programme, and the initial decision to proceed. In this regard he can be considered de facto to have been the original sponsor of the project. Such senior and influential support is obviously valuable in helping establish the credibility of the programme with stakeholders, and building a cadre of support. However, it is not clear that there was a great deal of structure established to underpin this involvement and ensure that the decision making was fully informed. The impression obtained from the reports available suggest a degree of casualness in the way approval was given incompatible with the scale and complexity of the undertaking.[45]
- throughout its life, there was someone fulfilling the formal role of 'Senior Responsible Officer' for the programme. However, during the period from the programme's launch in 2002 to 2006, five different individuals fulfilled this role at various times. One of these was the project director, which was probably something of a conflict if part of the role of the SRO was to hold the programme to account. Although from September 2006 until the programme's formal conclusion in 2011 the role remained held by the same person, Sir David

Nicholson, the Chief Executive of the NHS, there was nevertheless criticism by the Public Accounts Committee of his performance in this role. For example, he chose to delegate the task of chairing the programme board to his deputy, whereas this could have provided a good way of remaining connected with the programme as its official sponsor.[46]

- in addition, although a health service minister was given responsibility for maintaining oversight of the programme, the effectiveness of this arrangement is also debateable. A number of different people held this role over the lifetime of the programme, so there was a lack of continuity (Computer Weekly reported following the resignation of Lord Warner in 2006 that he was the eleventh minister responsible for NPfIT to relinquish the responsibility[47]), and the extent to which the individuals in question had had any prior exposure to IT projects is uncertain. At least publicly, there seems to have been a tendency of these ministers to interpret their role as being primarily to defend the programme against criticism.[48]

All of these point to at least some challenges in relation to the sponsorship, governance and oversight of the programme, and while it is not possible from the information that is publicly available to make a fully informed assessment of the operation of the full suite of such mechanisms and structures, given the importance of governance and the sponsor in leading, shaping, guiding and overseeing the achievement of the objectives of any project, the less than entirely successful outcome of the programme also points to problems in this realm.

Difficulties in this area of activity in relation to IT projects are not uncommon. In the first instance, effective sponsorship and sound governance of IT projects relies on at least a degree of understanding of these sorts of initiative in general, as well as of the specific undertaking in question, including the broader organisational context around it, the range of complexities and difficulties facing it, the possible options available to address these, and their implications. This requires a level of commitment on the part of the various participants – and particularly the sponsor. However, given the other pressures and demands facing them (since for governance to be effective these individuals need to be important and influential players in the organisation), it's not unusual for the sponsor and others involved in the project's governance to fail to devote the necessary time and focus to this activity. This is perhaps reinforced by a lack of appreciation of the importance of the governance function, and a tendency still to regard IT projects as activities that can largely be left to the IT department. Another pattern which is sometimes observed is for those concerned to become less active in their participation if and when projects run into trouble – which is unfortunate, as it is probably in such situations that active sponsor and governance board support and involvement is most vital.

In contrast, another tendency sometimes displayed by governance bodies and project sponsors is for them to seek to become too actively engaged in hands-on management of the project, thus usurping the role of the project management team. In practice, there is quite a delicate balance to be struck here. Just as a governance entity that is too remote and has insufficient understanding of the project gives rise to a range of issues - eg lack of connectedness with the sponsoring organisation, lack of oversight and lack of support when needed - too much governance body intervention in ongoing project activity can undermine the effectiveness of the project team, and involve the governance body in areas which may be beyond their real competence and expertise. Hence effective governance is also reliant on good working relationships between the governance body and the project team; transparency of information, so that the governance body are sufficiently well informed about project activities to make considered decisions where necessary, which also entails good 'staff work' to provide the right information in the right way; clarity of roles and authorities between the two groups; and the investment of sufficient time by all concerned (eg for briefings, preparation, discussions etc). It is also desirable for senior project personnel to participate in governance body meetings, but for their role to be circumscribed to some degree, so that for example while they contribute to discussions and provide information and input, they do not participate in any decisions made by the body.

These principles probably apply to most if not all IT projects, in that the commissioning organisation needs ultimately to institute appropriate mechanismsto ensure it is comfortable with the progress and direction of the initiative it has commissioned, and those undertaking the project need to know that what they are doing is what was intended by the commissioning organisation; they may also at times need help from the commissioning organisation to address problems and issues that they themselves cannot resolve. This said, the greater the scale of the project, then the greater the degree of formality and rigour likely to be required to ensure governance is as effective as possible.

RESOURCING, EXPERTISE AND CAPABILITY

Despite the budget it had available, the profile of the project, and the access it had to many of the leading providers in the industry, the case study points to a number of apparent resourcing problems encountered by the NPfIT. These included:

- a possible lack of in-depth expertise in health care IT on the part of some of the main vendors contracted to the programme;
- the need to offshore development activity by some software suppliers due to insufficient resources with the necessary expertise being available in the UK;
- a lack of sufficient resources in terms of both quantity and expertise among some NHS Trusts to undertake all the implementation activities required in association with the programme.

To these one might perhaps add insufficient familiarity with and understanding of complex IT initiatives on the part of ministers, senior Department of Health civil servants, and NHS managers, to equip them to exercise appropriate oversight and stewardship of the project; and possibly also shortcomings in terms of the diplomatic, political and media management skills required by senior NPfIT and supplier personnel to negotiate the myriad of challenges encountered, given the particular context of the project, not least the highly politicised and fragmented nature of the NHS (which admittedly might have been sufficient to try even the patience of Mother Teresa – although it seems unlikely that Mother Teresa would have known enough about IT project management to have been a serious candidate for a senior project role).

Again, though, the NPfIT is not unique among IT projects in struggling to access all the resources with the skills and depth of expertise required. This is perhaps another of those circular issues, in that without a thorough understanding of the difficulties and complexity that the project is going to encounter, then determining the right resourcing in terms of the nature, mix, quality and quantity of skills and experience will prove problematic – and there is a good chance of a mismatch. Given that one of the core theses behind this book is that much of the complexity implicit in IT projects is not fully appreciated, then it follows that there is a widespread tendency to under-resource them. This is perhaps compounded by the budgetary pressures to which almost all projects are subject to some degree and which are likely to cause organisations to underinvest in the resource needed to undertake the full suite of tasks required to complete a project with sufficient rigour and thoroughness. Likewise, tasks which require significant user involvement such as data preparation and migration, or acceptance testing are often subject to short-cutting, due to the pressure on such staff arising from ongoing operations.

Given that in many cases at least a proportion of the resources to be employed on the project in question are likely to belong to a third party supplier, the resourcing issue also often overlaps with the supplier selection one discussed previously. One of the considerations in the determination of the choice of supplier is the skills and experience of the personnel who will be made available to work on the project; it is not unknown for a supplier to present its 'A' team during the bidding and negotiation phase prior to the engagement being finalised, but for a different group of vendor employees to show up to undertake the work once a deal has been concluded. Organisations should therefore seek details of at least the key individuals the supplier would intend to allocate to their project prior to concluding any agreement. As NPfIT illustrates, even very large supplier organisations do not have an unlimited supply of first class talent.

Unquestionably, one of the most important resourcing decisions – if not the most important one – made by any project is the selection of the project manager. This plays back into our earlier discussion regarding IT project management and methodology, and the prevailing perception that the skillsets required are largely 'technical' in nature, with little acknowledgement of the broader suite of skills likely to be required – such as the diplomatic skills of a Mother Teresa. In fact it seems that successful IT project leadership in any given context requires perhaps three main areas of expertise:

- A high degree of familiarity with all the various aspects of IT projects – technical and non-technical.
- A high degree of familiarity with the type of activities which the project in question is seeking to address – sometimes referred to as 'Subject-Matter Expertise'. In the case of the NPfIT, this would be the healthcare sector.
- A high degree of familiarity with the particular organisational context in which the project in question is being undertaken - including its culture and its internal power dynamics. In the case of the NPfIT this would be the NHS, and perhaps also the Department of Health.

Clearly, it would be quite unusual to find this mix of knowledge and experience in one individual, and hence a common response is to adopt a 'double headed beast' structure at the top of many projects, where one individual, perhaps drawn from a supplier organisation, brings the IT project expertise, and someone else, drawn from inside the organisation undertaking the project, provides the subject matter expertise and organisational context. In my experience, whilst not without its challenges, with the right blend of people, personalities and skills, this can be a powerful and effective model. In hindsight, it might have been beneficial to have adopted something along these lines in the case of NPfIT, where as noted difficulties were experienced particularly around the interfaces between the project and the wider NHS and the government.

Ultimately, one might assert that having the right level and quality of resources, with the necessary expertise and experience, is the single biggest determinant of success for these sorts of projects. Obviously, this does not directly diminish the core level of difficulty faced by the project, although it may ensure that at many of the potential pitfalls are avoided and risks mitigated.

PROGRESS MEASUREMENT AND MONITORING

Another challenge which the NPfIT appears to have struggled with, and with only mixed success, concerns the accuracy of the information available to it regarding progress, project status and expenditures to date. The absence of up-to-date and definitive information, is a recurrent theme in the National Audit Office and Public Accounts Committee reviews.

Again, this is not entirely unusual for IT projects. One difference between an IT project and an engineering project like a bridge or a ship, for example, is that with an IT project there is normally little that can be seen physically in the way of tangible progress. While clearly there is more to the construction of a bridge or a ship than solely that which can be seen externally, this does at least provide an indication of the level of progress being achieved.

Under these circumstances, perhaps even more so than for engineering and construction projects, to be in a position to accurately assess the progress made requires a good plan, which includes all relevant tasks and a fair assessment of how long they are likely to take. The paradox here however is that as we have seen, a significant proportion of these tasks are 'non-technical' ones, which do not necessarily lend themselves to accurate projection of the likely time they will take to perform. As a result, even where an attempt is made to plan the project thoroughly (which isn't always the case), IT project plans may tend to be less definitive than those for engineering projects. This means that there is a less reliable basis against which to measure progress.

Linked to this, there is significant complexity in measuring the progress made, especially for 'non-technical' activities. This again often requires a degree of skill and judgement to make an informed and accurate assessment of actual progress. Even for the more technical activities, there is a need for some degree of assessment of the quality (as opposed to just the quantity) of the work done, so there is more to this than simply checking on the number of lines of code written.

The next question is how best to do this. One option is obviously to ask those responsible for the activities and deliverables in question to report on this. This also requires the establishment of some form of reporting routine, along with mechanisms and resources to consolidate the inputs received - this normally forms part of the suite of responsibilities of the project or programme office. The downside of an approach which relies solely on information from those accountable for the tasks in question is that there may be a tendency of those concerned to overstate the progress made and understate the work still to do. This tendency was observed at times on the NPfIT. The alternative is to put in place some form of separate monitoring process to provide independent assessment and verification of progress and status. This reduces the risk of inaccurate reporting, but obviously creates an additional project overhead, and to be done accurately requires that the individuals given responsibility for this have an appropriate level of understanding of the activities in question, and effective working relationships with those performing the tasks, neither of which are necessarily guaranteed.

Obviously, the larger the project, the more detailed the plan and the greater the number of tasks included, the more demanding the progress monitoring becomes. This is further complicated if the project is diverse and dispersed, as was the NPfIT, which meant that there were a multiplicity of sub-elements which needed to be properly planned, and then progress monitored against these plans. In addition, many different organisations were also involved in the programme, so to keep track of it in its entirety required information to be consolidated across all of these. To do this rigorously can entail a sizeable resource commitment and the creation of a significant bureaucracy - which in turn can result in considerable cost.

Tracking of expenditures should be more straightforward, as accounting systems exist to do this. This still requires the establishment of processes to ensure the total project budget is allocated appropriately to the different activities which make up the project, and individuals are given responsibility for managing each of these component elements. Spending then needs to be recorded accurately against all of these, and of course resources again need to be in place to do this. In addition, a means needs to be in place to consolidate the different component parts into an aggregated picture. Finally, mechanisms are required to accommodate change within the budgets, for example if there are changes to the scope of different activities, and additional money is made available to provide for these, or if funds are reallocated between different parts of the project.

MANAGING CHANGES

One of the principal problems that IT projects consistently encounter concerns the pressure to change the design or the scope of the system during the course of the project. This appears to be much more prevalent in the case of IT projects than building or engineering projects, where the design is almost always fixed prior to the commencement of actual construction. This said, there are many examples of such projects where design changes took place prior to the commencement of construction, which invariably resulted in major problems occurring and significant additional costs being incurred – one recent case being the new Scottish Parliament building, where the actual cost increased to £414 million compared to an initial estimate of between £10 and £40 million, partly as a result of design changes.[49]

In the case of IT projects, however, the pressure to change the scope and the design of the project often extends throughout the project's lifecycle. There are a number of factors that contribute to this. Firstly, as we have seen, the original project scope decision is often a somewhat subjective and judgemental one. Given this, sometimes the disadvantages arising from the original scope decision may become progressively apparent - at least to some - as the project unfolds, increasing the pressure to amend it (and very often to extend it). Similarly, as the project unfolds and the design and scope of the project becomes more tangible and visible - for example through more detailed demonstrations and testing - any gaps in the scope or inelegancies in the design become more evident to the client organisation and in particular its users. Thirdly, over the life of many systems projects, which can take many months and sometimes years, the organisation - and its wider environment - may be subject to considerable change, which may in turn have implications for the design or scope of the project. One particular variant of this is the newly appointed manager who adopts a different perspective from his or her predecessor, which necessitates changes to a project which is in train. But perhaps the main reason why changes to IT projects during their lifecycle are so prevalent is simply because the flexibility is there to accommodate such changes. What may sometimes be overlooked in this are the additional costs likely to be incurred, the additional time that will be added to the project, and the additional risks arising to its delivery - which obviously need to be set alongside any benefits arising. Studies of the causes of IT project failures invariably allude to 'Scope Creep' as one of the principal contributory factors.

As the case study shows, there were a number of changes in the scope of NPfIT over the course of the programme's existence. For example, the National Audit Office report in 2006 noted that:

> 'The Quality Management Analysis System (QMAS) to support the General Medical Services Contract, NHSmail (e-mail and Directory Services), PACS (Picture Archiving Communications Systems), bowel cancer screening and Payment by Results were added to the Programme. NHS Connecting for Health has also supported some other projects outside the Programme, such as the procurement of ambulance radios. There have also been increases to the scope of some of the projects being delivered within the Programme, for example the choice element of Choose and Book and the nomination of dispensing location and patient medication record within the Electronic Prescription Service'.[50]

It was also decided to increase the number of GP systems which would be made available under the programme. This was despite the magnitude of the existing commitment, and the acknowledgement of the risks associated with scope creep, which led to any such changes requiring sign-off by the project's Management Board. Subsequently a number of decisions were taken to reduce the scope of the programme (again this is not entirely unknown when projects run into difficulties). While there may have been a clear logic for these changes given the particular context and pressures facing the project, the impact of them on the project is not transparent from the publicly available record. In particular, the decisions to reduce the project's scope would seem inevitably to have led to a reduction in benefits (as noted by the Public Accounts Committee in 2011) - but if some assessment of this had been undertaken, it was not made available.[51]

In light of this, a key requirement for any IT project - regardless of its scale - is a means of managing the requests to modify the design of the system or change its scope as the project unfolds. Ideally, this involves a number of elements: a means of capturing requests for changes and describing accurately what is being asked for; a means of determining the different ways of meeting the request, their respective pros and cons, and the various modifications to the solution to which different options are expected to give rise; mechanisms for estimating the likely impact of these on overall project costs, benefits, timescales and risks; and finally some decision-making mechanism to determine on the basis of the information available how best to respond to the change requested. Of course, to do this with rigour is likely to require a substantial commitment of resources to perform the necessary analyses, and a degree of bureaucracy to orchestrate the process through to a considered decision. For at least some organisations there may be a limited appetite for this, and the internal power dynamics may be such that it is difficult to say no to changes requested by particular groups of users or which have support from certain influential stakeholders; likewise, in pursuit of 'delivery at all costs', a strong and powerful project manager or sponsor may be able to resist most change requests regardless of their validity. Whilst obviously reducing the risk of scope creep and the associated consequences, this however gives rise to an increased likelihood of user disaffection with the project, and the potential for disengagement and resistance.

BENEFITS

The NPfIT also serves to illustrate some of the common difficulties experienced by IT projects in relation to the issue of benefits. NPfIT appears to have struggled initially with the quantification of the benefits identified, and then with ensuring that the benefits identified were realised, and with their measurement.

In the first instance, difficulty with the quantification of benefits is not an issue confined solely to IT projects. For example, a new bridge may reduce journey times, congestion and pollution, but providing reliable forecasts of these, and then putting a financial value on them for use in the evaluation of project economics is unlikely to be straightforward (similar issues arise for example in relation to the proposed new HS2 high speed rail link).

In this situation, the approach adopted by NPfIT, as reported by the National Audit Office in 2006, was as follows:

'In its business cases for the components of the Programme, the Department put a financial value on benefits where it could, but, as the main aim is to improve services rather than reduce costs, it was not possible to do so in all cases. As a consequence, it was not demonstrated that the financial value of the benefits exceeds the cost of the Programme. The Treasury's guidance states that benefits should be valued when possible, but recognises that sometimes they cannot be. In this case, the Treasury has accepted the Department's approach and has approved all expenditure so far made and planned. Nonetheless, considerable efforts were made to specify and describe the high level benefits that the different projects within the Programme are intended to deliver for example in the agency's National Programme Implementation Guide, and documentation setting out the intended timeline and milestones for delivery of benefits'.[52]

This probably went further than in the case of many IT projects, where the difficulties in identifying and evaluating the various benefits mean that little attempt is made to do this, and as a result justification for the project may be based on a broad set of vague or aspirational objectives.

While this is of course the reality, it does have some serious implications. Firstly, it makes it quite difficult to evaluate different solutions in the same problem space which yield a different mix of costs and benefits. While the costs may be more readily quantifiable, it may not prove possible to arrive at even an indicative assessment of the different level and distribution of benefits associated with each different solution option. This makes it very difficult to identify the particular solution which yields the best outcome. This may contribute to a tendency to err on the side of ambition rather than of caution, since the broader the scope of the project, the wider the sweep of strategic benefits likely to arise, and in the absence of any definitive information to the contrary, despite any possible reduction in costs, it is harder to argue that a more circumscribed scope will be able to yield a proportionate level of benefits. Some of the difficulty here is perhaps evident in the criticism directed at the NPfIT by the Public Accounts Committee in 2011 following the decisions to reduce the coverage of the Detailed Care Record to only a sub-set of that originally intended, where it was stated that the original objective of the programme of a single standardised solution across the country would not now be achieved – however, while this was of course true, to assess this properly required the loss of this benefit to be measured against the reduction in costs and risks, and the increase in feasibility arising from the reduced scope.[53] In reality it seems that the way this decision may actually have been arrived at was not through a detailed assessment of the relative impacts on costs and on benefits, but rather it arose from the recognition that it would not be possible to deliver the originally proposed scope within the agreed budgets and contracts, and therefore the scope would have to be reduced in order to avoid exceeding the funds available to the programme. This points to the importance of judgement and pragmatism in the way these sorts of decision are taken, given the difficulties encountered in putting an accurate financial valuation against any benefits identified.

This said, the absence of readily financially quantifiable benefits does not prevent the identification of the benefits arising from the project: it simply means that it is harder to measure these in monetary terms. For example, the NPfIT was intended to result in reduced patient safety incidents (including deaths) associated with poor documentation. Whilst it may be highly problematic and subjective to put a financial value against this benefit, it is still clearly possible to identify the reduction in such incidents that are expected as a result of the project, and then to track these. Hence, while a project's true economics may be difficult, or even impossible, to ascertain definitively, the benefits associated can still be set out, and progress in the delivery of them can - and should - still be monitored. In truth, the difficulties around the financial quantification of benefits puts a greater premium on this activity, and equally on ensuring the required actions are taken to support and drive the delivery of the benefits arising from and associated with the project. In the case of IT projects, this will more often than not require changes in user and organisational actions and behaviour, so that the full potential of the new system and hence the full value of the investment made can be achieved. This is perhaps rather different from in our bridge example, where the users are to some extent 'passive' consumers of the solution, in that they will use the new bridge if it suits them to do so and won't if it doesn't. In the case of many IT projects, however, as we have discussed previously, the users are a critical part of the solution, and its successful delivery is heavily dependent on their actions.

Given all this, IT projects should ideally seek to do a number of things.

- Firstly, there should be as clear and comprehensive a statement as possible of the full suite of benefits anticipated. Ideally, this statement should ultimately be owned by the organisation, perhaps through the project sponsor, rather than the project, to reflect the fact that the end being sought is not simply to complete the project per se, this is merely an enabler of a set of changes and improvements arising. This is however often more complicated than it may appear. Identifying the full suite of benefits may be difficult, and require both a deep understanding of the problem space, and of the proposed solution. Also, there is often a reluctance on the part of the user community to sign-up to the set of possible benefits identified, in case they are subsequently held responsible for any failure to achieve them. This may also play into a situation where users are already suspicious of and resistant to the project.

- Linked to this, there should be the development of some set of mechanisms and measures to assess the delivery of the different benefits identified. This is likely to require the collection of baseline data against these various measures for the situation prevailing prior to the implementation of the new project so that there is something to compare against once the project has been implemented - so in the example of patient safety incidents associated with documentation and records referred to above, this would consist of the prevailing level of incidents of different types in different NHS entities and locations (often this information should be available from the financial case for the project, as it is likely to be required to make the case to proceed).

- The allocation of the responsibility for ensuring delivery of different benefits to relevant parties within the organisation. Again, these will often be drawn from the user community rather than from within the project, since this is likely to be a matter of leveraging the new system post implementation. Users may again be reluctant to take on this responsibility, not least because there is often a (justified) fear that the new system will not work properly – at least initially, and users will be left being held accountable for something which they cannot possibly deliver.

- Tracking of the benefits and ensuring their realisation post the implementation of the project and the dissolution of the project team. This of course requires resources to be available to do this. In practice, this is rarely done with any rigour, since once a new system is live (assuming things get to this point), the tendency is for everyone concerned to breathe a deep sigh of relief, and look to move on to new things. This puts a major onus on the project sponsor to ensure that the focus is maintained here, and that the full value of the investment made is indeed realised.

This again demonstrates that to approach the whole benefits area properly and effectively requires the establishment of a series of activities and processes, and the commitment of significant resources. Despite the sensible and pragmatic benefits framework the NPfIT established initially, the evidence suggests that in practice the actual measurement and delivery of them still proved highly problematic. Moreover, the pursuit of the delivery of benefits is also quite likely to give rise to some complex intra-organisational dynamics and tensions which require careful management, not least between the project team responsible for delivering the project per se, and the wider organisation and its stakeholders and users who ultimately have to employ the new system in such a way that the benefits from it can be achieved. This once more illustrates the need to ensure positive organisational ownership of and user engagement with the project.

INDEPENDENT REVIEW

In the maelstrom of day to day project life, it is easy for those involved to become so focused on the next deliverable that they lose sight of the bigger picture and the project's overall health. Moreover, it is not unusual for projects - and especially those which are struggling - to become rather defensive and less ready to present a truly accurate picture of their situation, and for the relationships between projects and their governance bodies and stakeholders to become frayed and adversarial.

Given these tendencies, projects benefit from being able to call on some form of independent review, as a means of providing an additional source of input to them, and some measure of objective assessment of their activities, which may be useful both to the project itself and to those responsible for its governance.

In the case of NPfIT, the programme appears to have received a large amount of independent input and scrutiny. For example a number of different third parties were identified as having contributed to various different deliverables and analyses, and of course there were regular independent progress reviews, such as 'Gateway Reviews'[54] - a series of short, focused, independent peer reviews into different parts of the programme at key stages, in accordance with an approach developed by the Office of Government Commerce – as well as those by the National Audit Office and the Public Accounts Committee.

Again, however, the effectiveness of at least some of this input seems open to question. From a distance, some of the third party contributions seem designed more to validate and confirm the direction proposed by the project, rather than providing an objective assessment of and input to it, while it is not apparent that the National Audit Office and Public Accounts Committee reviews, nor the Gateway Reviews (of over 30 reports undertaken, 9 were assigned a 'red' status, indicating that immediate action should be taken before proceeding further[55]), had much effect on the project's activities.

This illustrates some typical difficulties with such independent input. On the one hand, even though it may be independent, in the sense that it is at least one step removed from the project per se, this does not mean it will inevitably be entirely authoritative, objective and 'true and fair'. In the first instance, there may be issues relating to the expertise, knowledge and depth of understanding of the subject matter, the project, the organisation and its activities on the part of those engaged to provide the independent scrutiny. Ideally this should be as comprehensive as possible, but of course in reality few individuals or organisations outside those already directly involved in the project will possess this fully. Independence is often accompanied by distance. For example, in large organisations the Internal Audit units may frequently be asked to review periodically major IT projects, but they may not possess the resources with the depth of understanding of such undertakings to provide informed insight (inevitably those employees with most expertise in this area are normally to be found working on IT projects). On the other hand, while third party organisations may have extensive experience of these sorts of initiatives, they may lack a proper appreciation of the particular organisational context in which the project is taking place, and the full implications of this. Moreover, the engagement of any third party to provide such input necessarily involves some form of commercial arrangement, which may colour the input provided – for instance, the third party may see the review as an opportunity to increase its involvement and therefore revenues from the project in question, which may serve to influence its conclusions; alternatively, 'he who pays the piper calls the tune', and there may therefore be a tendency for any such review to support and reinforce the perspectives of those who commissioned it.

This plays into the nature of the relationship between the project and those providing the scrutiny, which may also depend partly on who commissioned the review in the first place - was it from within the project team itself, was it the sponsor, or was it someone unrelated to the project. If the former, there is a strong likelihood of co-operation on the part of the project team, although there is a greater risk of less objective input. In contrast, if the scrutiny takes place at the request of those removed from the project, for example as part of a corporately determined Internal Audit programme, there is an increased risk that the project will adopt a defensive and adversarial attitude towards the review. This is perhaps demonstrated in the apparent reaction and response - or perhaps more accurately, lack of response, since little tangible action seems to have arisen following the publication of the reports, which again may suggest something about how seriously they were taken - of the NPfIT to some of the external reviews to which it was subject. This in turn points to the importance of effective sponsorship and governance of the project as a means of ensuring both that the project is subjected to appropriate and high quality independent scrutiny, and that this is then acted upon by the project management team, rather than ignored.

Under these circumstances, one model that I have seen prove effective in this regard is where the project sponsor and the governance body commission any independent input and assessment of the project, in conjunction and in agreement with the project management team. At least a part of this input is provided by a third party or a small group of individuals already known to and trusted by the organisation in question, which is engaged on an ongoing basis, and they participate regularly in the routine processes and meetings of the project. However, they report to the sponsor and the governance body, not to the project manager. If necessary to satisfy wider corporate requirements, some participation from representatives from entities such as the organisation's Internal Audit unit can also form part of this arrangement.

EVENTS

Any project will inevitably undergo any number of events during its lifetime, the vast majority of which will be routine and mundane, and can easily be dealt with by the project in the normal course of its activities. However, as we saw earlier with the engineering and construction project mini-studies, over the course of any project there is always a potential for particularly significant things to happen which will have a major impact on the project. Given the scale and duration of NPfIT, it is hardly surprising that it was subject to a number of such events, including most notably the changes in key personnel, the withdrawal or replacement of some of the most important suppliers, the delays in delivery of some of the software applications, the modifications to the delivery model to increase the degree of local ownership, the reorganisation of the NHS, and the change in government following the 2010 election. Some of these events were clearly ones over which the project had negligible or no control or influence - such as the reorganisation of the NHS or the change in government, or the actions taken independently by some of the agents involved in the project, as in the case of the withdrawal of some of the suppliers, or the departure of key personnel – while others appear to represent conscious decisions on the part of the project – such as the change in the delivery model or those cases where the project made the choice to replace certain suppliers (as opposed to those where the supplier took the decision to withdraw). These latter cases were however driven by particular events and changing circumstances – hence the modifications to the delivery model followed from the pressures for increased local control over the project and changes in technology which made a more flexible solution more feasible, while the decision to replace certain suppliers resulted from perceived deficiencies in their performance.

One noteworthy aspect of this list of events is that in many respects none of them seems especially surprising given the context and nature of the project. For example, given the length of time it took, it was probably inevitable that there would be some changes in both key personnel and suppliers, some degree of reorganisation of the NHS, and even a change of government at some point during the project's life. While the precise form which any of these would take would of course be harder to determine in advance, since at least some of the types of events that projects may encounter may be anticipated, this puts them in a position to mitigate the likely impact of them if and when they occur, and in some cases perhaps seek to exert influence so that the events in question are avoided. Hence the penalties incorporated in the supplier contracts represented a strategy for avoiding the risk of the withdrawal of key suppliers (albeit one that ultimately proved unsuccessful, however). Likewise, succession planning arrangements could have been put in place to ensure there were individuals with the necessary capabilities available to provide cover in the event of the departure of key project personnel; and it would even have been possible to ensure connections were maintained with opposition politicians so that they were as well informed as possible about the project if and when they came into power.

Such activities - ie those designed to mitigate the adverse consequences of events upon the project should they occur, and to reduce the likelihood of such events happening in the first place, form the essence of project risk management. To do this well requires a comprehensive appreciation of the core complexities facing the project, such that the potential events likely significantly to impact the project can be determined with a degree of authority and appropriate actions instigated to mitigate their impact or – where possible – avoid them. This also entails the exercise of sound judgements on the part of the project, in terms of the balance of probability of particular situations occurring, and the practicability of possible responses. There is always a danger of over-investing in the risk management activity, given that by definition some risks will not ultimately manifest themselves, or will not have the projected impact, and even if they do occur, the project is still in a position to respond to the situations arising. This said, approached sensibly and done well, risk management can clearly contribute significantly to the ultimate success of a project – although it is often difficult to discern the full extent of this contribution, given that the extent to which the actions taken contributed to something not happening that otherwise would have done is not easily identifiable.

Of course, projects are unlikely to be in a position to prevent or mitigate the impact of all the events and changes to which they may be subject, so another critical activity that they need to undertake is to respond to these appropriately as and when they do occur. Again, the quality of the response is likely to be an important determinant of the project's success. This plays back into the earlier discussion regarding the quality, expertise, experience and capability of project management – and project governance, since some of the events and circumstances arising may be of a sort which require wider organisational action or guidance, beyond the scope of what the project itself is capable - the point being that the greater this is, the better placed the project to deal effectively with the various events, changes and situations to which it is ultimately subject.

CONCLUSION

This list of potential sources of complexity which may be encountered by IT projects - all of which were to some degree experienced by NPfIT - as set out in this chapter does not purport to be an exhaustive one. Nor have we sought to explore any of these sources of difficulty in microscopic detail. However, the chapter has hopefully served to demonstrate firstly the array and variety of such sources of complexity that IT projects may have to contend with. It is not being suggested that all IT projects will inevitably be subject to all of the sources of difficulty identified to the same degree – this will clearly vary depending on the nature of the particular project and the context in which it is being undertaken. For example, IT infrastructure improvement initiatives are unlikely to entail any significant user involvement; the introduction of a new stand-alone system will not face any integration challenges; a project undertaken in-house by the IT Department will not require either a procurement process to be run, or any investment in supplier relationship management. This said, many of the sorts of project undertaken by businesses and other organisations of all sizes, large and small, which involve the use of IT technology to support certain core operational activities, are likely to encounter a significant proportion of the sources of complexity listed. The fact that there are a substantial number of these is a clear contributory factor in making IT projects as hard as they are. It may also help explain why larger projects seem to become disproportionately more difficult than smaller ones, since the combination of scale and complexity contributes to an exponential increase in difficulty; and why projects which may be technically very complex but have fewer implications in terms of user involvement and organisational change seem often to prove more successful. Ultimately, all of the different sources of complexity that apply to any individual project need to be approached and addressed in some way or other for the project to be successful. If areas are left unresolved, overlooked or ignored, or even short-cut, this will certainly give rise to problems - as the NPfIT clearly illustrates. That's not to say that the problems arising will prove insurmountable, and will inevitably result in the failure of the project, but they will continue to threaten the success of the project until a satisfactory resolution is found. Ultimately, to be successful any project needs to achieve at least a passing grade in all areas.

Secondly, the analysis also shows that many of the sources of complexity encountered in the course of IT projects concern broader organisational issues rather than purely IT or technical ones. These often give rise to a myriad of difficult choices – none of which may be entirely ideal, in the way that (to quote just one example) the choice of a fixed price contract with a supplier comes with advantages and disadvantages, but so too does a time and materials one - from a wide array of options, with major implications for the organisation, which requires the exercise of significant organisational judgement. As such, it follows that many of the critical decisions that need to be taken in the course of any material IT project should be taken by the leadership of the organisation as a whole. This emphasises the importance of the wider organisation maintaining ownership of the IT projects it undertakes, rather than handing over responsibility for them to the IT department or to a third party supplier. The IT department will have an important part to play in these decisions, and in some cases may wish to recommend particular courses of action, but it should not be the ultimate arbiter. Likewise there is no reason why a third party should not provide input and advice to the client to assist them with their decisions. But ultimately, where the decisions are ones which have important organisational implications, then they need to be taken by the executive management of the organisation. Of course, one of the challenges here is to ensure that any such decisions taken are informed and wise ones. This places a responsibility on those who do not have significant IT project experience who are charged with making or contributing to these decisions to develop an appropriate understanding of the subject area and the difficulties and complexities involved - and equally on the other participants involved, such as the IT department, the project team, and potentially also the third party suppliers, to support them in this.

Thirdly, and somewhat linked to this previous point, the extent of the complexity encountered and the importance of choice in any IT project means that these are not really the rigid, linear, mechanical undertakings that they are often perceived to be, where a solution is specified to address a particular problem or opportunity, a plan is put in place, and provided the plan is adhered to, a successful outcome will arise. In reality this is simplistic. In fact, some authors (eg Cicmil, Cooke-Davis, Crawford and Richardson (2009); Curlee & Gordon (2011))[56] have suggested that projects (of all types, not specifically IT projects) are better viewed through the lens of 'Complexity Theory', which seeks to explain how order, structure, and pattern emerge from extremely complicated, apparently chaotic, situations. Taking such an approach, projects conform in many respects to what are referred to as 'Complex Adaptive Systems', which are characterised by possessing a large number of interacting elements, are adaptive and dynamic in the way they adjust to changes in their environment and those taking place internally, to the point where they can be considered 'self-organising', and which co-evolve with their environments, so that as they change, they change the environments in which they operate also. Certainly some of the features referred to are apparent in the NPfIT case study, such as in connection with the organisational and relationship dynamics within and surrounding the project (the significance of which is often under-stated by more traditional project management approaches), and the changes it underwent in the course of its life-time.

Similarly, it seems that in many respects IT projects (and/or the problems that they are seeking to address) have much in common with what some authors have referred to as 'Wicked Problems' (eg Rittel and Webber, 1973), and others as 'Messes' (Ackoff, 1974; Horn and Weber, 2007).[57] The principal characteristics of these sorts of problems are as follows:

- there is no definitive formulation or definition of the problem – hence there will be different views of the problem, and different views of the solution (which may be contradictory)
- there is no definitive 'right' solution, and hence a reliance on individual judgement and perspectives when determining whether any 'solution' can be considered adequate
- there is no immediate or ultimate test of a solution (hence it is difficult to determine whether it is adequate)
- there is no finite set of potential solutions/approaches to such problems
- all such problems are essentially unique
- all such problems are interconnected with other problems, and can be considered to be symptoms of another problem
- there is uncertainty and ambiguity
- the consequences of any particular course of action are difficult to imagine, and risks are difficult or impossible to assess
- there is typically great resistance to change
- problem solvers are often out of touch with the problems/potential solutions

Degrace and Stahl (1990) note the applicability of this concept to software development, while Lane and Woodman – referencing Heathrow Terminal 5 in particular - argue that most large, long and complex projects can be considered wicked problems.[58] And again, a number of these elements are visible in the case study – such as in the uncertainty regarding the problem/opportunity definition, the delivery model, the contracting strategy or the selection of suppliers, the different perspectives of all the different stakeholders, down to the ambiguity around the adequacy of the solution being implemented at the Nuffield Orthopaedic Centre.

Hence these different perspectives seem at least as valid as a 'classical' project management one in providing insights into IT projects and what they entail, and all the complexities, challenges, judgements and uncertainties involved in achieving even an 'adequate' outcome. Looked at in these terms, it begins to become much easier to comprehend why such undertakings prove often to be so hard, and why they might result in failure.

CHAPTER 5: WHAT CAN POSSIBLY GO WRONG? – ANOTHER LENS ON THE PROBLEMS ENCOUNTERED BY IT PROJECTS

It could of course be argued that the list of potential bear traps facing the unsuspecting IT project as set out in the previous chapter is somewhat exaggerated because of our choice of NPfIT as the source project for the analysis. My own experience however would suggest that this is not the case, and that in fact a large proportion of IT projects are likely to encounter a large proportion of the sources of complexity listed (and perhaps others that are not referred to). One way to seek to confirm this would be to present additional case studies, but as an alternative to this, the following sections provide a listing of some of the difficulties encountered during some of the projects with which I have had some degree of personal involvement (either as a participant, an advisor, a member of a governance board, or an interested observer – unfortunately, I can't claim that I was merely a spectator in the case of those projects which proved to be the biggest basket cases...but then, you learn more from your mistakes than your successes). The various difficulties are organised into ten core themes, namely:

1. Project Objective, Pre-Project Preparation and Set-up
2. Strategy, Planning and Dependencies
3. Resourcing, use of third parties, and delivery model
4. Organisational/stakeholder/user engagement
5. Governance
6. Project management
7. Technical aspects
8. Organisational change and readiness
9. Benefits
10. Project oversight and review

This is of course another list – in fact it's ten lists, for which apologies. However, this does serve to illustrate the diversity of difficulties that different projects run into, many of which echo those experienced by NPfIT. This to some degree contrasts with other analyses of the causes of IT project failures, which often focus on a small handful of key problem areas. In reality, there are a myriad of different factors which cause the problems experienced by different projects, and which may ultimately contribute to project failure.

1. PROJECT OBJECTIVE, PRE-PROJECT PREPARATION AND SET-UP

- Insufficient clarity regarding the project's over-arching objective and intent – instead there is only a vague set of general aspirations
- Lack of alignment/support among executive team – (eg where it was someone's pet project). Some express support, but may be happy to see failure. Others may be openly antagonistic, especially if/when things start to go wrong
- Pursuit of a 'pure' solution at the expense of the ruthlessly pragmatic leads to over-ambitious, infeasible solution
- Lack of appreciation of what the initiative is really going to take to deliver – naivety, over-optimism, ignorance (may results in organization losing interest when it gets hard)
- Unrealistic timescales, cost estimates, expectations re benefits due to inadequate planning and preparation
- Inadequate financial case – poor definition of the organisational problem to be addressed, failure to evaluate options, lack of consideration of trade-offs between the size of the prize and the complexity, sophistication, cost and risk entailed in the solution
- Project jumps too quickly to solutions (eg a particular software package) without sufficient analysis/wider organisational engagement – choice may not be appropriate, or there may be better ways of meeting the requirements – end up doing the wrong project
- Insufficient time/effort spent in preparation; fall victim to the tyranny of urgency – inadequate analysis, leading to superficial appreciation of what's being contemplated, insufficient funding of project
- Failure to appreciate the full range of requirements that need to be satisfied
- Failure to appreciate all aspects of change that will follow from what is being proposed – including wider organisational implications, structural and process changes, dependencies/contentions with other initiatives etc - leading to potential unintended consequences
- Lack of 'permission' from some key stakeholders for all requisite elements of the project (such as some of the wider implications, especially where these were not properly understood in advance)
- Failure to determine rigorously which initiatives should be within scope and form part of the project, and which should be excluded or form part of a subsequent project

- Attempt to use a complex IT project to address an immediate organisational problem – but delivery timescale of project too long to provide a viable solution within the timeframe required

2. STRATEGY, PLANNING AND DEPENDENCIES

- Absence of a clear over-arching strategic framework covering the project and how it fits with the wider development of the organisation
- Absence of a clear over-arching IT roadmap covering the project and how it fits with other IT activities
- Seeking to undertake a number of different projects and attendant organisational change initiatives at the same time; places unrealistic demands on the resources and capabilities of the organisation, and leads to complex interdependencies and contentions between initiatives
- Scope of project poorly defined – leading to overlaps with other projects in the wider activity set, or gaps that it is assumed the project will address which it is not seeking to address
- Scope of project too big – places unrealistic demands on the resources and capabilities of the organisation, and leads to too long a time period before delivery, resulting in loss of engagement and support from wider organization
- Scope of project is too small – project fails to deliver material value, requires additional projects to deliver benefits, increases reliance on manual processes or interfaces to other systems
- Unrealistic project time-lines based on aspirations rather than viable plans underpinned by analysis
- Failure to understand interdependencies/contentions between project and other initiatives
- Failure to understand project dependencies on items/activities which lie outside the scope of IT (eg changes at a broader organisational level)
- Lack of clear prioritisation of project compared to other IT and wider organisational initiatives
- Failure to communicate priorities clearly to all relevant parties
- Failure by some individuals to acknowledge priorities
- Project takes too long/longer than expected - causes lack of momentum, loss of interest and support; increased likelihood of staff turnover, material

organisational/technology change which the programme then has to accommodate

- Short term imperatives divert focus, budget, resources etc from strategic project
- No means for accommodating short term imperatives alongside the project – gives rise to opposition, as project is seen as an impediment to achieving other organisational priorities
- Organisation unable to accommodate the demands of the IT project alongside all the other things it has to accomplish
- Plans are overly rigid/insufficiently flexible (flexibility is needed because 'the plan never survives contact with the enemy')
- Plans are developed at an unrealistic level of detail which means that they become unrealistic/unmanageable as soon as anything changes
- Plans fail to take account of the constraints on the pace and level of project activity imposed by the wider organisational environment and competing priorities

3. RESOURCING, USE OF THIRD PARTIES, AND DELIVERY MODEL

- Organisation lacks sufficient expertise to deliver a project of the nature, scale and complexity in question – this covers a wide range of skills that are needed, but starts at the top of the organisation in terms of sponsorship and support for the initiative
- Project leader is an experienced, highly competent individual from within the organisation, but has no significant previous experience of/expertise in IT projects – therefore doesn't appreciate the full suite of complexity likely to be encountered, and doesn't know what 'good looks like' – leads to at best sub-optimal project set-up and management
- Other key project personnel likewise have no prior experience in IT projects
- Under-estimation of project complexity, results in under-resourcing in terms of expertise and quantity of personnel – can lead to too much being asked of individuals, they get overstretched and out of their depth, and may end up being damaged – meanwhile the project struggles
- Arrogant project leadership unwilling to consult or listen to advice
- Insufficiently experienced project leadership 'don't know what they don't know' – and don't know how to access what they don't know

- Over reliance on third party vendors/consultants/partners for advice, support and delivery – but these organizations have their own agendas, which are not necessarily always wholly consistent with optimum project delivery
- Host organization does not have the expertise to manage the activities of third parties or evaluate advice received from them
- Over-reliance on off-shoring, coupled with lack of expertise in managing off-shore vendors
- Inappropriate use of off-shoring for certain types of activity (eg development of highly functionally complex applications)
- Poorly designed Project Organization and Delivery Model
- Lack of clear accountabilities and reporting relationships between different participants in the project
- Absence of structures to resolve disputes between different stakeholders/interested parties within the project or impacted by it
- Lack of involvement of sufficient numbers and quality of IT resources where project orientation was organisational change led
- Lack of adequate involvement of organisational and change management resources where project orientation was IT-led
- Operational teams reluctant to release key personnel to the project, as they are perceived as critical to ongoing business activity – results in project being under-resourced, or resourced by less knowledgeable personnel
- Competition/lack of co-operation between different third parties within the project team
- Competition/lack of co-operation between different sub-teams within the project
- Poor choice(s) of third party supplier(s)
- Poor relationships with third party supplier(s) – including tension, lack of co-operation
- Inadequate evaluation of capabilities and financial situation of third party suppliers
- Third party lacks certain key expertise
- Third party allocates less experienced/lower quality resources to work on project

- Loss of key expertise (eg due to transfer/resignation/personal circumstances)
- Problems arising from design of contractual relationship with third party – may result in client struggling to exercise control/influence over third party

4. ORGANISATIONAL/STAKEHOLDER/USER ENGAGEMENT

- Lack of genuine Stakeholder support from all relevant Stakeholders
- Failure to engage all relevant organisational constituencies and obtain the necessary support for the project's value proposition – may give rise to the development of a cadre of influential 'blockers'
- Some key stakeholders remain unconvinced that the problem in question was a genuine organisational priority
- Inappropriate choice of Executive Sponsor
- No real interest or commitment from Executive Sponsor (who may have been chosen because of his/her role in the organization, may have been 'press ganged' into taking on the position, or may be concerned at being associated with a potentially risky initiative due to the impact on his/her career)
- Sponsor's support erodes if/when the going gets tough
- Weak organisation lead appointed to take on day to day management of the initiative, lack of credibility across the organisation, unable to build the necessary support
- Failure of project/project sponsor/leadership to recognize that they need to build the necessary support for the initiative and overcome/remove any blockers – reliance on authority of Sponsor
- Failure to engage or neutralize a particularly powerful/vocal individual or group of stakeholders opposing or not supporting the project
- Initiative seen by wider organisation as just an IT project, and therefore of no particular concern to them -leading to lack of interest, and lack of engagement – resulting at best in sub-optimal outcomes
- IT department perceives initiative as an IT project, no attempt to engage wider organisation
- Underestimation of impact of project on wider organisational activities
- Underestimation of wider impact of project on roles, responsibilities and organization structure

- Underestimation of impact of project on organisational processes
- Poor requirements gathering, lack of requirements sign-off by wider organisation – leads to incomplete definition of requirements, potential future user engagement issues and need to make changes to solution
- Insufficient understanding/acknowledgement of diversity of organisational requirements (eg in different geographies)
- Organisation seeks to engineer old processes into new solution, leading to increased project costs and inefficiencies
- Organisation demands unrealistic solution quality, performance, response times etc which project is unable to achieve
- Project commits to unrealistic solution quality, performance, response times etc leading to organisational disappointment when these are not achieved
- Line organisation have unrealistically high expectations about the nature of the new solution (especially immediately after go-live)
- Users demand low value fixes post implementation, fail to take ownership of driving adoption of new ways of working and benefits delivery from the investment
- Responsibility for initiative handed back to line organisation too soon after implementation: too many problems still requiring resolution, lack of expertise on hand to address them
- Organisation too slow to take over responsibility from project team, leads to increased costs, inappropriate reliance on project, failure to drive next phase of improvement
- Antipathy between client organisation and project, gives rise to culture of blame and recrimination
- Changes in Executive Sponsor or organisational leadership results in loss of momentum/change of direction
- Changes in key stakeholders leads to loss of support for programme

5. GOVERNANCE

- Ineffectual Project Governance – lack of wider organisational ownership/oversight of project
- Governance Board members lack the expertise required to oversee a project of this sort and complexity

- Governance Board is effectively powerless because project is really only answerable to one senior individual
- Project team fails to take account of governance input
- Sponsor fails to take account of wider governance board input
- Governance Board inadequately underpinned by quality staff work, provision of comprehensive and accurate information on which to base decisions
- Governance Board doesn't fully understand its role, discusses the wrong things
- Governance Board 'second guesses' the project team
- Governance Board makes decisions that they are not qualified or in a position to make
- Governance Board is really only an Advisory Board – no real authority to make decisions
- Project team does not appreciate how to interact with the Governance Board and use it to maximum effect
- Governance Board unrepresentative of stakeholders
- Governance Board membership is too junior, therefore can't speak for all stakeholders
- Accountabilities/authorities of Governance Board and its members insufficiently well defined
- Lack of clarity re escalation processes/decision making where there are disputes/ contentions between different Stakeholders
- Lack of clear decision rights within Governance Boards

6. PROJECT MANAGEMENT

- Lack of adoption of 'gated' decision-making process results in premature decision making without sufficiently comprehensive analysis
- Failure to adhere to stage gates, results in key issues remaining unresolved even though project has progressed to next stage: as project ramps up, cost and time taken to resolve them increases
- Lack of adoption of or adherence to a significantly rigorous project methodology
- Ineffective Scope Control and Change Management

- Failure to take a value perspective when changes are being requested/approved – results in significant low value changes being incorporated
- Failure to manage the unavoidable trade-offs between Scope, Schedule and Budget
- Insufficient transparency of status reporting – leading to an inaccurate view of status
- Overly rigid adherence to plan, rather than constant review of activity and correction
- Underestimation of complexities of, and importance of, reference data clean-up and conversion
- Weaknesses in data clean-up/conversion, and ongoing data management
- Poor budgetary control
- Underestimated testing requirements
- Poor testing model and processes
- Failure to manage dependencies on/contention with other initiatives
- Organisation lacks familiarity with development approach adopted and isn't fully equipped to manage this effectively
- Poor issues management
- Inadequate risk management
- Ineffectual contingency planning
- Poor implementation/cutover planning
- Project takes too long – lack of delivery, loss of interest and support, cuts in budget
- Significant changes take place in wider organisation during life time of project, which project struggles to incorporate
- Poor expectations management
- Poor Early-Life Support management
- Problems with transition from project mode to ongoing support model
- Problems arising from different geographical location of different participants in the project

7. TECHNICAL ASPECTS

- Project is overly process-focused, lack of appreciation of the costs and complexities of providing the systems to support the processes proposed
- Lack of strong, knowledgeable IT leadership and expertise within the project (eg IT project management, technical and functional architecture, software development, environment management)
- Insufficient understanding of the software applications selected (functional cover, degree of fit with organisational requirements, complexities of implementation, ability to customize, consequences for organisational processes and structure, ability to support post implementation etc)
- Underestimation of the complexities and costs of configuration (even of highly configurable applications)
- Underestimation of the complexities and costs associated with integration of individual applications with other applications
- Under-investment in the hardware required to support the solution being proposed – resulting in significant performance problems
- Creation of highly complex technical architecture to support the solution (at best, results in additional expense to build and then maintain – at worst, proves infeasible)
- Inadequate technical/performance testing
- Inefficient organization of technical environments (eg for development and test)
- Failure to recognize project dependency on expertise in legacy systems (eg in terms of need to extract data for conversion, and/or build interfaces to new systems)
- Poor set-up of security structures consistent with agreed roles and responsibilities to support smooth solution operation
- Lack of economic, and potentially realistic, upgrade path for the solution post implementation (eg due to degree of customization, or the complexities of integration)

8. ORGANISATIONAL CHANGE AND READINESS

- Failure to understand all the components of Organisational Change entailed by the new solution: eg impacts on operating processes; impact on roles, responsibilities and organisation structure; impact on certain organisational activities
- Failure to appreciate and then undertake effectively all the components of wider organisational involvement necessitated to implement the new solution eg design of accurate test scenarios; participation in User Acceptance Testing; data cleansing and migration; process mapping (old and new); education in the new operating processes; familiarisation and training; benefits realisation planning and delivery
- Failure to simplify organisational activities prior to implementation of new solution – lost opportunity, also resulting in additional costs because it leads to automation of unnecessary complexity
- Less rigorous management of Organisational Change and Readiness aspects of programme than technical implementation aspects
- Poor appreciation of 'As Is' processes leading to incomplete appreciation of full suite of changes required in transition to new processes and activities
- Lack of complete clarity around full extent of proposed new ('To Be') processes
- Inadequate contingency planning for potential eventualities during and immediately after go-live

9. BENEFITS

- Inadequate benefits management/realisation approach
- Failure adequately to identify the benefits arising from the project as part of the initial decision to proceed
- Failure to establish rigorous benefits realisation plan, or mechanisms to track benefits delivery
- Inadequate benefits management activity post implementation
- Failure to drive full benefit delivery eg through process and behaviour change
- Excessive focus on potential future financial benefits at microscopic level of detail

- No real organisational ownership of proposed benefits
- Users/stakeholders unwilling to commit to future benefits because of potential consequences for them if they fail to deliver

10. PROJECT OVERSIGHT AND REVIEW

- Inadequate independent project assurance mechanisms
- Absence of a Quality Plan
- Inadequate Governance Board review
- Reliance on Internal Audit department to provide independent assurance, where Internal Audit lack the expertise to provide this
- Reliance on Third Party to provide independent assurance, where the Third Party fails to provide an entirely objective assessment of programme health, as they are either too closely aligned with the project management, and therefore their input is insufficiently critical; or alternatively perceive the assurance activity as a means of generating potential future sales revenue through increased direct involvement in the programme, and therefore provide overly critical input
- Project leadership/sponsor fails to take account of assurance input

As noted, this list – which again should not be considered an exhaustive one - is derived from my own experience, but it's apparent that many of the problems identified are consistent with those emerging from the NPfIT. All of this tends to support the contention that despite its scale, the NPfIT provides a good example on which to base some general conclusions about IT projects, and that the sorts of issues encountered by NPfIT and described in Chapter 4 are indeed ones which are likely to be faced by many and even most other IT projects, large and small.

CHAPTER 6: WHY THEY FAIL - THE PSYCHOLOGY OF IT PROJECTS

The foregoing analysis should have served to show that an IT project is a complex, multi-faceted undertaking, embracing a diverse mixture of different activities and intricacies – only some of which are actually technical matters relating directly to 'Information Technology' per se; in reality, a greater proportion of the challenges encountered probably relate to the various human and organisational dynamics surrounding the project. Linked to this, it's apparent that IT projects can – and do - run into all sorts of different difficulties. In fact, there seems to be a definitive propensity on the part of such projects to fall into a large proportion of the potential 'bear traps' that are laid out ahead of them for them to fall into.

But as noted at the outset, the fact that they are complex undertakings likely to encounter such a variety of difficulties should not necessarily give rise to failure - or an increased incidence of failure – as long as the level of difficulty was met by an appropriate level of response (this said, the more complex the project, the greater the potential for the response to be insufficient). The challenge, therefore, for any IT project, is to understand the degree of complexity entailed and then respond accordingly. In line with our 'opposing forces' concept discussed previously, ultimately, for the project to succeed, the strength of the response needs to be at least equivalent to the strength of the complexity. If the complexity exceeds the response, the project will fail. If the response exceeds the complexity, then the project will cost more, take longer, and consume more resources than it needed to. Given the number and proportion of projects that run into difficulties, however, it is apparent that very often the response is not adequate. This raises the obvious question – why is this?

Whilst as the previous chapter has shown, there are any number of specific factors which can cause projects to have problems, it seems that at a more fundamental level, there are a small number of deeper-seated and interconnected underlying 'tendencies' which give rise to a mismatch between the strength of the response relative to the level of complexity inherent in a project. In particular, these include:

1. A tendency to underestimate or to fail to appreciate the level of complexity involved in any IT project

2. A tendency to overestimate the degree of understanding of the complexity encountered and the ability of the individual concerned and the wider organisation involved to address it
3. A tendency to launch into IT projects without adequate preparation
4. A tendency to treat IT projects as primarily and substantially technical activities
5. A tendency for senior managers to distance themselves from such projects, especially during their execution
6. A tendency to under-resource the project, particularly in terms of the skills and expertise required
7. A tendency for IT managers and vendors to encourage organisations to commit to overly-ambitious projects
8. A failure to learn lessons from the problems experienced by other projects

It will probably come as no surprise to the reader (assuming anyone has got this far) to hear that in my view, much of this stems from the first item on this list, the tendency on the part of those who commission IT projects to underestimate or to fail fully to appreciate the complexity, and the nature of the complexity, implicit in any particular project (see for example Royal Academy of Engineering/British Computer Society 2004). [1] Without such an appreciation, there is an inevitable likelihood of committing to projects which are overly ambitious (see Collins, 1998) [2], to under-resource the project teams required to deliver them, and to neglect many of the senior management responsibilities that go with their delivery.

There is perhaps another level to this lack of appreciation of complexity, insofar as those involved often 'don't know what they don't know' in relation to IT projects. This links to the remarks made by Donald Rumsfeld, the then US Secretary of Defence in 2002 regarding what he referred to as 'unknown unknowns'. His comments are worth quoting in full – they were as follows: 'We know there are known knowns; these are things we know we know. We also know there are known unknowns; that is to say we know there are some things we do not know. But there are also unknown unknowns, the ones we don't know we don't know'.[3] Rumsfeld's remarks (which were of course made in a somewhat different context from that which concerns us here, namely that of the Iraq war) were treated with a degree of humorous disdain by many commentators, but from a project perspective they ring very true indeed (they are, for example quoted in Sharon Doherty's book on the construction of Heathrow Terminal 5). [4] The key point is that where we know there is something that we do not fully understand (ie known unknowns), actions can be taken to address our lack of knowledge, and potentially turn these situations into 'known knowns'. In contrast, where we have no appreciation of a shortcoming in our knowledge, there is no reason for us to take any action; no intervention or advance preparation can be undertaken in respect of something of which we are entirely unaware. Linked to this, and perhaps even more problematically, studies also show that there is a widespread human tendency to believe that we have a more comprehensive understanding of the complexities, difficulties and risks prevailing in any situation than we really do, to underestimate the impact of or the complexity associated with things of which we are ignorant, and to overestimate our abilities to deal with any complexities that may be encountered (see Taleb, 2007).[5] If this is true, it serves to exaggerate and exacerbate the impact of the lack of appreciation of the complexity.

This may help explain why organisations often appear to enter into such initiatives without undertaking the necessary preparation and analysis to put them in a position where they have as comprehensive an appreciation as possible of the difficulties they are likely to encounter, and know that the project they are undertaking is the right one under the circumstances. Whereas objectively speaking, where managers lack a solid appreciation of the subject matter, the logical response would be to undertake the research needed or seek out appropriately qualified advice to ensure that the complexities and risks are made explicit and understood (cf 'Time spent in reconnaissance is seldom wasted'), in practice, organisations seem frequently to enter into such initiatives quite lightly, even casually, without considering profoundly the real questions, issues and challenges confronting them, the different options that might be available to them, the implications of these options and their respective advantages and disadvantages. They seem all too ready and all too quick to leap straight to one solution, namely to launch a new IT project, without really considering the alternatives, without being sure that this really is the best way of addressing the perceived organisational requirements (and in some cases in ignorance of whether it will actually meet them at all), without any deep appreciation of what such an undertaking is likely to entail, in terms of things like resources and capacity, cost and timescale, and without understanding the risks and rewards of such an undertaking.

However, given the tendencies described above, if managers fail to recognise the limits of their understanding, and underplay the potential complexities involved, undertaking the type of preparatory activities described or seeking out additional input is likely to be considered unnecessary. If little of the complexity is recognised, neither is the need for such analysis. In fact, under such circumstances, such activity may be perceived as wasteful - and costly – procrastination. Senior managers are very often men and women of action, and may not necessarily be overly imbued with patience, or interest in the complexities of delivery (on this theme, a lead partner in an IT consultancy once said to me that senior managers don't really want to know what these projects entail, they just want to know that they are doable – and will go on asking until they get the answer they are looking for). It is also quite common for such an initiative to be established as the 'pet project' of some senior executive, who has unilaterally determined that this is the way for him/her to deliver on his/her objectives and intentions. Moreover, having decided upon a particular course of action, and being in positions of authority, such managers – many of whom of course tend also to be self-confident and persuasive individuals - are often able to convince others of the wisdom of the course of action proposed, and to override any opposition, even where this may be better informed. Hence a shared prevailing wisdom – a sort of 'Groupthink' propensity[6] – may develop within the organisation's senior echelons around the project. Clearly, if a broad constituency of support has already developed – perhaps including some parties, such as the IT department or external consultants, which can be considered 'informed' – continued deliberation is likely to be considered unnecessary. Faced with a perceived need – and with a solution to this need identified in the shape of the IT project in question, and at least a degree of influential support for the proposed course of action - the preference is often for tangible activity to address this. Again such a 'bias for action' is clearly not unique to IT projects –impatience and the desire to see progress may apply to all manner of different activities. In reality, however, while there may be situations where time is of the essence in relation to IT projects – for example if a critical existing system has reached the point where it is proving very difficult to maintain, or will no longer be supported by the vendor (although in this latter case there are usually ways of extending the support arrangements, albeit at a price) – this is perhaps more the exception than the rule. By and large, implementation of a new IT system is not normally the best way of solving an immediate problem facing an organisation, because of the length of time the project is likely to take. Hence, in most situations there is no real reason why a more considered review of the options should not be undertaken, overcoming the risk of an imperfect appreciation of the full suite of complexities facing the project. Obviously there will be costs involved in undertaking such an analysis, but these are likely to be fully justified in terms of the increased understanding achieved, and the future savings due to the avoidance of potential pitfalls. Moreover, this also provides a means to broaden support for the initiative and build greater alignment with other executives and stakeholders who would otherwise be opposed to or have only lukewarm enthusiasm for the initiative, thereby further increasing the likelihood of success.

To leap so quickly into action is to miss the biggest single point of leverage in the entire project, which of course comes right at the very start – in fact, and perhaps more accurately, before what might be regarded as the start of the undertaking, when such crucial decisions are taken around whether to commit to the project, and if so, what form it should take, and how to set it up to maximise the chances of success. None of this is of course rocket science. Any project management textbook will set out in detail the various stages of the ideal project life cycle, and emphasise the vital importance of preparation and planning. But such discipline is clearly frequently lacking in the case of IT initiatives.

Likewise, and still related to this incomplete and inadequate understanding of the full range of complexities likely to be encountered in the course of an IT project, is a propensity on the part of at least some senior managers to regard such projects as largely technical activities, rather than broader-based exercises in organisational change (a perspective that is perhaps at times encouraged by IT departments because it gives them greater autonomy and control of the agenda).[7] This has several consequences. Firstly – since they are rarely technical experts, and therefore would presumably have little to contribute to a largely technical endeavour – it absolves managers from significant involvement in the initiative in question. This has a number of follow-on implications, which are discussed further below. Secondly, primary responsibility for the project can be passed either to the IT department to undertake, or can be contracted out to a third party supplier or consultant. This may then reinforce the neglect of the broader organisational change aspects and relationship dynamics of the project, and may also reduce the extent of engagement of the wider organisation in the initiative. Although some IT departments may have a good appreciation of the importance of these issues, they may not be sufficiently well-placed within the organisation or have the authority and influence to be in a position to build the engagement required. Being external, this is of course potentially even more difficult for a third party. Linked to this, if these are predominantly technical activities, then they should be capable of being delivered by a standardised, 'mechanical' methodological approach, where success will inevitably ensue as long as the methodology is applied with the necessary rigour. The establishment of standard methodological frames for use in IT projects may contribute to this perception – and these obviously have value, but while they may be very helpful in assisting in the organisation and conduct of an IT project, as discussed previously, use of the methodology alone is insufficient to guarantee success. Finally, by treating IT projects as substantially technical activities, there is an inevitable tendency to downplay or discount many of the other constraints, challenges and subtleties facing the project, and see the only limitations on the project as being technical ones – this again leads to a propensity to commit to overly ambitious undertakings which are under-resourced.

As noted, perhaps because they see them as largely technical activities where they have little to contribute, and perhaps also because they see themselves as having performed their key role in ensuring the project was kicked off in the first place, it is not unusual for senior managers to distance themselves from such projects once they have commenced. However, the Royal Academy of Engineering/British Computer Society emphasised the importance of executive sponsorship as a critical success factor in the successful delivery of complex IT projects (a perspective which was reinforced in the 2012 Standish CHAOS Manifesto)[8], and saw the frequent absence of this as a major cause of failure. There appear to be three key aspects of such leadership which are critical. The first of these is to demonstrate support for and commitment to the project in question, so as to encourage organisational engagement with it and alignment behind it. Without this, it is easy for others to regard the undertaking as not being of any great importance. This becomes increasingly significant if and when the project runs into difficulties – as of course many projects do at some point. Secondly, there is also a need to ensure that all parts of the organisation work together in support of the project's delivery, and that inter-departmental tensions and disagreements are effectively resolved. Given their nature, most IT projects will span internal boundaries within an organisation, and hence disputes (eg between user departments and the IT department, or between different user departments) are highly likely to occur. Appropriate resolution of these will very often not be possible without senior intervention. Thirdly, as we have seen previously, IT projects normally give rise to a complex set of choices and dilemmas – many of which extend well beyond purely technical matters - where there is not necessarily an obvious right answer for the organisation. Given this, senior management involvement in determining the best course of action under the circumstances is highly desirable. Without this, there is an increased likelihood that any choices made will be organisationally sub-optimal.

Another internal organisational dynamic which is not uncommon in this regard is for senior management support for the initiative to decay over time if the project proves more problematic than originally envisaged.

A further manifestation of the failure to grasp the full complexity of the project being undertaken is a tendency to under-resource the initiative, notably in terms of the level and skillsets of the people allocated to work on it, as well as the budget made available to it. It follows that if those commissioning IT projects lack a full appreciation of the challenges involved, and regard the initiative as simpler than it really is, then it will be resourced at the level perceived to be appropriate, rather than the one that is actually required. In terms of our 'opposing forces' construct, this means that if a project of – say – factor 6 complexity (on a scale of 1 to 10, with 10 being the NPfIT) is regarded as having only factor 4 complexity, the resources made available to the project, and the appointments made, will reflect the perception of a factor 4 project. As a result, the individuals chosen may likewise lack the appreciation of the additional complexities associated with a factor 6 project. Related to this, a common practice is to appoint an established manager with a good understanding of the organisation, its activities and processes – but negligible previous exposure to IT projects – to lead the project, perhaps with some support from an IT professional or an external consultant. Again, without an established frame of reference for the activity, without a clear sense of 'what good looks like', and lacking the appreciation of the complexities, risks and pitfalls inherent in IT projects, there is often a propensity for the individual in question to downplay or neglect these as the project progresses. Such individuals are also less well-placed to deal with the unknowns (in Donald Rumsfeld's parlance this would include both 'known unknowns' and 'unknown unknowns', since it is depth of experience that best equips anyone to respond to both of these), because they 'don't know what they don't know', and there is a high risk of 'unconscious incompetence'.

At the same time, although the suppliers and consultants working with the project may have the knowledge and experience to diagnose some of the problems being encountered, the structure of their contracts may mean that it is not necessarily in their interests to raise these with the client organisation. Moreover, suppliers and consultants may also struggle to understand some of the complexities encountered by a particular project, particularly where these relate to the unique circumstances and the internal dynamics and culture of the client organisation. As third party outsiders they may at times find it difficult to get their voices heard – for example the customer may be suspicious of the third party's motives in raising the concerns, given that they are both participants in a commercial arrangement; or there may be internal organisational political considerations which mean that the messages being conveyed by the supplier are not necessarily what the organisation wishes to hear, and therefore chooses to turn a deaf ear to them.

Once projects are in difficulties – as is highly likely if they are under-resourced in the way described – another set of dynamics may come into force. One of these involves a reluctance on the part of project teams to share information with the wider client organisation regarding the difficulties being experienced, perhaps in the hope that the problems can be overcome without this, and/or because they are aware of the reaction that this may provoke from those who were responsible for commissioning the project. Hence a common pattern is for the project's situation to continue to deteriorate before the client organisation becomes aware of the prevailing situation.

This bias on the part of at least some senior managers to fail to recognise or to underplay the complexity inherent in many IT projects may be reinforced by the actions of IT departments, IT project professionals, and third party vendors and consultants, all of whom have an interest in projects proceeding. This is because such projects provide challenging and potentially rewarding work for IT and project people – after all, for IT project people, this is what they do, and if there are no projects, they'll be out of a job; while for supplier organisations and consultants, these projects provide the source of much of their revenues. Hence, these groups may also have an incentive to overstate the case for proceeding, and to underplay the difficulties to be encountered. These forces again tend to encourage a sort of 'Groupthink'[9], where there is broad alignment among a community of key interested parties in support of a particular project, and where any voices of dissent tend to be ignored or overridden.

On one level, the continuing incidence of problems experienced by IT projects is perhaps surprising, given that by now there ought to be enough evidence available to demonstrate that these are generally difficult and risky undertakings. For instance, if you asked the average man or woman in the street for their perspective on IT projects, the reaction would probably be quite similar to that of a plumber asked for a quote to fix a leaking pipe. Tricky, and several times more expensive than the number you first thought of. But type 'IT project failures' into Google, and up pops a listing of a multiplicity of recent articles and reports – many of which identify the same set of factors to account for the high incidence of unsuccessful initiatives as are referenced in earlier analyses. Other than perhaps some signs of slowly improving performance emerging from the Standish data[10], there is little to suggest that the reports of high profile project problems and disasters have caused organisations significantly to modify their approach to such initiatives if and when they themselves embark upon them, or to do so with greater circumspection; equally neither are there obvious signs of improved practice on the part of the providers. This perhaps points to the deep-seated nature of some of the factors referred to above - if those concerned have misplaced faith in their ability, if they fail to appreciate the complexities, if they 'don't know what they don't know', then there is again no incentive to look to fill a knowledge gap that they would not recognise they had, and hence for them to seek to learn lessons from others' experiences; moreover organisations and practitioners are often imbued with a sense of overconfidence and superiority that causes them to believe that they will never make the same mistakes or run into the same difficulties as experienced elsewhere (I recall visiting a reference site where the company in question had recently rolled out the application we were interested in, and being told that it was a great package, but had proved very difficult to implement, and thinking, 'That's okay, we know how to do these things, that won't be a problem for us'…only to find out subsequently for ourselves just how difficult it was to implement).

IT departments and suppliers may likewise share a degree of reluctance to learn and disseminate the lessons emerging from these experiences, since the status quo continues to provide them with a healthy income stream, which might be negatively impacted by an improvement in performance.

Much of this is not unique to IT projects. In their review of 258 transport infrastructure projects (essential reading for all advocates of the HS2 rail link), Flyvbjerg, Bruzelius and Rothergatter (2003) point to a consistent pattern of the underestimation of costs and the overstatement of benefits in pre-project projections compared to actual outcomes.[11] As a result, they conclude that '...over-optimistic forecasts of viability are the rule for major investments, rather than the exception'.[12] Whilst they acknowledge the contribution of shortcomings in methodologies, weaknesses in the historical data record used in forward projections, unexpected changes in external factors, and other what might be considered 'legitimate' sources of forecasting error in accounting for some of this variation, they argue that this consistent and statistically significant pattern of underestimation of costs and overestimation of benefits is due to more than just random error. They conclude that the differences arising are ultimately attributable to '...project proponents succeeding in manipulating forecasts in ways that make decisions to go ahead with projects more likely than decisions to stop them'.[13] Hence, for example, consultants and contractors who contribute to estimates and forecasts have a vested interest in having their proposals accepted. This extends to the tendering process, where there is again a systematic tendency to bid low, since contractual penalties for producing over-optimistic tenders are generally very small in relation to the overall contract value, and moreover difficult to enforce. Also, if budgets are constrained, as they normally are, and projects are competing for funds with other potential investments, then the chances of receiving funding are increased if the viability of the project is overstated (it may be argued that if all the other potential projects seeking funding are doing this, then a project not doing so places itself at a disadvantage). There also appears to be a perception in some quarters that low estimates help keep actual costs low.

Flyvbjerg, Bruzelius and Rothergatter also identify a number of what might be considered behavioural factors that encourage this bias – notably the fact that politicians and decision makers often feel a desire to leave a mark, or a 'monument', in the form of a major and lasting piece of infrastructure – moreover, given the timescale of many such projects, they will often be out of office by the time the project is due to complete, and if it goes awry, there will be no adverse personal consequences; engineers simply like building things, and taking on more ambitious and complex engineering projects to prove to themselves that they are capable of doing them; and officials and bureaucrats sometimes see such undertakings as a way of raising their status and extending their influence.[14]

Finally, they also identify two other factors which contribute to the results observed. The first of these is a failure to learn lessons from previous experiences.

From their analysis of over 100 major transport infrastructure projects since 1920, Flyvbjerg, Bruzelius and Rothergatter show that there is no trend in the degree of cost overruns among these projects over time. Today's project is every bit as likely to exceed its cost estimates as was yesterday's. Hence, there was no indication that there had been any collective learning about project viability over the period.[15] Secondly, they argue that these results also point to major weaknesses in the analysis and management of project risk[16] (which as discussed previously is closely related to what I've been calling 'complexity').

(In parentheses, it is perhaps worth noting that Flyvbjerg and his colleagues were focused on transport infrastructure projects, a large proportion of which tend to be in the public sector, and some authors – eg Myddelton (2007)[17] - have argued that project failures occur disproportionately in public sector projects where there may be less pressure to demonstrate a definitive return from the investment, and some of the controls and imperatives facing private sector organisations undertaking projects are less prevalent. If this really is the case it would presumably apply equally with regard to IT projects. It isn't really possible to validate this theory, as private sector organisations are not always keen to share information publicly about the projects they are undertaking, especially if they run into difficulties, but it's clear that from the information that is accessible regarding private sector projects, there are plenty of examples where things have not gone as well as may have been wished or intended - eg the Channel Tunnel, Wembley Stadium, or the Boeing 787 Dreamliner (see also the 'Why Projects Fail website 'Catalogue of Catastrophe' maintained by Calleam Consulting Ltd).[18] It is also apparent that similar human dynamics, such as the wish to leave a mark, the desire on the part of practitioners to undertake ambitious and difficult projects because these are interesting and challenging things to do, and the commercial motivations of suppliers are frequently just as evident in the private sector. In the case of IT projects specifically, Flyvbjerg and Budzier (2011) in the study referred to earlier of 1471 projects concluded that there was little difference between projects in different types of organisations (this said, 92 per cent of the projects in their sample were in public agencies).[19] My own experience is exclusively in the private sector, and I can personally testify to involvement in a number of IT initiatives best described as 'problematic' – but then perhaps again this was just me...).

Returning to the discussion of the human and psychological factors that may be at play in this regard, military history is also replete with examples of commanders who underestimated the opposition and overestimated their own abilities and those of the resources they had available, to their considerable detriment (see Dixon 1976). Dixon identifies a number of other characteristics associated with what he refers to as 'military incompetence'. These include: an inability to profit from past experience, a failure to make adequate reconnaissance, a tendency to reject information which is unpalatable or which conflicts with preconceptions, a suppression or distortion of bad news, a tendency to abdicate from the role of decision maker, and an undue readiness to find scape-goats for setbacks.[20]

Similarly, David Owen (2007) identifies a number of characteristics of what he calls the 'hubris syndrome', which he argues afflicts some politicians (including Tony Blair, who was of course responsible for giving the green light to proceeding with the NPfIT, although this is not one of the examples of hubristic behaviour on his part referred to by David Owen). These include: excessive confidence in their own judgement and contempt for the advice or criticism of others; restlessness, recklessness and impulsiveness; a tendency to allow their 'broad vision' to obviate the need to consider other aspects of a course of action, such as its practicality, cost, and the possibility of unwanted outcomes; and a consequent type of incompetence in carrying out a policy, where things go wrong precisely because too much self-confidence has led the leader not to bother worrying about the nuts and bolts of a policy.[21] In his book 'Ego Check' Mathew Hayward (2007) discusses some famous examples of unrealistic self-belief among business leaders, and the consequences of this for the organisations they led.[22] Nassim Nicholas Taleb (2007) likewise shows how widespread is the tendency for human beings in any number of situations to fail to consider adequately the risks that they are likely to encounter, to develop rationalisations to convince themselves of the correctness of their analyses, which may or may not have real merit; and to ignore or dismiss contrary information, views and analyses.[23] Janis (1972, 1982) and others have discussed the propensity of groups to display something of a herd mentality in arriving at shared consensus in response to complex situations.[24]

Finally, a review of transformation programmes of various sorts (half of which involved some IT aspects) undertaken by Capgemini in association with the Economist Intelligence Unit reported that, 'The first stages of developing transformation projects do not seem to pose significant problems: two-thirds of the executives questioned say they perform well in identifying the need for change, setting objectives or convincing their shareholders. They therefore pay great attention to the preliminary studies when justifying the launch of a major transformation project. However, executives are much less confident about maintaining strong momentum throughout the transformation process'.[25] Executives seem to be saying that there was nothing wrong with the strategy, the problems were in the execution and delivery. But looked at another way, this statement implies that transformation programmes were frequently initiated which proved beyond the capabilities of the respective organisations to deliver – that is to say, they were overly ambitious (one might be inclined to note that there is not much point in developing strategies and approaches which are infeasible and cannot be implemented).

It may be that some of these tendencies are in fact more in evidence in relation to IT projects (and perhaps also organisational transformation projects) than engineering and construction projects, not least because the broad technical challenges associated with the latter are better understood. As a result – and perhaps because there are rules and regulations, such as building regulations, in place in most countries that need to be complied with – the likelihood of an organisation undertaking an engineering or construction project without significant preparation and hence a solid appreciation of the difficulties likely to be encountered, and without reasonably detailed plans in place, seems low. In contrast, organisations seem much more likely to embark casually on an IT project. Again, this all points to naivety and a lack of appreciation of the difficulties and complexities inherent in such undertakings.

Ultimately, the conclusion that I – and hopefully also we – arrive at here seems irresistible. Projects struggle and fail – and this goes for all projects – not really because they are hard (even though they very often are), but because the quality of the response to the difficulties they encounter is inadequate. This must be the case, because by definition if the response was sufficient to address the difficulties, the project wouldn't fail. A number of factors contribute to the inadequacy of the response, but at the source of these is a widespread propensity on the part of those who commission IT projects to underestimate and/or to fail fully to appreciate the complexity and complexities inherent in the undertaking.

CHAPTER 7: NEGOTIATING THE COMPLEXITIES

On the one hand, this is perhaps quite a bleak assessment of the IT projects landscape – not so much that such undertakings are complex, but that there appear to be some quite visceral and fundamental human predilections at play which lead to a widespread tendency to underestimate the complexity inherent within them, and perhaps also to overestimate the individual and collective ability of those involved to address this complexity. On the other hand, it seems to me that in the same way that the first step towards overcoming alcoholism is to acknowledge that there is a problem, by recognising these tendencies, and by being much more cognisant of the multi-faceted nature of these sorts of undertakings, and of all the different potential sources of complexity (non-technical as well as technical), organisations put themselves in a much stronger position to succeed when they embark upon them. This is therefore the first step to project success. Obviously, this is only the first step, and as noted previously there are any number of other project activities in which the organisation has to achieve a passing grade in order ultimately to achieve this. From my own experience however, while I don't believe there are any panaceas which can guarantee this, there do seem to be things which organisations can do to increase the chances of at least a good result, and (with apologies for contributing yet another list to the already overstocked inventory of 'IT project essential things to do') these are set out below. These are again targeted primarily at those who commission IT projects, and those who then sponsor, direct and orchestrate them once they have been commissioned.

- **Understand what you are getting yourself and your organisation into** – everything we know and hear about IT projects point to them being hard, and prone to failure, so anyone embarking on one would be well-advised to ensure they have as good an appreciation of what they are likely to have in store as possible. You might therefore want to read this book - or if not this book, then other books (such as Collins, 1998 – although the case studies are perhaps a bit dated now, they still seem valid, and it's a lively read)[1] or other sources of information about IT projects (there is plenty of material readily available via a simple Google search – while the quality of some of this is perhaps questionable, it's nevertheless all good context), so that you understand what you are letting yourself in for – namely in all likelihood an extremely complex, multi-faceted, non-linear, 'wicked' and 'messy' undertaking involving significant adaptive, organisational change and human dynamics-related elements and a much smaller IT technical component than might be anticipated.

- **Ensure the organisation owns and supports the project** – just like any other activities that the organisation undertakes, these projects should be in pursuit of an organisational aim (otherwise, why would the organisation wish to undertake them?). As a result, the organisation – starting with the senior executives responsible (and not the IT department) - needs to own them, understand them, believe in them, and buy in to the intent and the value proposition - which probably isn't the 'base case', but instead a rather battered, less optimistic version of the value proposition, which acknowledges the potential for things going awry – the key question being whether those concerned would still be willing to commit to the project, and would subsequently still support it even if and when the going gets tough – because if not, you're probably better off not proceeding. You're in for a marathon, not a sprint (to coin a phrase), and need to be prepared for this. Of course, it is easier to commit to these things if there is an imperative which makes them unavoidable (for example if the existing system is on its very last legs); where there is no imperative, only some degree of strategic intent and/or a positive value proposition, it is that much more essential that the support for this be rigorously tested. Without such support, any project is likely to struggle. At the same time, as we have seen, many of the complexities that the project will encounter will raise organisational dilemmas with no definitive right answer where the resolution will be a question of judgement, and where the response can – or at least should - only be determined by the organisation's leadership. This applies even if the project is a highly technical infrastructure initiative with no direct user impact – the organisation should still understand the logic and the benefits case for the project, and should exercise appropriate oversight of its initiation, progress and delivery. But as we have seen, the majority of IT projects involve a lot more than just IT (to the point where some commentators have suggested that there is no such thing as an IT project per se, only 'IT-enabled organisational change projects'). Without effective organisational leadership therefore there is a risk that projects will be undertaken, or decisions taken in association with projects, which the organisation ultimately would not support. This requires at least a degree of understanding of IT projects and activities on the part of the executive of the organisation (see above), and the establishment of sound governance arrangements (see below).

- **Put on the cloak of humility...** – I haven't seen this one on any of the other lists, but it seems to me that one of the key ingredients for success is to approach such undertakings with a degree of humility, recognising the limitations of one's understanding and knowledge of the subject matter, being prepared to listen and to learn, expecting this to be every bit as difficult for your organisation as it seems to be for other ones, acknowledging that there will always be unknowns (known and unknown), and appreciating that all projects are unique, and that even if the organisation in question can point to other successfully completed projects, this doesn't guarantee that the next project will inevitably succeed.

- **Treat what everyone tells you with a degree of caution...** – because lots of people will offer you advice and input, and the likelihood is that much of this will be driven by particular agendas, and/or will not be particularly well-informed (this goes for some of what you may read as well – though not this book of course); so there is a need to make good judgements about what people are telling you, and whose advice you decide is most valuable and detached (rather than closest to what you would like to hear).

- **...as well as any financial projections** – because all the evidence points to the vast majority of these sorts of undertakings costing more, taking longer and delivering less than projected; so why should your initiative be any different? Hence, the use of a single 'most likely' outcome as the basis for the financial case is best avoided. Given the tendency for over-optimism, a more realistic approach is to take account of a range of different – and more pessimistic – scenarios in the projections. Collins (1998)[2] recommends multiplying all cost estimates by 3, while Flyvbjerg and Budzier (2011)[3] suggest stress testing the impact of major project cost overruns and benefits delivery shortfalls on the overall viability of the organisation, and using techniques such as 'reference class forecasting' (which incorporate the results of similar projects undertaken in other organisations in project forecasts) to ensure the integrity of projections. This may also link with the use of a 'stage-gated' project approval process, with cost ranges rather than single point estimates established at each stage, reflecting the degree of uncertainty prevailing at the time of the stage gate, and approval at each stage being based on the high end range cost projection, not the midpoint one (see below).

- **Remain ruthlessly pragmatic throughout** - there is a trade off between the purity and sophistication of the solution, and the complexity of delivery; there is a widespread tendency (not least among users, IT departments and suppliers) to seek to increase the scope of projects so that they can deliver greater benefits, but with this comes increased cost and risk. You need to be honest, pragmatic and ruthless in the decisions you take around scope, budget, timing, quality, and risk. This applies throughout the life-time of the project: how much user involvement is required; how much process change is appropriate compared to how much system modification; how much testing should you do; how 'perfect' does the solution need to be before it can go live? There is always a trade-off to be made here between benefit (which often comes in the form of reduced risk and increased confidence) and cost. Ultimately, this is a matter of judgement, which may vary from one organisation to another – and also within organisations – depending on the particular context and the appetite for risk.

- **Put in place a stage-gated approval process** – some of the key elements of such an approach were discussed previously. This has a number of advantages in connection with IT projects. Firstly, it prevents the organisation from adopting a particular solution to a given problem/opportunity without at least some consideration of the options (both in terms of solutions and of definitions of the problem/opportunity). As such, it forces the organisation to undertake some appropriate analysis, and contributes to an increase in understanding. It prevents the risk of the 'pet project', where a single influential individual forces the initiation of a particular undertaking without broader support, because it necessitates a degree of scrutiny and analysis of any proposals prior to any course of action being decided upon. It also helps overcome the risk of linearity in the project definition process, because each separate stage entails a degree of revalidation at the next level of detail of the conclusions emerging at the previous stage. This means that there is an increased likelihood that the organisation will choose to pursue the right project, rather than the one that they first thought of. Through the process of narrowing down of options and deepening the understanding of them, it also increases the opportunity to surface more of the different sources of complexity facing any particular potential solution before that solution is committed to fully. This should lead to a reduction in the number and severity of the unknown unknowns (as the analysis will start to reveal at least some of these, and turn them into known knowns, which can be managed, or known unknowns, which can be explored further).

- **Fools rush in where angels fear to tread**– clearly, to undertake the sort of analysis referred to above is likely to be quite time consuming (and will also involve some costs), so in their enthusiasm to press ahead as quickly as possible, and perhaps under pressure from suppliers and other interested parties to commit to a particular course of action, organisations and those commissioning projects will often persuade themselves that they can short-cut this activity. Of course they can, but to do so is dangerous, in that it increases the probability of making poor choices in terms of the project definition and solution, and reduces the understanding of the complexities facing the project and the wider project 'landscape' prior to its full commencement.   This is accompanied by a significant increase in project risk. Moreover, if the complexities are not identified and unearthed at this stage, there remains every likelihood that they will become apparent later; by this time, the project may be in full flow, the rate of spend will be much greater, and therefore the time and cost involved in dealing with the situation encountered will likewise be greater too.   So short-cutting the analysis is likely to prove a false economy, that will come back to bite you subsequently. Hence, part of the intention during this early stage of the project's life is 'to go slow to go faster later'.   There is no substitute for doing things properly; ultimately, you have to achieve a passing grade on every aspect of the project. Similarly, Kotter (1995)[4], writing in a slightly different context in relation to organisational change – but only slightly different if one accepts that IT projects are a form of organisational change project, notes that 'The change process goes through a series of phases that, in total, usually require a considerable length of time. Skipping steps creates only the illusion of speed and never produces a satisfying result.'

- **Set-up is crucial** – as I've tried to show in this book, IT project success is about much more than the IT, much more than the selection of the IT solution (just as engineering projects are about much more than the engineering and the physics). A major point of leverage in determining project success comes in the way the project is set up, for example with the right people, third parties, structure, governance model, organisational engagement and stakeholder management, phasing and so on. This again takes thought, understanding and time to do properly – and requires people who appreciate what's involved here...which brings us on to...

- **Accessing the right project leadership** – in my experience, the closest thing to a panacea in connection with any IT projects is being able to call on someone (ideally more than just one) who really knows what 'good looks like' in this regard. This is not about having IT skills per se, nor about project planning and management skills, but rather what I'd call 'full life cycle IT project leadership' skills, which cover the whole gamut and sweep of activities and challenges and complexities referred to in this book, from the point where the project is merely a tiny glimmer in the organisation's eye, through to the party to celebrate its ultimate success (party planning skills are probably optional), and have an appreciation of how best to approach and deal with them. Hence it is not a place for the gifted amateur. A big part of this also involves being able to work successfully with the executives responsible for commissioning the project, and all the other stakeholders inside and potentially outside the organisation, to help ensure the project is set up properly in the first place, and then steered forward towards delivery. The latter is fundamental – it's the understanding of the delivery complexities that is required to ensure the organisation does not commit to something which is unachievable or beyond its capability. Unfortunately, these people do not grow on trees. And there is the question of how to know what to look for if you haven't previously had a great deal of exposure to this area of activity. Which again points to the importance of those who commission IT projects taking the steps to increase their understanding of the subject matter before they commit to anything (see above). This said there are organisations and consultancies (large and small) who can provide people with the breadth of skills required. Avoid the salesmen and the strategists, though – the former will tell you whatever they think you want to hear, and while the latter may be able to give you a nice shiny strategy, they often lack a real appreciation of the complexities involved in delivering this. The sort of individual one is looking for can usually point to a variety of battle scars from previous endeavours, and combines a high level of confidence in their own expertise and abilities with a degree of humility about the potential challenges to be overcome (not least because they know that there are always likely to be unknown unknowns). A personal recommendation from someone known and trusted is often the best way to find these people.

- **Choosing the right supplier(s)** – potentially linked to this, another key decision point for any project is the selection of the supplier or suppliers to participate in the project. As well as being critical for the delivery of the project, if it is proposed that the supplier(s) will provide long-term support for the solution implemented, such a decision will also represent the start of a long-term commercial relationship with the supplier(s) in question. Either way, any such choices, and the basis of the commercial arrangements with the supplier(s), are not something to be entered into lightly. At the same time, selection of a renowned supplier with an established reputation is not a guarantee of project success, since: 1. All projects are unique so the fact that the third party in question has been successful previously does not mean that they will be this time; 2. You may not get the supplier's 'A' team – and in fact you may very well get the 'D' team; 3. You can't delegate responsibility for some of the most challenging aspects of the project to a third party.

- **There is no substitute for good governance** – project governance provides the means by which the sponsoring organisation maintains accountability for, oversight of and involvement with the project. But there is more to this than simply arranging a monthly meeting for the project team to discuss things with the sponsor (although this is of course a start). To be effective, those participating in the governance process need to have an accountability for successful project delivery (otherwise talk is cheap, and it is easy for those involved to bandy round opinions – and usually IT projects attract plenty of opinions, especially if they're struggling - and input without any responsibility for the consequences); linked to this, they also need to have a good appreciation of the subject matter – otherwise the input may not be particularly well - informed and knowledgeable. This brings us back to the point made earlier regarding the need for those who commission IT projects to educate themselves about such undertakings; in addition, it places an onus on the project team to provide the information the governance board needs to make informed decisions. Moreover, thought is required around what decisions the governance board needs to take, and what decisions should be the responsibility of the project team. There is a danger of over-enthusiastic governance boards involving themselves in detailed project management issues, where they may not have the understanding to make informed decisions. This also erodes the accountability of the project management team. One way of resolving this tension is where issues require decisions on the part of the governance board, the project team makes a recommendation which the governance board then endorses or rejects. If the recommendation is rejected, the project team then has to come up with a revised recommendation. Clear decision rights among the board members – in terms of who ultimately makes decisions, who makes recommendations, who provides input, who has the right of veto – is also very helpful.

- **Transparency, transparency, transparency** – Good governance needs to be underpinned by reliable and accurate management information on project status, issues and risks. However, you may sometimes have to work quite hard to get this, because of the tendency to suppress bad news discussed previously. Given this, it is desirable for sponsors and senior stakeholders not to rely solely on the formal information flow from the project team, but also for them to keep their ears to the ground, and maintain a broader network of connections with those inside and connected with the project to help inform their sense of how things are progressing. Another vehicle is the periodic use of independent expert assurance and scrutiny to provide a detached, objective assessment of project well-being. This said, you need to make sure that those concerned really are expert, and really are objective.

- **Don't walk away** – don't imagine that at any point in the project's life the wider organisation and the senior executives within it, and particularly those responsible for commissioning the project, can walk away from it, and hand over its subsequent progression to the delivery team, the IT department, or worse still, a third party. Organisational ownership, and senior executive sponsorship, of the initiative is required all the way through.   As the project unfolds, things will happen – many unexpected - which will require an organisational response. 'The plan never survives contact with the enemy', there will be changes – these things take time, the world will not stand still during this period, issues will arise. Some of these will give rise to decisions which will have wide implications for the organisation, which the project team per se is not equipped or in a position to take (for example, unless they are really trivial ones, the project team should not be responsible for making decisions around changes in scope - these have potential implications for project economics and the balance of risk and reward, which require an organisational decision, not a project one; moreover, if the project acts as arbiter in such situations, and chooses to reject a user request for changes, this is likely adversely to impact the prevailing dynamics between the project and the users in question, which is avoided if the decision is made by the governance board; likewise the go-live decision is one that should be taken by the organisation, not by the project). Delivery of the project will make demands of and have consequences for the wider organisation, and not least the users, and lead to changes, which the executives of the organisation need to understand and be comfortable with; and there will be situations where the project team will need support and guidance from the leadership of the organisation in dealing with particular situations, resolving disagreements, managing stakeholders, overcoming resistance and so on. Hence there is a need for constant and continual attention, otherwise the project is likely to be blown off course, and it may hit the rocks. The involvement of the executive leadership of the organisation will be especially important if and when the project runs into difficulties, as is all too often the case, even for projects which are well configured and well managed. Under these circumstances, there is an organisational decision, not just a project one, to be taken about the right course of action, and those responsible need to be in a position to make an informed and considered judgement about this, rather than act hastily or be swayed by those who shout loudest. This requires good project governance. Moreover, if the executives responsible do choose to delegate responsibility for the project, or even visibly reduce their engagement with it at some point, it is worth reflecting on what sort of signal this may send to the rest of the organisation about the project's significance (especially in light of the importance of the role of the user community in many projects).

- **Use of an established project management approach does not guarantee success...** – this helps, but it isn't sufficient. As I've tried to show, many of the things that can make IT projects so difficult, such as wrestling with the organisational culture, managing relationships, engaging with users and stakeholders, building alignment, making good organisational decisions and so on do not necessarily lend themselves to conventional project management techniques, nor are project managers in a position within the organisation to undertake them. This leads back once more to the critical importance of the role of the organisation's wider leadership in the success of the project, and emphasises the point that senior managers cannot distance themselves from such initiatives.

- **The go-live and its aftermath is likely to be messy** – taking a new system live is very often a fraught process: there is normally a lot to be done in a short space of time, people are under pressure, it is not unusual for unforeseen problems to occur (where the 'cutover' to the new system is particularly complex, it is helpful to have undertaken some form of rehearsal previously; also it is desirable to have established a fall-back plan in the event that things go seriously awry). Likewise, there is a high probability of problems being experienced with the operation of the new system following its implementation. For example, there are usually practical set-up problems - users forgetting passwords or not being able to send things to print to their usual printer, while there may well be operational situations which were not covered by the test scenarios employed, so new problems may become evident; users frequently forget at least some of their training, and may seek to use the new system in the same way they did the old one, which leads to them getting into difficulties. Very often it may take several weeks or even months for the new solution to achieve stability. This has many parallels with the Heathrow Terminal 5 start-up experience. Given the potential for such problems to arise, prudent preparations include the establishment of additional support arrangements and appropriate investment in the development of contingency plans. The risks involved can result in a reluctance to 'step into the unknown' and implement the new system, but there is again a balance to be struck between the cost of delay and the additional confidence that can be gained as a result of a deferral. Moreover, the decision to go live helps focus project activities, and it is often only once it is in live operation that it becomes possible to understand what is really required – particularly in terms of organisational processes – to get the full value out of the new system. Again, this is ultimately a matter of judgement.

- **It's not over until the benefits lady sings** – in my experience, most projects are declared complete once the new system has been implemented, or once it is considered reasonably stable. But really this is premature. Since the purpose of undertaking the project is to enable some broader organisational end, the project should only be considered complete once this end has been achieved, or at least is well advanced. Moreover, driving the benefits delivery is hard and requires focus; it is not surprising that many projects fail to deliver the benefits projected if this is neglected. So, once again, you have to stick with it, and put in place mechanisms to support this.

In short then – understand what you're getting into (you may want to read this book), approach with caution, don't jump to conclusion or to judgement, prepare thoroughly, get expert help (you may need to get expert help to identify the expert help), set things up properly, stay connected, ask good questions, make well-informed, pragmatic decisions, and see it through right to the end (did I mention reading this book?). Then have a party – because you and everyone involved will deserve one.

CHAPTER 8: CONCLUSION – WHY IT PROJECTS ARE HARD, AND WHY THEY FAIL

So, have I succeeded in answering the two questions that I asked myself at the start of this book? Namely, 'Why are these things hard?', and 'Why do they fail?'

I guess the reader (assuming anyone's got this far) ultimately needs to be the judge of this, but my answer to the first question would be that they are hard because they are complex. The fact that projects are complex is not a particularly original observation, and to some extent such an explanation might still be considered somewhat tautologous, and so – using in part the example of the NHS National Programme for IT (NPfIT) - I've tried to make explicit many of the different sources of complexity that IT projects are likely to have to confront, and which lead to them being hard. That's not to say that all IT projects will encounter all of these complexities, but it's probably reasonable to assert that a large proportion will encounter some of them, and some will encounter most of them. What is also important to note is that many of these complexities are 'non-technical' in nature, and don't necessarily have much to do directly with IT – things like selecting and working with suppliers, engaging with users and other stakeholders, establishing good project governance and so on. Often these sorts of issues involve a significant human behavioural/relationship element. Moreover, IT projects also frequently entail 'wicked' or 'messy' aspects, where the decisions which the organisation commissioning and undertaking the project has to make have no obvious right answer, but instead give rise to different sets of implications and consequences, all of which have advantages and disadvantages. As a result, the difference between success and failure in an IT initiative is less a matter of applying a particular methodology with rigour, and more a matter of judgement. Ultimately, all IT projects have to achieve at least a 'passing grade' in dealing with all the different sources of complexity that they face.

It's perhaps possible to argue that the evolution of technology will reduce (and is already reducing) at least some of the difficulties inherent in IT projects, and that in future the track record of performance will improve. Certainly as discussed earlier, the advent of cloud computing seems to have reduced the IT infrastructure burden for certain types of undertaking that are in a position to take advantage of this; likewise, more sophisticated data warehousing, mining and reporting tools may have helped to make it easier than hitherto to store, search for, recall and analyse information without imposing a rigid classification framework; and improved integration technologies may make it easier to join different systems together than previously. No doubt there are plenty of other areas of technology advances which those who know about these things can point to that will reduce some of the difficulties IT projects are likely to face. However, this only extends so far. Given that as we have seen IT projects are only partly about the IT, significant aspects of them are unaffected by improvements in technology, and are unlikely to become any less 'hard' for the foreseeable future, if ever.

The fact that IT projects are hard does not entirely answer the second question, and explain why they should frequently fail – or at least struggle. Obviously, the need to achieve a passing grade on multiple dimensions 'sets the bar' quite high for every project (and for some projects – like NPfIT sets it very high indeed), but as long as the complexity is met by an equivalent level of response, then even though hard, the project should still ultimately be successful. The reason why so many IT projects struggle, therefore, must lie in the quality of the response, which frequently proves insufficient to address all the demands and the complexities encountered. Given this conclusion – which seems self-evident when you think about it - the question arising is why this should be: this was discussed at some length in Chapter 6, but in my view the short answer is because of a common failure on the part of organisations of all shapes and sizes – and those inside organisations who commission IT projects - to understand the potential sources of complexity that the project is likely to encounter, and an associated tendency to underestimate these – particularly in the case of those organisations and individuals who are less familiar with and less experienced in undertaking such projects. This points to the critical importance of all concerned appreciating what is involved in the successful completion of any IT project before they commit to it; which brings us back to understanding the potential sources of complexity. Hopefully, this book helps in this regard – and at least if and when I sit down again with a management team who are contemplating a roll of the IT project dice, I'll have something to back up my assertion that 'these things are hard'. Reflecting on this, I think people know they're hard, but they don't know why they're hard – and understanding this is the key. Because if you do, you will know what you are getting yourself and your organisation into, and you will be much better placed to deal with what you are about to receive. Insofar as there is a panacea for success in these sorts of undertakings, it seems to me that this is as close as you are likely to get.

NOTES AND REFERENCES

Introduction

1:...in the kingdom of the blind – attributed to Desiderius Erasmus, 1466-1536, quoted in 'Adegia' (1536) – see William Barker (Compiler): The Adages of Erasmus (2001), University of Toronto Press, Scholarly Publishing, 2nd Revised edition, 384pps

2:...a little knowledge – the version 'a little learning is a dangerous thing' generally attributed to Alexander Pope (1688-1744); found in 'An Essay on Criticism' (1709) – see poetry.eserver.org/essay-on-criticism.html (extracted 11/07/2013)

3: Arthur Sullivan and William Schwenck Gilbert: ...HMS Pinafore: or The Lass that Loved a Sailor. An Entirely Original Comic Opera, in Two Acts. Bacon and Company, 1879, 31pps

4: definition of 'hard': requiring a great deal of effort or endurance; performed with or marked by great diligence or energy; difficult to resolve, accomplish or finish; difficult to understand or solve – see oxforddictionaries.com/definition/English/hard

5: Computer Weekly 22/09/2011: The world's biggest civilian IT project finally looks to have failed, but is the NHS IT failure a surprise? (Karl Flinders) (http://www.computerweekly.com/blogs/outsourcing/2011/09/the-worlds-biggest-civilian-it-project-finally-looks-to-have-failed-but-it-is-no-surprise.html) (accessed 06/11/13)

6: Computer Weekly 23/09/2011: The NHS IT project is dead, but why do large IT projects so often fail? Part 2 (Karl Flinders) – subsequent articles in this series published in Computer Weekly on 26/09/2011, 28/09/2011, 30/09/2011, 04/10/2011, 05/10/2011, 07/10/2011, 11/10/2011, 13/10/2011, 17/10/2011, 20/10/2011, 24/10/2011, 27/10/2011, 31/10/2011, 03/11/2011, 10/11/2011, 15/11/2011, 17/11/2011, 22/11/2011, 24/11/2011, 29/11/2011, 01/12/2011, 13/12/2011, 16/12/2011, 10/02/2012 (http://www.computerweekly.com/blogs/outsourcing/2012/02/bill-curtis-is-chief-scientist.html) (accessed 06/11/13)

7: The Standish Group (1995): CHAOS (https://cs/nmt.edu/ncs328/reading/Standish.pdf) (accessed 20/08/2013)

8: The Standish Group (2012): CHAOS Manifesto – The year of the executive sponsor (versionone.com/assets/img/files/CHAOSManifesto2012.pdf) (accessed 20/08/2013)

9: M.Block, S.Blumberg and J.Laartz: Delivering large-scale IT projects on time, on budget and on value October 2012 (www.mckinsey.com/insights/business_technology/delivering_large-scale_it_projects_on_time_on_budget_and_on_value)

10: B.Flyvbjerg and A.Budzier: Why your IT Project May Be Riskier Than You Think Harvard Business Review, September 2011 (hbr.org/2011/09/why_your_it_project_may_be_riskier_than_you_think/)

11: House of Commons Committee of Public Accounts (2013): The dismantled National Programme for IT in the NHS. Nineteenth Report of Session 2013-2014. Published 18th September 2013. London, The Stationery Office Ltd.

12: Independent 1/12/2013: Obamacare: US healthcare site overhauled in rush to salvage policy – and reputation (David Usborne)

http://www.independent.co.uk/news/world/americas/obamacare-us-healthcare-site-overhauled-in-rush-to-salvage-policy--and-reputation-8976019.html

Chapter 1

1: Megastructures: The Collection – The Secrets of the World's Greatest Architectural Achievements . ITV DVD, 2009. ITV Studios Home Entertainment (see also natgeotv.com/uk/ megastructures (accessed 11/07/2013)

2: Deborah Cadbury (2004): Seven Wonders of the Industrial World. Harper Perennial, London, 400pps

3: Bell Rock lighthouse mini study based on:
        D. Cadbury (2004), Chapter 2 pps 63-106
        Bella Bathurst (2005): The Lighthouse Stevensons, Harper Perennial, London, 284pps, especially Chapter 4, pps 66-105
        Bellrock.org.uk: A Reference Site for the Bell Rock Lighthouse (www.bellrock.org.uk) (accessed 11/07/2013)

4: financial conversions to modern day equivalents undertaken using www.measuringworth.com

5: Robert Stevenson (1824): Account of the Bell Rock Lighthouse, Constable, Edinburgh

6: Great Eastern mini study based on:
        D. Cadbury (2004), Chapter 1, pps 13-61

L.T.C. Rolt (1989): Isambard Kingdom Brunel, Penguin, London, 449pps, especially Chapters 13, 14 and 15, pps 304-421

Sally Duggan (2003): Men of Iron – Brunel, Stephenson and the inventions that shaped the modern world, Pan Books, London, 206pps, especially Chapter 8, pps 151-173

7: Brooklyn Bridge mini study based on:

D. Cadbury (2004), Chapter 3, pps 107-151

David G. McCullogh (1983): The Great Bridge. Simon Schuster, New York, 636pps

8: Tacoma Narrows Bridge Disaster – see www.enm.bris.ac.uk/anm/tacoma/tacoma.html (accessed 11/07/2013)

9: London Heathrow Airport Terminal 5 mini study based principally on:

Sharon Doherty (2008): Heathrow's Terminal 5: History in the Making. John Wiley and Sons, Chichester, 358 pps

10: EC Harris: Effective integration and partnering delivered T5 on time, on budget. www.britishexpertise.org/bx/upload/Member_projects/EC_Harris_T5.pdf (extacted 11/07/2013)

11: Chris Clayton (2008): The Heathrow Tunnel Collapse. University of Southampton, Advanced Course in Risk Management in Civil Engieneering, LNEC Lisbon (http://riskmanagement.lnec.pt/pdf/papers/Nov21_apresentacoes/20_presentation_Clayton.pdf) (extracted 11/07/2013)

12: Nuno Gil (2008): BAA: The T5 Project Agreement Manchester Business School, University of Manchester (https://research.mbs.ac.uk/infrastructure/Portals/0/docs/BAA%20The%20T5%20Project%20Agreement%20A%20Online.pdf) (extracted 11/07/2013)

13: House of Commons Transport Committee: The opening of Heathrow Terminal 5 (2008). Twelfth Report of Session 2007-2008. Published 3rd November 2008, House of Commons, London, The Stationery Office Ltd - Willie Walsh evidence: question 162

14: Colin Matthews evidence: p8 and question 278, House of Commons Transport Committee (2008)

15: Union resentment: p7, and questions 198-203, House of Commons Transport Committee (2008)

16: This account is based on the report undertaken by the House of Commons Transport Committee (2008)

17: Doherty, 2008, p145

18: House of Commons Transport Committee, 2008, Ev12, question 96

19: House of Commons Transport Committee, 2008, Ev5, question 29

20: Business Traveller, 02/06/2011: Heathrow's T5C opens for business (http://www.businesstraveller.com/news/heathrowa-s-t5c-opens-for-business) (accessed 26/07/2011)

21: Change in T5C requirements – see Letter from British Airways to BAA, 24/01/08, www.caa.co.uk/docs/5/ergdocs/heatgatnov07/ba_annex5.pdf (extracted 26/07/2013)

22: Business Traveller, 02/06/2011: The Interview: BA's Operations Manager James Wooldridge (http://www.businesstraveller.com/news/the-interview-baa-s-operations-manager-james-wo) (accessed 26/07/2011)

23: Passenger/flight numbers – see www.heathrowairport.com/about-us/company-news-and-information/company-information/facts-and-figures (accessed 26/07/2013)

Chapter 2

1: definitions of a project - see for example B.Smith (1985): 'Project concepts' in Effective Project Administration, Institution of Mechanical Engineers, quoted in J.Rodney Turner (1993): Handbook of Project-based Management: Improving the Processes for Achieving Strategic Objectives, McGraw Hill, Maidenhead, England, 540pps; and Project Management Institute http://www.pmi.org/en/About-Us/About-Us-What-is-Project-Management.aspx (accessed 29/07/2013)

2: learning by doing – see for example R.C. Schank (1995): What We Learn When We Learn By Doing. Institute for the Learning Sciences, Northwestern University, Technical Report No. 60 (cogprints.org/637/1/LearnbyDoing_Schank.html) (accessed 29/07/13); K.Anders Ericsson, Ralf Th. Krampe and Clemens Tesch-Romer (1993): The Role of Deliberate Practice in the Acquisition of Expert Performance. Psychological Review, vol 100, no. 3, pps 363-406; David A. Kolb (1984): Experiential learning: experience as the source of learning and development, Prentice Hall, Englewood Cliffs, New Jersey

3: Bella Bathurst (2005): The Lighthouse Stevensons, Harper Perennial, London, 284pps

4: 'events dear boy...' see E.M. Knowles (2006): What they didn't say: a book of misquotations. Oxford University Press, pp vi, 33

5: management of risk and uncertainty – see J. Rodney Turner (2009): The Handbook of Project Based Management: Leading strategic change in organisations, 3rd edition, McGraw Hill, Chapter 1

6: Bell Rock Lighthouse – see note 3 to Chapter 1

7: Footbridge replacement project – this account is based on the following:
- o Bucks Free Press, 23/10/2011: Demolished Denham footbridge may be replaced (James Nadal) http://www.bucksfreepress.co.uk/news/9321197.Demolished_Denham_footbridge_may_be_replaced/ (accessed 28/10/13)
- o Buckinghamshire County Council, 21/12/2011: A40 Oxford Gardens Footbridge Removal and Replacement with PUFFIN Crossing – Report to Cabinet Member for Planning and Transportation http://democracy.buckscc.gov.uk/documents/s22131/PT20.11%20Report.pdf (and associated appendices) (accessed 28/10/13)
- o getbucks.co.uk, 07/02/2012: Months of roadworks on busy A40 (Jack Abell) http://www.getbucks.co.uk/news/local-news/months-roadworks-busy-a40-5706279 (accessed 28/10/13)
- o getbucks.co.uk, 01/05/2012: Traffic problems on A40 in Denham (Jack Abell)
  - o http://www.getbucks.co.uk/news/local-news/traffic-problems-a40-denham-5705444 (accessed 28/10/13)
- o The Society for All British and Irish Road Enthusiasts (SABRE): Something wicked comes the A40 way (various posts) http://www.sabreroads.org.uk/forum/viewtopic.php?f=1&t=26567&sid=3b59d24f063dec313da276bb801df902&start=0 (accessed 28/10/13)

Chapter 3

1: ...biggest computer project: Sean Brennan (2005): The NHS IT Project – the biggest computer programme in the world...ever!, Radcliff Publishing, Oxford 225pps (re background to the project, see especially Chapters 6 and 7, pps 49-89)

2: see Brian Randell et al (2010): The NHS's National Programme for Information Technology (NPfIT): A Dossier of Concerns (http://homepages.cs.ncl.ac.uk/brian.randell/Concerns.pdf) (accessed 20/09/13) for a compendium of documentation relating to the project

3: see Brennan (2005), especially Chapters 6 and 7, pps 49-89 for a discussion of the background to the project

4: Department of Health (2002): Delivering 21st Century IT support for the NHS: National Strategic Programme
http://webarchive.nationalarchives.gov.uk/20130107105354/http://www.dh.gov.uk/prod_consum_dh/groups/dh_digitalassets/@dh/@en/documents/digitalasset/dh_4067112.pdf

5: NHS entities:
       Hospital Trusts – National Audit Office (2000): The Management and Control of Hospital Acquired Infection in Acute NHS Trusts in England. Report by the Comptroller and Auditor General, published 17/02/2000, London, The Stationery Office Ltd
       GPs – GHK in association with ICM Research (2011): Programme of Research Exploring Issues of Private Healthcare Among General Practitioners and Medical Consultants: Population Overview Report for the Office of Fair Trading, p45 (www.oft.gov.uk/shared.oft/market-studies/Population-Overview-Report-1.pdf) (accessed 20/09/2013); Daily Hansard, Written Answers, 7th July 2008, Column 1284W (www.publications.parliament.uk/pa/cm200708/cmhansrd/cm080707/text/80707w0033.htm) (accessed 20/09/2013)

6: McKinsey involvement – Computer Weekly 02/07/2007: Another ministerial spokesperson for the NHS IT programme moves on (Ted Ritter) (http://www.computerweekly.com/blogs/public-sector/2007/07/another-ministerial-spokespeop-1.html) (accessed 20/09/2013)

7: Anecdote re projected length of time project would take: House of Commons Committee of Public Accounts (2011): The National Programme for IT in the NHS: an update on the delivery of detailed care records systems. Forty-fifth Report of Session 2010-2012. Published 3rd August 2011. London, The Stationery Office Ltd. (http://www.nao.org.uk/wp-content/uploads/2011/05/1012888. pdf) (accessed 20/09/2013) - question 146, ev13

8: Table – F.Burns (1998): Information for Health: an information strategy for the modern NHS 1998-2005 A national strategy for local implementation NHS Executive, London http://webarchive.nationalarchives.gov.uk/20130107105354/http://www.dh.gov.uk/prod_consum_dh/groups/dh_digitalassets/@dh/@en/documents/digitalasset/dh_4014469.pdf) (accessed 20/09/2013); Brennan (2005): The NHS IT Project; Department of Health (2002): Delivering 21st Century IT Support for the NHS

9: NHS entities:
Hospital Trusts and GPs – see note 5
Strategic Health Authorities: Brennan (2005) p25

NHS entities contd:

Primary Care Trusts: The Primary Care Trusts (Establishment and Dissolution) (England) Order, 2006 (www.legislation.gov.uk/uksi/2006/2072/made) (accessed 20/09/2013)

Foundation Trusts: British Medical Journal, The first wave of foundation trusts 3rd June 2004 (http://www.bmj.com/content/328/7452/1332) (accessed 20/09/2013)

Total number of trusts: National Audit Office (2008): The National Programme for IT in the NHS: Progress since 2006. Report by the Comptroller and Auditor General, HC 484-I Session 2007-2008, 16 May 2008 (http://www.nao.org.uk/wp-content/uploads/2008/05/0708484i.pdf (accessed 20/09/2013) - see table p8

10: Risk assessment score - Public Accounts Committee, 2011, question 144, ev 13

11: Cost – see Brennan (2005), p5; £20bn figure quoted in House of Commons Committee of Public Accounts (2007): Department of Health: The National Programme for IT in the NHS. Twentieth Report of Session 2006-2007. Published 11th April 2007. London, The Stationery Office Ltd (http://www.publications.parliament.uk/pa/cm200607/cmselect/cmpubacc/390/390.pdf) (extracted 20/09/2013) - see question 48, Ev 8

12: Components of programme – Brennan (2005), Chapter 9, pps 101-108; National Audit Office (2006): Department of Health: The National Programme for IT in the NHS. Report by the Comptroller and Auditor General, HC 1173 Session 2005-2006, published 16th June 2006. (http://www.official-documents.gov.uk/document/hc0506/hc11/1173/1173.pdf) (extracted 20/09/13) – see pages 10,11

13: Additions to programme – National Audit Office (2006), p10

14: Launch of programme - National Audit Office (2006), p1

15: Connecting for Health - National Audit Office (2006), p1

16: Appointment of Richard Granger – Brennan (2005), p5

17: Establishment of programme office - National Audit Office (2006), p30

18: Delays in appointment of COO - National Audit Office (2006), p29

19: Appointment of Professor Aidan Halligan – Brennan (2005), p5

20: Appointment of Professor Sir John Pattison – Computer Weekly (01/12/2003): Health service's £2.3bn programme loses its head (Tony Collins) (http://www.computerweekly.com/news/ 2240053725/Health-services-16323bn-programme-loses-its-head) (extracted 03/06/2013)

21: Changes to SROs – National Audit Office (2006), p44

22: Connectivity with wider NHS – National Audit Office (2006), p44

23: Ministerial oversight - National Audit Office (2006), p29

24: Cluster level organisation – Brennan (2005), pps109-110

25: Other NHS organisational entities involved – Parliamentary Office of Science and Technology (POST) (2004), New NHS IT, Postnote Number 214, February 2004, London (www.parliament.uk/briefing-papers/POST-PN-214.pdf) (extracted 20/09/2013)

26: Care Record Development Board – National Audit Office (2006), p31

27: Input from trusts – Brennan (2005), p26

28: Foundation trusts – House of Commons Public Accounts Committee (2009): The National Programme for IT in the NHS: Progress since 2006 Second Report of Session 2008-09, published 27th January 2009, The Stationery Office Ltd, London (http://www.rcc.gov.pt/SiteCollectionDocuments/ProgressITinNHSsince2006.pdf) (accessed 20/09/2013) – see question 20, Ev 3, question 23, Ev 3-4

29: GPs – Public Accounts Committee (2007), question 65, Ev 10

30: Roll-out phases – Brennan (2005), pps 130-131

31: Contracting – Brennan (2005), pps 123-125; National Audit Office (2006), p34

32: Output-Based Specification (OBS) – National Audit Office (2006), pps 30-31

33: Contracting – Brennan (2005), pps 119-123; National Audit Office (2006), pps 2, 35-37

34: 'Vigorous' - National Audit Office (2006), pps 2, 35

35: Praise for contracting process: National Audit Office (2006), pps 2, 35-37; The Observer 13/02/2005: A £6bn question for the NHS (Simon Caulkin) (http://www.theguardian.com/business/2005/feb/13/theobserver.observerbusiness21) (accessed 20/09/2013)

36: Criticisms of contracting process - Public Accounts Committee (2007), question 8, Ev 2; Outsource Magazine 24/09/2010: The End of NPfIT (Alistair Maughan) (http://outsourcemagazine.co.uk/the-end-of-npfit/) (accessed 20/09/2013); Guardian 24/08/2006: Yet another setback for Blair's vision of a hi-tech NHS (Bobbie Johnson and Sarah Hall) (http://www.theguardian.com/society/2006/aug/24/ health.epublic) (accessed 20/09/2013); House of Commons Committee of Public Accounts (2013): The dismantled National Programme for IT in the NHS. Nineteenth Report of Session 2013–14. HC 294 Published 18/09/2013, London, The Stationery Office Limited (http://www.publications.parliament.uk/pa/cm201314/ cmselect/cmpubacc/294/294.pdf) (extracted 23/09/2013), question 114, Ev 9; Parliamentary Office of Science and Technology (POST) (2004)

37: Favouring large companies - ehealth insider 12/10/04: NPfIT procurement unfriendly for SMEs, says OFT (http://www.ehi.co.uk/news/EHI/887/npfit-procurement-unfriendly-for-smes-says-oft) (accessed 20/09/2013)

38: Main contracts - POST (2004); Brennan (2005), p5 and p124

39: Lockheed Martin withdrawal - Observer 31/08/03: Americans ditch £10bn NHS project (Conal Walsh) (http://www.theguardian.com/technology/2003/aug/31/internet.politics) (accessed 20/09/2013)

40: Surprise at some contractors – Brennan (2005), p119-125

41: Table: National Audit Office (2006) pps 14-23

42: Table: National Audit Office (2006) p12

43: Challenges - Parliamentary Office of Science and Technology (2004)

44: 'Gushing' – Public Accounts Committee (2007), question 78, Ev 11

45: Conclusions – National Audit Office (2006), p6

46: Ministerial support – National Audit Office (2006), p29

47: Sound project management – National Audit Office (2006), pps 29-30, also QinetiQ Ltd (2005): NHS Connecting for Health Process Capability Appraisal prepared for National Audit Office by QinetiQ (http://www.nao.org.uk/wp-content/uploads/2006/06/05061173_Qinetiq.pdf) (extracted 23/09/13)

48: Meeting users' needs – National Audit Office (2006), pps30-31

49: Confidentiality – National Audit Office (2006), pps31-33

50: Competition for contracts – National Audit Office (2006), pps 35-36

51: Testing suppliers' ability to deliver – National Audit Office (2006), p36

52: Approach to suppliers – National Audit Office (2006), p37

53: BT/Fujitsu and IDX - National Audit Office (2006), p37

54: CSC and iSoft - National Audit Office (2006), p38

55: BT and N3 - National Audit Office (2006), pps38-39

56: GP systems - National Audit Office (2006), pps40-41

57: Inform users and win support - National Audit Office (2006), pps44-45

58: Awareness and understanding - National Audit Office (2006), pps45-48

59: Keeping public informed - National Audit Office (2006), p48

60: Costs - National Audit Office (2006), pps4-5

61: National Audit Office (2006), p6

62: Delivery delays/changes to timings - National Audit Office (2006), p12

63: Heterogeneous nature of NHS - National Audit Office (2006), p24

64: Business change programme - National Audit Office (2006), pps43-45

65: Medix survey - National Audit Office (2006), p47

66: Changes to leadership - National Audit Office (2006), p44

67: National Audit Office (2006), pps6-7

68: Letter from academics – see B. Randell et al (2010), p37

69: Health Minister response – see Computer Weekly, 10/10/2006: Experts strike new NHS warning note (Tony Collins) (http://www.computerweekly.com/news/2240103597/Experts-strike-new-NHS-warning-note) (accessed 23/09/2013)

70: Gateway failures - e-health insider 23/06/2009: CfH publishes OGC Gateway Reviews (Jon Hoeksma) (http://www.ehi.co.uk/news/EHI/4956/cfh-publishes-ogc-gateway-reviews) (accessed 23/09/2013); Computer Weekly 23/06/2009: 16 key points in Gateway Reviews on NHS IT scheme (Ted Ritter) (http://www.computerweekly.com/blogs/public-sector/2009/06/16-key-points-in-gateway-revie.html) (accessed 23/09/2013); full list of reviews available at http://www.connectingforhealth.nhs.uk/about/foi (accessed 23/09/2013)

71: Hutton frozen out – British Medical Journal (2004), May 15; 328(7449): 1145-6: National Programme for information technology is sorely needed and must succeed – but is off to shaky start (Michael Humber) (http://www.ncbi.nlm.nih.gov/pmc/articles/PMC411076/) (accessed 23/09/2013)

72: iSoft problems – The Guardian 21/08/2006: 'No believable plan' for completion of iSoft work on NHS overhaul (Simon Bowers) (http://www.theguardian.com/society/2006/aug/21/health.egovernment) (accessed 23/09/2013); e-health insider 21/08/2006: 'No believable plan' for completion of iSoft Lorenzo (http://ehi.co.uk/news/EHI/2080/'no-believable-plan'-for-completion-of-isoft-lorenzo) (accessed 23/09/2013)

73: Accenture withdrawal – Guardian 29/09/2006: US firm replaces Accenture on health service IT work at 'no cost' to taxpayer (Simon Bowers) (http://www.theguardian.com/business/2006/sep/29 /epublic.usnews) (accessed 23/09/2013)

74: Second letter from academics – Computer Weekly 10/10/2006: Experts strike new NHS warning note

75: BT contract reset – National Audit Office (2008), p41

76: Public Accounts Committee (2007)

77: Progress – Public Accounts Committee (2007), pps 5,12-14, Ev84-85,110

78: 'patchy' performance of PAS systems - Public Accounts Committee (2007), p14

79: Nuffield Orthopaedic Centre – Public Accounts Committee (2007), letter from Sir John Bourn to Mr Richard Bacon, ev 92-95

80: Public Accounts Committee (2007), pps3-4

81: Loss of suppliers - Public Accounts Committee (2007), p6

82: Only two suppliers - Public Accounts Committee (2007), pps5-6

83: Shortage of capacity - Public Accounts Committee (2007), p5, question 55, Ev8

84: 'Sham' - Public Accounts Committee (2007), question 60 Ev 9

85: 'hundreds of pages of text…' - Public Accounts Committee (2007), Ev 31

86: Involvement of clinicians - Public Accounts Committee (2007), pps 4,5,17, question 19 Ev4, question 59 Ev 9, Ev 27-32

87: Low priority - Public Accounts Committee (2007), p6

88: Six responsible owners - Public Accounts Committee (2007), p20

89: Narrow focus on IT - Public Accounts Committee (2007), p6

90: Local responsibilities - Public Accounts Committee (2007), p6

91: Relationships between suppliers and local NHS - Public Accounts Committee (2007), Ev 112-113

92: Implications of delays - Public Accounts Committee (2007), pps6-7

93: Costs and benefits record - Public Accounts Committee (2007), p5

94: Decentralisation measures – National Audit Office (2008), p33

95: New operating model - National Audit Office (2008), p33

96: Transfer of funds - National Audit Office (2008), p33

97: Grouping of Strategic Health Authorities - National Audit Office (2008), p33

98: Additional supply capacity - National Audit Office (2008), p42

99: Increased medical professional involvement - National Audit Office (2008), p38

100: Patient lead - National Audit Office (2008), p34

101: Richard Granger resignation – Guardian, 18/06/2007: NHS director general of IT quits after repeated system delays (Simon Bowers) (http://www.theguardian.com/business/2007/jun/18/ health.politics) (accessed 23/09/2013); ZD Net: Top 10 Richard Granger quotes (http://www.zdnet.com/top-10-richard-granger-quotes-3039287615/) (accessed 23/09/2013)

102: National Audit Office (2008)

103: NAO summary conclusions - National Audit Office (2008), pps 7-15

104: Progress - National Audit Office (2008), p24; National Audit Office (2008), Volume 2: Project Progress Reports

105: Implementation of Summary Care Record - National Audit Office (2008), p21; T. Greenhalgh et al (2008): Summary Care Record Early Adopter Programme. An independent evaluation by University College London 30/04/2008 (http://discovery.ucl.ac.uk/6602/1/6602.pdf) (extracted 23/09/2013)

106: Implementation of Detailed Care Record - National Audit Office (2008), pps 8, 21-23

107: Trusts' reservations - National Audit Office (2008), p23

108: Programme costs - National Audit Office (2008), pps 9, 24-26

109: Benefits - National Audit Office (2008), pps10, 29-30

110: Service availability - National Audit Office (2008), pps 10, 30-31

111: Five main challenges - National Audit Office (2008), pps 11-13

112: Strong leadership and governance - National Audit Office (2008), p32

113: Local ownership programme - National Audit Office (2008), pps 33-34

114: Accurate view of progress and costs - National Audit Office (2008), pps 4, 25, 32-33

115: Maintaining patient confidence - National Audit Office (2008), pps 34-37

116: Securing support of NHS staff - National Audit Office (2008), pps 37-39

117: Managing suppliers effectively - National Audit Office (2008), p41

118: Relations with Local Service Providers - National Audit Office (2008), p41

119: Deploying and using systems effectively - National Audit Office (2008), pps 42-48

120: Fujitsu withdrawal – Guardian 29/05/2008: NHS ends key contract in computerised medical records project (http://www.theguardian.com/society/2008/may/29/nhs) (accessed 23/09/2013)

121: Securing increased clinician support – Public Accounts Committee, 2011, p11, also question 130 Ev 12, questions 153-155 Ev 14, question 315 Ev 27

122: Public Accounts Committee (2009)

123: 'Very disappointing...' - Public Accounts Committee (2009), p5

124: Six deployments - Public Accounts Committee (2009), p9

125: Lorenzo reviews – National Audit Office (2008), pps 22-23; Public Accounts Committee (2009), Ev 24

126: Connecting for Health optimism - Public Accounts Committee (2009), p11

127: Lorenzo deployment Morecambe Bay - Public Accounts Committee (2009), p11

128: September projected go-live at Morecambe Bay - Public Accounts Committee (2009), Ev 29 (Memorandum from Department of Health to the Committee, dated 15/09/2008)

129: Actual Lorenzo go-live at Morecambe Bay – e-health insider 06/11/2008: Soft launch of Lorenzo at Morecambe Bay (Lyn Whitfield) (http://www.ehi.co.uk/news/ehi/4309/soft-launch-of-lorenzo-at-morecambe-bay) (accessed 23/09/2013)

130: 'Continuing delays...' - Public Accounts Committee (2009), p5

131: Roll-out approach untested - Public Accounts Committee (2009), p5

132: Millenium problems - Public Accounts Committee (2009), pps 10, 16, question 149 and 153 Ev 16

133: Changes to interaction between trusts and LSPs - Public Accounts Committee (2009), question 242 Ev 21-22

134: Doubts re 2014-15 completion - Public Accounts Committee (2009), p5

135: Allowing trusts to adopt alternative systems - Public Accounts Committee (2009), p6

136: Foundation Trusts - Public Accounts Committee (2009), pps 14-15

137: Fujitsu departure - Public Accounts Committee (2009), pps 12-13

138: Overall leadership - Public Accounts Committee (2009), p16

139: New appointments – Computer Weekly 07/08/2008: New health IT leaders with joint salaries of £400k (Ted Ritter) (http://www.computerweekly.com/blogs/public-sector/2008/08/new-health-it-leaders-with-joint-salaries-of-400k.html) (accessed 23/09/2013)

140: Not providing value for money - Public Accounts Committee (2009), p6

141: Uncertainties re local costs - Public Accounts Committee (2009), p6

142: Benefits issues - Public Accounts Committee (2009), p6

143: Difficulties in gaining clinician support - Public Accounts Committee (2009), pps 6, 16

144: Changes to working practices without consultation - Public Accounts Committee (2009), p16

145: Data security concerns - Public Accounts Committee (2009), pps 7, 17-18

146: Mr David Nicholson comments - Public Accounts Committee (2009), question 11 Ev 2, question 32 Ev 5

147: Revisions to BT contract in South – National Audit Office (2011): Department of Health: The National Programme for IT in the NHS: an update on the delivery of detailed care records systems. Report by the Comptroller and Auditor General, HC 888 Session 2010– 2012, 18/05/2011, London, The Stationery Office (http://www.nao.org.uk/wp-content/uploads/2011/05/1012888.pdf) (extracted 23/09/2013), pps 10, 28

148: Trusts permitted to build on existing systems - National Audit Office (2011), p8

149: Interoperability toolkit - National Audit Office (2011), p8, Public Accounts Committee (2011), question 270 Ev 23; Connecting for Health website: Interoperability Toolkit – Background and Overview http://www.connectingforhealth.nhs.uk/systemsandservices/interop/overview (extracted 23/09/2013)

150: Reconfiguring contract for London - National Audit Office (2011), pps 9,23

151: Press release – Department of Health (09/09/2010): The future of the National Programme for IT (http://webarchive.nationalarchives.gov.uk/+/www.dh.gov.uk/en/MediaCentre/Pressreleases/DH_119293)

152: Contracts still to be honoured... – e-health insider 10/09/2010: Little change on LSP Contracts: Connelly (Sarah Bruce) (http://www.ehi.co.uk/news/ehi/6230/little-change-on-lsp-contracts:-connelly) (accessed 23/09/2013)

153: Remaining spend - Public Accounts Committee (2011), p3

154: National Audit Office (2011)

155: Deliveries versus problems - National Audit Office (2011), p16

156: Table - National Audit Office (2011), p17

157: Table - National Audit Office (2011), pps 9, 11

158: Exclusion of GP practices/Ambulance trusts - National Audit Office (2011), p9

159: Progress in London – National Audit Office (2011), pps 24-25

160: London costs – National Audit Office (2011), p23

161: Progress in South - National Audit Office (2011), p31

162: Costs in South - National Audit Office (2011), p30

163: Changes to CSC contract - National Audit Office (2011), p34

164: Lorenzo defects - National Audit Office (2011), p35

165: Lorenzo roll-out criteria – e-health insider 04/10/2009: Connelly sets benchmark for November (Jon Hoeksma) (http://www.ehi.co.uk/news/ehi/5353/connelly-sets-benchmark-for-november) (accessed 23/09/2013)

166: First full scale roll-out – Computer Weekly 09/06/2010: NPfIT pushes forward with first Lorenzo deployment at an acute trust (http://www.computerweekly.com/news/1280092969/NPfIT-pushes-forward-with-first-Lorenzo-deployment-at-an-acute-trust) (accessed 23/09/2013)
167: Lorenzo deployments - National Audit Office (2011), p34

168: Lorenzo release 2 - National Audit Office (2011), p34

169: Mental health trusts - National Audit Office (2011), p34

170: Interim systems - National Audit Office (2011), p35

171: Implementations in other Trusts - National Audit Office (2011), pps 11, 35

172: GP systems - National Audit Office (2011), p35

173: Further functionality required - National Audit Office (2011), p12

174: Costs - National Audit Office (2011), p7

175: Cost uncertainties - National Audit Office (2011), pps 14-15

176: Outstanding work remaining - National Audit Office (2011), pps 10, 15

177: Reorganisation of NHS - National Audit Office (2011), p15

178: Quality of information provided - National Audit Office (2011), p7

179: Overall conclusion - National Audit Office (2011), pps8,13

180: Department of Health response - National Audit Office (2011), p14

181: Public Accounts Committee (2011)

182: Unable to deliver original aim - Public Accounts Committee (2011), p5

183: Networked architecture - Public Accounts Committee (2011), question 124 Ev 11

184: Greater flexibility - Public Accounts Committee (2011), question 130 Ev 12, question 151 Ev 13, question 154 Ev 14, question 216 Ev 19, question 291 Ev 25

185: New technology - Public Accounts Committee (2011), question 124 Ev 11

186: Ability to opt out - Public Accounts Committee (2011), p12, question 306 Ev 26

187: 'monolithic to modular...' - Public Accounts Committee (2011), question 61, Ev5

188: Future uncertainties - Public Accounts Committee (2011), pps 3, 5, 11

189: No reduction in costs - Public Accounts Committee (2011), p5

190: 'clearly overpaying' - Public Accounts Committee (2011), p3

191: Cost comparisons - Public Accounts Committee (2011), p8-9

192: Ongoing CSC negotiations - Public Accounts Committee (2011), pps 3, 11

193: Effective CSC monopoly - Public Accounts Committee (2011), p5

194: Value of spend to date - Public Accounts Committee (2011), p5

195: Size of Connecting for Health central team - Public Accounts Committee (2011), question 187 Ev 16

196: Failure to provide information - Public Accounts Committee (2011), pps 4, 6

197: Security Issues - Public Accounts Committee (2011), p6

198: Weak management - Public Accounts Committee (2011), pps 6, 9, questions 113-116 Ev10

199: Chaired by deputy - Public Accounts Committee (2011), question 187 Ev 16

200: Oversight by Major Projects Authority - Public Accounts Committee (2011), p6

201: Trusts understanding of implications - Public Accounts Committee (2011), p6

202: Body like Connecting for Health - Public Accounts Committee (2011), p12

203: Project inherently risky - Public Accounts Committee (2011), p7

204: Risk assessments - Public Accounts Committee (2011), questions 139-142 Ev 13

205: Payment by results - Public Accounts Committee (2011), question 125 Ev 11, question 312 Ev 27

206: 'One size fits all' unworkable - Public Accounts Committee (2011), pps 3, 5, 7, question 119 Ev 10

207: Lack of clinician support - Public Accounts Committee (2011), p7, question 129 Ev 12

208: Disagreements re Clinical 5 – e-health insider 05/10/2009: Readers back reformed NPfIT (Lyn Whitfield) (http://www.ehi.co.uk/news/ehi/5264/readers-back-reformed-npfit) (accessed 23/09/2013)

209: No further deployment – e-health insider 11/05/2011: No CSC deal until NAO reports – PM (Lyn Whitfield) (http://www.ehi.co.uk/news/ehi/6873/no-csc-deal-until-nao-reports---pm) (accessed 23/09/2013)

210: Dismantling... – Department of Health press release (22/09/2011): Dismantling the NHS National Programme for IT (https://www.gov.uk/government/news/dismantling-the-nhs-national-programme-for-it) (extracted 23/09/2013)

211: Resignation of Christine Connelly – e-health insider 22/06/2011: Christine Connelly resigns as NHS CIO (Jon Hoeksma) (http://www.ehi.co.uk/news/acute-care/6970/christine-connelly-resigns-as-nhs-cio) (accessed 23/09/2013)

212: Media coverage – eg Mail Online 22/09/2011: £12bn NHS computer system is scrapped...and its all YOUR money that Labour poured down the drain (Daniel Martin) (http://www.dailymail.co.uk/news/article-2040259/NHS-IT-project-failure-Labours-12bn-scheme-scrapped.html) (accessed 23/09/2013)

213: New CSC contract – ZDNet 04/09/2012: NHS finally seals CSC deal with £1bn of savings and no compulsory Lorenzo roll-outs (Jo Best) (http://www.zdnet.com/uk/nhs-finally-seals-csc-deal-with-1bn-of-savings-and-no-compulsory-lorenzo-rollouts-7000003694/) (accessed 23/09/2013)

214: House of Commons Committee of Public Accounts (2013): The dismantled National Programme for IT in the NHS. Nineteenth Report of Session 2013-2014. Published 18th September 2013. London, The Stationery Office Ltd.

215: Component programmes continuing – Public Accounts Committee (2013), p8

216: CSC contractual situation - Public Accounts Committee (2013), pps 8-9

217: Benefits statement – National Audit Office (2013): Department of Health - Review of the final benefits statement for programmes previously managed under the National Programme for IT in the NHS. Memorandum for the House of Commons Committee of Public Accounts, June 2013, (http://www.nao.org.uk/wp-content/uploads/2013/06/10171-001_NPfiT_Review.pdf) (extracted 23/09/2013)

218: Total costs - Public Accounts Committee (2013), pps 8-9

219: 22 Trusts taking Lorenzo - Public Accounts Committee (2013), p9

220: Fujitsu dispute- Public Accounts Committee (2013), p9

221: Benefits - Public Accounts Committee (2013), pps 10-11

222: Paperless NHS - Public Accounts Committee (2013), p6

223: Sir David Nicholson comments - Public Accounts Committee (2013), questions 119-120, Ev 10

Chapter 4

1: NHS employees: BBC News, 22/03/2011: Staff census shows NHS workforce hits 1.4 million (Dominic Hughes) (http://www.bbc.co.uk/news/health-12819538) (accessed 25/09/2013)

2: Impact underestimated - National Audit Office (2006), p24

3: S.Noles & S.Kelly (2007): The Definitive Guide to Project Management. Financial Times/Prentice Hall, London

4: Public Accounts Committee (2011), question 144 Ev 13

5: Boston Big Dig - see en.wikipedia.org/wiki/Big_Dig (accessed 25/09/2013); Megastructures DVD (2009)

6: 'when eating an elephant...' – www.brainyquote.com/quotes/quotes/c/creightona207381.html (accessed 25/09/2013)

7: Fractal – oxforddictionaries.com/definitions/English/fractal (accessed 25/09/2013)
8: Project stage gates – see for example en.wikipedia.org/wiki/Phase-gate_model (accessed 25/09/2013); PRINCE2 advocates the use of project stages – Office of Government Commerce (2009): Managing Successful Projects with PRINCE2. Stationery Office Books

9: 'no plan survives contact with the enemy' - www.brainyquote.com/quotes/quotes/h/helmuthvon182561.html (accessed 25/09/2013)

10: 'time spent in reconnaissance...' - see Peter G. Tsouras (ed) (2005): The Book of Military Quotations. Zenith Imprint

11: 'fools rush in...' - Alexander Pope (1709): An Essay on Criticism

12: 'how best to eat the elephant' – see note 6 above

13: Morecambe Bay roll-out – e-health insider 06/11/08: Soft launch of Lorenzo at Morecambe Bay (Lyn Whitfield)

14: Decreases in support – e-health insider 21/11/06: Survey shows waning medical support for NPfIT (http://www.ehi.co.uk/news/EHI/2279/survey-shows-waning-medical-support-for-npfit) (accessed 25/09/2013)

15: Rephasing of Lorenzo – Public Accounts Committee (2009), pps 5-6, Ev24

16: Adequate steps taken – National Audit Office (2006), pps 30-31

17: Broad spectrum of stakeholders - National Audit Office (2006), p31

18: Criticism by medical professionals – Public Accounts Committee (2007), p17, question 19 Ev 4, question 58 Ev 9, question 217 Ev 23, also Ev 27-32

19: Frank Burns quote – Brennan (2005), p86; Disagreements re Clinical 5 – e-health insider 05/10/2009: Readers back reformed NPfIT (Lyn Whitfield) (http://www.ehi.co.uk/news/ehi/5264/readers-back-reformed-npfit) (accessed 23/09/2013)

20: Software development - there seem to be surprisingly few overviews of software development as an activity in its entirety – the most comprehensive account is perhaps contained in Steve McConnell (2004): Code Complete: A Practical Handbook of Software Construction. 2nd Edition, Microsoft Press, 950pps

21: reference sites – Tony Collins with David Bicknell (1998): Crash: Leaning from the World's Worst Computer Disasters. Simon and Schuster UK, London, p107

22: less centralised architecture – Public Accounts Committee (2011), question 124 Ev 11

23: 'most dangerous word' – Collins (1998), p64; 'not overridingly important' – Collins (1998), p122

24: Importance of organisational change aspects: Parliamentary Office of Science and Technology (2004): New NHS IT; National Audit Office (2006), p43; Public Accounts Committee (2007), p6

25: Change in effectiveness of NHS – Brennan (2005), especially Chapter 2, pps 7-22

26: Adaptive challenges – RA Heifetz and M Linsky (2002): Leadership on the Line Staying Alive Through the Dangers of Leading Harvard Business School Press, Boston, 252pps

27: Literature on organisational change – eg JP Kotter (2012): Leading Change. Harvard Business Review Press; W. Bridges (2009): Managing Transitions– Making the most of change. Nicholas Brealey Publishing, London; J.Hayes (2010): The Theory and Practice of Change Management. Pelgrave Macmillan (to name but three)

28: NAO positive of procurement- National Audit Office (2006), p7, and Appendix 2: Lessons learned from the procurement and management of the National Programme which may be of benefit to other departments, p53

29: 'Managing suppliers effectively' – National Audit Office (2008), pps 40-42

30: Public pronouncements – see ZDNet 19/06/2007: Top 10 Richard Granger quotes (http://www.zdnet.com/top-10-richard-granger-quotes-3039287615/) (accessed 25/09/2013)

31: Differences in costs – Public Accounts Committee (2011), questions 236-241 Ev 21

32: J.McDonagh and D.Coghlan (2001): The Art of Clinical Inquiry in Information Technology-related Change – Chapter 37 in P.Reason and H.Bradbury (eds) (2001): Handbook of Action Research Participative Inquiry and Practice, Sage Publications, 468pps

33: Cloud computing – see Christopher Barnatt (2010): A brief guide to cloud computing: An essential introduction to the next revolution in computing. Robinson Publishing; Amanda Fox and David Patterson (2013): Engineering Software as a Service: An agile approach to using Cloud Computing. Strawberry Canyon LLC

34: Software testing – see Cem Kaner, James Bach and Bret Pettichord (2001): Lessons Learned in Software Testing: A context driven approach. John Wiley; Brian Hambling (ed) (2010): Software Testing: An ISTQB-ISEB Foundation Guide. 2nd Edition. British Computer Society

35: Parliamentary Office of Science and Technology (2004): New NHS IT

36: Biometric identifiers - Parliamentary Office of Science and Technology (2004): New NHS IT

37: Implementation complexities – National Audit Office (2008), pps 42-47; Nuffield Orthopaedic Centre – Public Accounts Committee (2007), letter from Sir John Bourne to Mr Richard Bacon, ev 92-95

38: Parliamentary Office of Science and Technology (2004): New NHS IT

39: Sir David Nicholson comments - Public Accounts Committee (2013), questions 119-120, Ev 10

40: PRINCE2 (2009)

41: 'sound project management' – National Audit Office (2006), p29

42: QinetiQ review - QinetiQLtd (2005): NHS Connecting for Health Process Capability Appraisal prepared for National Audit Office by Qinetiq

43: J.McManus and T. Wood-Harper (2008): A study in project failure. British Computer Society (http://www.bcs.org/content/conwebdoc/19584) (extracted 25/09/2013)

44: Royal Academy of Engineering and The British Computer Society (2004): The challenges of complex IT projects (http://www.ceid.upatras.gr/tech_news/challengesIT.pdf) (extracted 25/09/2013)

45: degree of casualness – see Public Accounts Committee (2011), question 146 Ev 13

46: Delegation of chairing programme board - Public Accounts Committee (2011), question 187 Ev 16

47: Computer Weekly 14/12/2006: Lord Warner, minister in charge of the NHS's National Programme for IT "retires". (http://www.computerweekly.com/blogs/public-sector/2006/12/lord-warner-minister-in-charge.html) (extracted 25/09/2013)

48: Defend the programme – Computer Weekly 10/10/2006: Experts strike new NHS warning note (Tony Collins)

49: Scottish Parliament building cost increase: The Holyrood Inquiry (2004): A Report by the Rt Hon Lord Fraser of Carmyllie QC on his Inquiry into the Holyrood Building Project (http://www.holyroodinquiry.org/FINAL_report/report.htm) (accessed 25/09/2013)

50: Scope changes identified by National Audit Office – National Audit Office (2006), p10

51: Impact of scope reductions on benefits – Public Accounts Committee (2011), p5

52: Approach to measurement of benefits - National Audit Office (2006), p26

53: Impact of scope reductions - Public Accounts Committee (2011), p5

54: Gateway Reviews: Office of Government Commerce: OGC Gateway Review for Programmes and Projects (http://webarchive.nationalarchives.gov.uk/20100503135839/http:/www.ogc.gov.uk/what_is_ogc_gateway_review.asp) (accessed 25/09/2013)

55: Gateway review failures: The Register 19.06.2009: NPfIT failed nine Gateway Reviews (Kable)

56: S. Cicmil, T. Cooke-Davis, L. Crawford and K. Richardson (2009): Exploring the complexity of projects: Implications of Complexity Theory for Project Management practice. Project Management Institute; W.Curlee and R.L. Gordon (2010): Complexity Theory and Project Management. John Wiley

57: H. Rittel and M Webber (1973): Dilemmas in a General Theory of Planning, pp. 155–169, Policy Sciences, Vol. 4
http://www.uctc.net/mwebber/Rittel+Webber+Dilemmas+General_Theory_of_Planning.pdf (extracted 23/10/2013);
R.L. Ackoff (1974): Redesigning the Future: A Systems Approach to Societal Problems. John Wiley & Sons;
R.E. Horn and R.P. Weber (2007): New Tools For Resolving Wicked Problems: Mess Mapping and Resolution Mapping Processes, Strategy Kinetics L.L.C.
http://www.strategykinetics.com//New_Tools_For_Resolving_Wicked_Problems.pdf (extracted 23/10/2013)

58: P. DeGrace and L.H. Stahl (1990): Wicked Problems, Righteous Solutions: A Catalogue of Modern Software Engineering Paradigms Yourdon Press Computing, 272pps; R. Lane and G. Woodman (undated): 'Wicked Problems, Righteous Solutions' – Back to the Future on Large Complex Projects http://www.leanconstruction.org/media/docs/RighteousSolution.pdf (extracted 23/10/2013)

Chapter 6

1: Royal Academy of Engineering and The British Computer Society (2004): The challenges of complex IT projects

2: Tony Collins with David Bicknell (1998): Crash – Learning from the World's Worst Computer Disasters, especially pps 25-53
3: Donald Rumsfeld quote:
www.brainyquote.com/quotes/quotes/d/donaldrums148142.html (accessed 25/09/2013)

4: Sharon Doherty (2008): Heathrow's Terminal 5: History in the Making, p245

5: Nassim Nicholas Taleb (2007): The Black Swan The Impact of the Highly Improbable. Penguin, London; especially Chapter 10, pps 137-164

6: Groupthink – see I.L. Janis (1971): 'Groupthink' Psychology Today 5 (6) 43-46; I.L. Janis (1972): Victims of Groupthink: a psychological study of foreign policy decisions and fiascos, Houghton Mifflin, Boston; I.L. Janis (1982): Groupthink: Psychological Studies of policy decisions and fiascos, Houghton Mifflin, Boston

7: IT department autonomy: Joe McDonagh and David Coghlan (2001): The Art of Clinical Inquiry in Information Technology-related change, Chapter 37, pps 372-378 in Peter Reason and Hilary Bradbury (eds): Handbook of Action Research: Participative Inquiry and Practice, Sage Publications, London

8: Executive sponsorship - Royal Academy of Engineering and The British Computer Society (2004): The challenges of complex IT projects; The Standish Group (2012): CHAOS Manifesto – The year of the executive sponsor

9: Groupthink – see Page 3 above

10: Evidence of improving performance - The Standish Group (2012): CHAOS Manifesto – The year of the executive sponsor

11: Bent Flyvbjerg, Nils Bruzelius and Werner Rothengatter (2003): Megaprojects and Risk An Anatomy of Ambition Cambridge University Press

12: Overoptimistic forecasts –Flyvbjerg, Bruzelius and Rothengatter (2003), p 43

13: Manipulating forecasts – Flyvbjerg, Bruzelius and Rothengatter (2003), p45

14: Behavioural factors – Flyvbjerg, Bruzelius and Rothengatter (2003), pps 45-48

15: failure to learn lessons - Flyvbjerg, Bruzelius and Rothengatter (2003), pps 16, 18

16: Poor risk analysis/management – Flyvbjerg, Bruzelius and Rothengatter (2003), pps 73-85

17: Public versus private sector project performance – D.R. Mydellton (2007): They Meant Well Government Project Disasters. The Institute of Economic Affairs, London

18: Calleam Consulting: Why Projects Fail – Catalogue of Catastrophe (calleam.com/WTPF/?page_id=3) (accessed 25/09/2013)

19: B. Flyvbjerg and A. Budzier (2011): Why your IT project may be riskier than you think. Harvard Business Review, September 2011

20: Norman Dixon (1976): On the psychology of military incompetence. Pimlico/Random House, London, especially pps 152-153

21: David Owen (2007): The Hubris Syndrome. Bush, Blair and the Intoxication of Power. Portico Publishing/Methuen, London, especially pps 1-3

22: Mathew Hayward (2007): Ego Check: Why executive hubris is wrecking companies and careers, and how to avoid the trap. Kaplan Publishing, Chicago

23: Nassim Nicholas Taleb (2007): The Black Swan

24: I.L. Janis (1972): Victims of Groupthink: a psychological study of foreign policy decisions and fiascos; I.L. Janis (1982): Groupthink: Psychological Studies of policy decisions and fiascos

25: Capgemini Consulting in co-operation with The Economist Intelligence Unit (2007): Trends in Business Transformation Survey of European Executives (http://www.corporate-leaders.com/sitescene/custom/userfiles/file/Trends%20in%20Bus%20Trans%20Survey%20April%202007%20-%20Capgemini.pdf) (extracted 25/09/2013)

Chapter 7:

1: Tony Collins with David Bicknell (1998): Crash – Learning from the World's Worst Computer Disasters

2: Tony Collins with David Bicknell (1998), p23

3: B. Flyvbjerg and A. Budzier (2011): Why your IT project may be riskier than you think. Harvard Business Review, September 2011

4: John P. Kotter (1995): Leading Change: Why Transformation Efforts Fail. Harvard Business Review, March-April 1995 (http://89.248.0.102/upload/Topplederprogrammet/Internsider/Kull9/Litteratur/2.1%20Leading%20Change%20-%20Why%20Transformation%20Efforts%20Fail%20by%20JP%20Kotter.pdf) (accessed 25/09/2013)

Index

313

314